MORE TRUTH
WILL SET YOU FREE

MORE TRUTH
WILL SET YOU FREE

DEREK O'NEILL

Bianca Productions™
San Antonio, Texas, USA

TABLE OF CONTENTS

TEACHINGS

Acknowledgement and Dedication

I 'd like to acknowledge all religions as valid at the core essence. I would like to acknowledge all people and beings as cells in the one divine body. I'd like to acknowledge the sorrow, the suffering, the bliss, and the happiness as being the path to true happiness. I'd like to acknowledge that all the beings in all the worlds are within and not without, and all the beings and all the worlds can and should be happy.

This book is dedicated to all sentient beings. You are about to realize that enlightened is who you are, and in fact all that we are here to do is to remove the sense of delusion in which we all live, not to obtain enlightenment.

I would like to thank all my teachers, my wife Linda O'Neill, my children Orla and Gavin, Sri Satya Sai Baba, His Holiness The Dalai Lama, His Holiness the Karmapa, Mother Amma, Ramana Maharshi, Sri Aurobindo, Paramahansa Yogananda, Bill Gates, Warren Buffet, The Rockefellers, President Obama, my Mother, Father, family, dogs, cats, flowers, plants, and yes, most important, the fly that has just landed on my nose.

INTRODUCTION

"I have to give away that which I need most: love, love, love."
— DEREK O'NEILL

This book is a collection of stories. I love to tell stories; they are the glue that holds all of these teachings together. A story is just that, nothing more, nothing less. The real treasures in this book are the teachings, which pepper the stories like spice for a good stew. I suppose the stories teach as well, but you have to remember that they are told from the perspective of the teller. There are many parts to a story, including the listener, the words, the teller, the being that lives inside the teller, and the spark of awareness that creates the whole thing. They are all connected in an "inner-net" of thoughts, feelings, emotions, and consciousness. The spark of awareness that creates everything is the life-force energy that I call God. The being that lives inside the teller is the observer, the consciousness that hopefully awakens every morning, that sees the dreams while the mind is asleep, and that is aware. Some people may call this the soul. The teller is the mind, the ego that loves to tell the story over and over again. The words are the story itself, whether it's a great sacred truth or an emotionally charged melodrama. The listener is you, who have all of these parts inside yourself, just like the teller.

It is not important that you believe the stories just because I told them. You have to do your own homework, kick the tires, and discover for yourself

1

what is truth and what is rubbish. I love to tell the story of an experience my niece had while visiting some friends in New York City. I have been teaching in New York City for several years, and for some hilarious reason, far beyond my understanding, some of my students love to put photographs of me up on their walls. So, my niece was visiting a friend, who took her over to a party with some of these delightfully insane students of mine. When she got there, the first things she saw were the photographs of me on the wall. So she immediately rang up her parents and went on and on about these crazy fools that had photographs of Uncle Derek on their walls. To her, I am just a slightly daft uncle, whom the family has tolerated out of some warped sense of family loyalty. Each has his or her own opinion of me—that is what makes this life so entertaining!

As I write this book, I find myself back in India in a town called Puttaparti in Southern India. This is where my teacher Sathya Sai Baba lives, surrounded by hundreds of thousands of devotees. Many who love him call him "Swami," which is a respectful name for a holy man. With the support of his followers, Swami has built a very modern city, including a super specialty hospital where all medical treatment is free. Open-heart surgery, or whatever you need, is absolutely free. While I am here I learn that a colleague, friend, and acquaintance of mine is here in this super specialty hospital. He is about to change consciousness and drop his mortal coil to the ravages of cancer. I sit here now by his bedside, and we laugh and cry at the adventure and struggles, the good times and the bad times that we both have experienced during our sojourn here on this planet.

As I look at this being transcending back into light, I can't help but wonder how he really does feel. Even though he shares with us his sorrows, fears, regrets, anguish, and happiness, I look at him and think, "How does a man who is a Druid (a priest in the ancient Celtic religion) from Ireland, who has studied Druids most of his life, end up here in Puttaparti in a hospital room? What adventures, matters, and consciousnesses have conspired so that he should end his last breath here in Puttaparti, India, and not Ireland, England, or France?" I'm about to sit with this man as he goes through his last struggle in this lifetime, the struggle for survival. Hopefully, as I speak to him and share what I have learned, he will stop the struggle, relax into the process of returning to light, and know there is a God, that there is light in the tunnel that will arrive for him. There will be people there, loved ones who have passed before him and discovered for themselves that from light comes light, and to the light we all travel from the moment of the hatching of the egg and the struggle.

This book is about one man's struggle in life, or struggle for life. We all have won the Olympic contest and the Gold Medal. The Gold Medal of these Olympic Games is life. When our Mother and Father came together, they did an act and seeds were created. These seeds raced toward the winning line, the goal line, and you were born, which means that you are already a winner. You won the race. The ironic problem is, of course, that with winning the race comes another kind of struggle, and that is what this book is about. It is about the struggle of life and one man's learning all of the lessons that come along with the struggle. Then something really amazing happens; the struggle stops, just out of the blue. After receiving all of the lessons and experiences you will find retold in my story, I began to accept everything as the same. There is no good or bad anymore, there just is. With that acceptance comes this calmness and peace that I believe all on this planet can actually attain, once they stop their struggle.

The problem is that people don't know how to stop their struggle. That is why, hopefully, as you read this book, you will begin to realize that the events described in it are very similar perhaps to your own life. The blueprint is the same for everyone's life. The only difference is the story. Everybody's story is different, but the truth is, the blueprint is always the same. It is a struggle for survival, a struggle to be heard, a struggle to be seen, and a struggle to be loved. Then, at the end, it is a struggle not to die. As you read this book, every time you say, "Yes, yes, this is me, this sounds like me," you and I will connect. Since I am in this space of non-struggle, peace, and calmness, the connection will help you heal. Just the connection will do it. No ritual ceremonies or secret waving of hands over candles at midnight is necessary. All it takes is the connection of "AHA!" I hope to meet you out in the Land of Consciousness, as I now call it, and I hope that by reading this book you will have some "AHA" moments, moments of calm and peace, as you begin to give up the struggle. We were born as lead, but when we calm ourselves and quit the struggle, we turn to gold. Truly this is the philosopher's stone.

Part of my wish for all of you is that you realize your true power. Quit giving it away and putting people on pedestals that don't belong there. Whether it is your tribe, your parents, your loved ones, your children, whomever you have put on a pedestal needs to come down. You have created your reality, and I have given you lots of reasons to believe that in this book. You are every bit as powerful as anyone else on this planet; you just don't believe it yet. When you are overjoyed because someone you have put on a pedestal looks at you or gives you a gift, while diving into deep depression when you are ignored, you have given all your power away. Life is a journey into the highest and most powerful part of yourself, your heart. You can skip and laugh along the path or you can be dragged by your ankles, scratching and clawing the whole way. So take everyone off the pedestals and have fun!

CHAPTER 1

WHO IS DEREK O'NEILL?

L et me introduce myself and we can begin this journey of discovery together. My name is Derek O'Neill, or so they told me. They put that tag on me when I was born, and I have been carrying that around for quite awhile. I found it pretty useful in introducing myself for jobs; I could never get the job when they said, "And your name is?" and I half-jokingly said, "God." So, it's been much easier to carry the Derek O'Neill tag. Without those tags, we would not survive here and things might get a bit confusing.

The idea of letting go of all those tags is worth some thought because you could finally get to see who has been hiding behind the tag. When you have self-esteem issues, it is like you are looking at the price tag on something and saying it is a bit too much. That is you showing you that you have abundance issues. You should just say yes. What you are buying is a tool to bring love to this planet because you'll look and feel better. When you look and feel better, then you are better. So, off you go to buy a few diamonds and stuff like that. I am talking about "Die-minds," not the shiny glitter, tinsel, and trash kind. "Die-minds." Let go of the attachment to your tag from time to time and find out who you really are. This is the process of taking the tag, your "price tag," off and learning how to stop struggling.

This being named Derek was born in 1964 in Dublin, Ireland, in a place known as the Liberties. I was born in a triangle of three churches: one was called Christ Church; the next, Whitefire Street Church; and the third, St. Patrick's Cathedral. Threes are very important on this planet, as are triangles. Some threes you may be aware of are the Father, Son, Holy Ghost; and Mother, Father, Child. One three you may not be aware of is positive, negative, and ground. Electricians are very familiar with this three; these are the wires that make electricity flow on this planet. When God, love, and you combine, miracles happen. But I am getting ahead of myself. Being born amidst three churches was highly auspicious.

DANCING A JIG

The day of my birth was quite the riot, I was told. My mother was at a dance and she was jiving (a very energetic dance) when I decided to begin to make my appearance. I laugh when I imagine my mother so active right up to the time of my birth. My head began to crown on the dance floor. I always laugh and say that is where I got my rhythm, as I worked as a professional dancer later on in life. I was lucky in that the dance was only ten minutes from the maternity hospital, so my mother danced right on over there for what she thought would be an easy birth. That was not to be, and my birth became a real struggle, with complications, hemorrhages, and other problems. That birth was my body's first experience on this planet and foretold a number of very important lessons I was to learn about the way life is here. I originally was conceived with a twin brother, but he was miscarried. He was a very evolved soul, who only wanted to stick his toe into physical form. We have a riot together, even today.

I muddled through and was born with jet-black hair down to my shoulders. This caused a bit of a stir at the hospital because in 1964 the Beatles were becoming famous. The staff would joke with my mother that I was the fifth Beatle because I had such long black hair. The nurses all wanted to feed and care for me, which suited my mother just fine. The trouble was that I didn't want to eat. I wouldn't eat for anyone. When they fed me formula, I would throw it all back up. They tried pumping my mother's breast milk and feeding me that, which I promptly threw up. This went on for weeks, and the doctors were worried I would not get enough nourishment. Despite the lack of food, I was growing like a weed and was apparently healthy. No one could understand how I could be healthy and growing without being able to keep any food in my stomach.

6

I later came to understand that I was a "light baby" or a "prana baby." This kind of a baby does not need to eat solid food because it gets nourishment and energy right out of the surrounding environment. I did not need food like other babies. There are stories of people not needing food for years and years, like the woman who lived on nothing but the Holy Communion given at Mass for 40 years and stayed fit as a fiddle. Of course, in Ireland in 1964, no one knew about these kinds of babies. The doctors, in their ignorance, decided to force-feed me intravenously, and that is how I began to take worldly nourishment. So on the day I was born the struggle began—the struggle called life.

EARLY LIFE

Seemingly, I was a very happy baby. You could leave me in a corner and I would sit there "goggling" without causing too much hassle for anyone. I lived a perfectly happy childhood just being. We lived on a street called John Dylan Street in Dublin. I lived with four brothers and two sisters, and we were always causing hilarious problems for my parents. One time, my brother was playing with matches and set a mattress on fire. The house was nearly gutted, but among us we were able to put the fire out. Another time, I was playing and somehow a wire coat hanger got stuck in my eye. It went right through the corner of my eye. As I came running out of the bedroom, my sister saw me and went hysterical. She saw me running around with a coat hanger hanging out of my eyeball and panicked. She lifted me up and put me on a gas cooker, which she didn't realize was still hot. So, there I sat with a coat hanger in my eyeball and my "arse" sizzling away. Hilarious! Yes, struggle, I think they call it the struggle of karma (destiny—cause and effect), of not understanding.

We lived in that house for several years, and as I was growing up, I would go across the street and play in St. Patrick's park that was right beside St. Patrick's Cathedral. One day a very important event happened. The event would cause me to later investigate certain aspects of my life and was the first of a number of events that would end my struggle and help me to understand how powerful our mind is, how powerful our thoughts are, and how powerful we are.

WASPS

When I was about five years of age, I went over to the park to play, even though my mother had told me not to go there because "bad men" hung out in the park and it wasn't safe. My mother would threaten me with all sorts of hell and brimstone if I went over there, but I was pulled there, it seemed, and I went anyway. Of course, being a boy, threats and warnings never stopped me. I was playing in the park and the next thing I noticed was my uncle coming through the back gate of the park. I knew that if he saw me and told my mother, my mother would give me quite a decent hitting, or seeing to at the least. I decided to run for the bushes and hide. When I jumped into the bushes, I didn't know that I had just jumped into a wasp's nest. I was ducking down, so focused on hiding from my uncle, that I didn't even hear the buzzing around me. Then I felt the first sting. My uncle had just walked past, so I couldn't move or he would catch me. Then I felt more stings coming on again and again and I ran out of the bush with the wasps after me. A woman, who was pushing her baby in a baby carriage, came to my rescue. Or perhaps it was more karma. She took the baby's blanket and after a short chase, caught me and wrapped me in it to protect me from the wasps. What she didn't realize was that she had wrapped a number of wasps in the blanket with me, and they gave me a proper going over. The woman took me from the park to nearby Adelaide Hospital. The hospital staff put iodine and other medicine on the wasp stings and kept asking me where I lived. I told them that I lived on the other side of the park. They told me they would take me home, but I was so afraid of my mother seeing them pull up to the house that I decided to run out of the hospital and went home by myself. She punished me for having all of the bee stings, but I never told her I got them in the park.

TALLAGHT

My father worked for Jacob's Biscuits. Not long after the baby blanket experience, his factory closed and a new one opened out in the country in Tallaght. He was given the option either to move to Tallaght with his family and keep his job in the new factory, or lose his job all together and have to find a new one. At that time in Ireland that wasn't a real option, so we moved to Tallaght. We moved out into the countryside from everything my mother knew and loved. I know that during the time we lived in Tallaght, my mother absolutely hated living there. She was far from the life she knew in Dublin City Center and as she said, far from her friends, neighbors, and everyone else she had learned to trust. She made it clear to all who would listen that she wanted to spend her life in Dublin.

The move may not have pleased my mother, but it was a godsend to me because it was there in Tallaght that I was introduced to martial arts at a very young age. I took to martial arts like a duck to water. I would go on to earn a place on the Irish Olympic Martial Arts team. I also studied many different forms of martial arts that introduced me to an understanding of the mind from an Eastern philosophy perspective. My teachers were not only Irish, but also Japanese, Chinese, and Korean. I learned martial arts from a variety of different cultures and experiences.

For me, Tallaght was great. It was out of the city, in nature. We lived right beside the River Dodder, and I would be there playing all day, every day, when I got the chance. That is where I started seeing auras of people, plants, and animals. The strange thing was that at such a young age, I didn't realize that everyone couldn't see and experience the things that I was experiencing. I assumed everyone could see what I saw. I never gave much thought to what I was doing—like sitting by rivers for hours on end, and having experiences that now boggle my mind, that I was lucky to have had.

I would sit by the river, and birds would land on me without fear. I would sit there, feeding and playing with the birds until someone would come up and the birds would fly away. As long as I was alone, the birds would stay, eat, play, and simply be. I would sit and watch the fish jump out of the water right in front of me. These were amazing experiences! People would find me by the side of the river, sitting perfectly still, doing this thing called the lotus position (sitting crossed-legged). I didn't know they had a name for it until much later. Now, with wisdom comes stiffness, unless you do yoga! Then the stiffness isn't as bad. I used to sit for hours and hours, five or six hours sometimes. My brothers and sisters used to call it the "bleep state." Many times I would be sitting by the river with dozens of birds perched on my shoulders. It was the craziest thing. I didn't know it was unusual; I thought it was normal. Even when I talked to people, I would say, "You are in the blues," and they usually would agree that they were depressed. What they didn't understand was that I was talking about the colors of the energy field around them, their aura. I was talking "auric" talk. I didn't even realize what an aura was until I was much older. Even though I didn't realize it at the time, I now know that all of these experiences were setting me up for something that would happen much later in my life. This later experience would boggle my mind beyond belief and bring me to the edge of my faith in the existence of God.

CHAPTER 2

My First Spiritual Experience

At about age five I had what I would now call my first spiritual experience. My family would call it my first weird experience. At the time I was unaware of the experience because when you are a child, you are still connected to God. You don't even realize that you are in the world unless, of course, you are one of those unfortunate souls who decide to pay off all of your karma with parents that won't love you. I know none of you had those types of parents. Your parents loved you, supported you, and never did anything mean or abusive at all, didn't they? Of course they did. I am joking, of course. Your parents did the best they could, as you will come to understand. As long as you hold onto being a victim, believing that your parents were monsters, you are ill. If you let go of all that judgment, the illness goes with it.

So, I was at home playing when some people brought a baby in the house. The baby was only a few weeks old and had whooping cough. I asked the grown-ups, "Can I hold the baby?" They told me that I was only a baby myself and it wouldn't be safe. I kicked up such a racket that they finally put me on the sofa and stacked cushions around me so that I could hold the baby safely. I held the baby for only a short while and then gave it back to the mother. When I gave it back, I had the whooping cough and the baby was clear and healthy. This was the first registered or recorded healing experience of my spiritual career. I didn't understand what had happened because I assumed that this happened to everybody. It was nothing. It was like, "That was grand! You love somebody and they get better." All I did was love the baby and it got better. What do you mean, "You can't do that?" Well, I was in for a spiritual awakening, and that spiritual awakening was coming.

VISIONS

I remember having visions, as a child, and saying things to my mother like, "Such and such a person will die tomorrow." She would slap me to shut me up because the mantra (saying) in those days was, "Children should be seen and not heard." I was to learn much later on that the reason my mother hit me for saying these types of things was because she was psychic too. In fact, she had psychic visions as well but was terrified of their negative effect and how people treated her when she spoke of them. She did not want to be treated like some kind of "weirdo." She hit me because she was afraid people would treat me the same way they treated her, and she wanted me to shut down and not connect with the visions. She did a great job of it because I did shut down for a period of time.

I believe we all have these psychic experiences. That is another story as we go further into this journey. I believe you have had these psychic visions as well. Some people call them good feelings, intuitions, or just knowing. All of these things refer to psychic experiences. When you begin to believe in these feelings, when you follow your gut instinct, this is when you begin to let the struggle go and begin to follow the lead-to-gold journey. You follow it without the victim-hood, without the problems, and without the issues. I am not telling you these stories to make myself out to be brilliant. I am telling them to remind you of the experiences you have had that have gone unnoticed. When you begin to notice them, this is when the awakening within you begins to take off with some speed.

As my mother and I walked this journey of seeing and pretending not to see, one Saturday morning, while I was watching television, I experienced something that would happen a lot: the room would disappear, and I would be looking into another dimension or something. This is what I call "Tell-A-Vision." It was as if watching the television brought me into a trance state that helped to open up a part of me that I had forgotten about. While in the trance, I saw a vision of my mother having or being involved in an accident with a bus. The accident was due to take place that evening. I knew that every Saturday evening at 7:00 p.m. my mother would take a bus and go into Dublin City to be with her old friends. She would stay there Saturday night and return the following Sunday. I knew that she was going to get onto that bus that night, that the bus would crash, and she would die. I loved my mother and there was no way I was going to let her die.

I decided to pretend that I had pains in my stomach and all sorts of things to get my mother's attention so that she wouldn't get on that bus. It wasn't working; she was still going to get on the bus. So just before she was due to go out, I knew I had to take drastic action. God and I had some words, and I went into the bathroom and found my father's Wilkinson Sword razor. This kind of razor had a sharp razor blade inside it that was in the top of the razor. I opened it, unscrewed the top of the razor, and removed the blade. I came out of the bathroom with the blade on my wrist and started screaming. I shouted, "Nobody loves me, I hate everybody," and "I want to die!" Then I went running back into the bathroom. I should have gotten an Oscar for that performance.

The door to the bathroom wasn't much and was only held closed by a flimsy latch. My parents tried to shoulder and kick their way through the door, but God was holding that door shut. Nothing they tried could open the door. This caused such a commotion that my mother missed the bus. I learned later that the bus did crash that evening, people were hurt and killed, and my mother was meant to be on that bus.

As all actions have consequences, I was to learn a very valuable lesson from interfering with my mother's karma in this event. Later on I studied many spiritual teacher's books about karma, cause and effect, and learned that we can't interfere with people's karma. Only God and enlightened beings with God's love can change karma through Grace. So, by keeping my mother off that bus, I was going to have to collect the karma for that action. For some reason, from that day forth my mother got even angrier with me. At times she acted like a possessed woman. She would hit me, scream at me, and then love me. She was a very loving woman, a woman who would give you her last pound. She would give our toys to other children so that the others would not feel left out. She even gave away our clothes to people who needed them.

She was a beautiful soul, but a soul that was struggling. Her soul was struggling with her own past. The traumas of her past that she hadn't dealt with in her life caused her to become an alcoholic. "Alcoholic," is another of these tags that people give each other. I just call them people who don't want to deal with their life. There I was, a child who was born to a woman who was an alcoholic. By the time I was born, my father looked like an innocent by-stander, and my mother looked like a raging anti-Christ. When she drank, she would scream, shout, and cause arguments all over the place. So I blamed my mother for a lot of the disharmony in our home. My mother had several jobs and made good money. So I blamed money as being the cause of my mother's drinking. I was a child and thought like a child about these things. Later on I found out that one of the reasons I wouldn't allow money to come into my life was because of what I thought money had done to my mother's life.

My mother was a very loving mother. Absolutely wonderful! I have the scars to prove it. On an average day, I would get a plate broken across my head because I wouldn't eat my cabbage. There is a saying in Ireland: "Mad as a brush." I never knew what it meant, even though I was always being hit with one. I had many a brush broken over my back. Then came the ultimate event. We were wishing in the New Year and wondering about the prospects of it all when my mother stabbed me. Let me tell you, she was my greatest teacher. I just didn't realize it because I was too pissed off. When you start to open spiritually, you will see you have been prepared. What she had been preparing me for was this experience, which is the experience that brings me here today.

Even though she was drinking when I was born, I did not learn until later in life that she never drank until she was the age of 32 or so. At that time she came home after working three jobs and caught my dad in bed with her best friend. The only way she could handle the pain of that discovery was to start drinking. So my childish impression that my mother was causing all of the problems in our home and my father was an innocent victim was not true. In fact, if anyone was the victim, it was my mother.

So there I was having all of these experiences, seeing auras and visions, watching people heal, and I began to realize that I couldn't go to some places because all the people there thought I was too strange. That was when I started to close down, to be "normal." That was when I stopped seeing the things that God wanted me to see. This would last until I was 18 years old and I met my wife Linda. She opened it all back up and ever since then, it has all been so easy.

CHAPTER 3

SEXUAL ABUSE

I t seems that one of the struggles I was born to experience in this lifetime was sexual abuse. I remember being sexually abused for the first time around the age of 6 by a man in a park. I didn't even register that the man was sexually abusing me when he was touching and feeling me. I didn't register the experience as a bad thing because it didn't really have an effect on me. I now understand that when people register an event as very nasty and bad and remember it as a traumatic experience, it will have a huge negative effect on their life. However, due to the fact that I had no emotions attached to the event, it had no effect on me. It just was.

When I was between the ages of 10 and 12, a schoolteacher sexually abused me. In those days the word of a schoolteacher was always taken as the truth. The schoolteacher was always right and never did anything wrong, so I thought it would be pointless to tell anyone about the abuse. As it turned out, the abuse was a blessing in disguise because I went to school as little as possible, always "on the hop." My mother never took me to school, which made it easy to skip class. She always had a hangover from her nightly wrestling match with a bottle of alcohol. Since she never took me to school, I would go out into nature and enjoy my time sitting by the rivers. My family began to call me "Nature Boy" because I was forever alone, sitting by the rivers for hours and hours.

During this time I developed a stammer. I am sure this was because I wasn't able to express what I was feeling, the fear of being abused by this teacher. One day the whole thing came to a head. I asked the teacher, "Could I go into the bathroom to use the bathroom?" He said, "Yes." While I was in the cubicle, he came in behind me and trapped me there. While he had me trapped, he took down my trousers and started sexually abusing me. By then I had learned some martial arts, and I struggled and managed to knee him in the testicles. It was just enough to get away. I went running out of the bathroom, out of the classroom, and all the way home.

By the time I got home, my brother, father, and mother were all in the house. I told my father and mother what had happened. They began to scream at me, and my father started to swing at me for saying such a thing. My big brother stopped him and said, "Listen to what he's saying; look at the state of him. He hasn't come home like this for nothing. You have to go up and find out what's happened."

With my brother's intervention, my father and brother brought me back to the school. When we reached the school, we went to the classroom. My father knocked on the door and out came the teacher.

The teacher said, "Oh, Mr. O'Neill, I don't know what got into Derek. I went to use the bathroom, and I accidentally walked into the cubicle he was using, and he just started to scream and shout and ran home."

When he heard this, my father started to hit me.

I screamed at my father, "That's not true. That's not true. That's not what happened. The teacher grabbed me. He was touching me. He pulled down my trousers."

The teacher lied to my father, and my father believed it. Luckily for me, my brother did not believe him.

I said, "He's doing it to other boys in the class as well. Look, he's doing it to such and such a boy and another such and such a boy."

My brother said, "We want to talk to these boys."

The teacher said, "No."

My brother then pushed the teacher aside and went into the classroom. He called the boys by name and asked them if the teacher had done anything to them. They started to cry and said that the teacher had been abusing them as well.

Now my father believed me, and we went up to the principal's office. My father and brother charged right in, to find the principal sitting at his desk. They started telling the principal what the teacher was doing to me and other boys. The teacher was trying to defend himself. My brother was screaming at the principal that the teacher was a monster, a sex abuser. The principal calmed everyone down and said that he would deal with the situation. I was asked to leave the office and sit outside, which I did. What happened in the office after that I never found out. When my father and brother came out of the office, they put me into our car and told me that the matter would be addressed. That was the end of the matter. When I returned to school three or four days later, the teacher was gone, and another teacher had taken his place. The new teacher was tougher, unkind, and unsmiling. I didn't know whether my situation had gone from bad to worse.

Weeks and months went by. We got word that the teacher had died of cancer and the matter was finally closed. I continued to go to school on the odd day. I don't know whether this experience caused me to dislike school so much or whether I just loved being in nature. Between the two, life made sure that I spent much more time with nature than I ever did with schooling.

The last postscript to my experience with this teacher did not happen until many years later when, at age 18, I traveled to Galway to participate in the "All Ireland Judo Championships." I traveled by train with the other boys and girls who were going to compete. I went off to get myself something from the train shop. I walked by a seat and was floored when I saw the teacher—the teacher that was supposed to be dead—the teacher who abused me when I was younger. He was sitting there in that seat, reading the paper. The seat beside him was empty. I went and got a bottle of Coke. I just stood there in shock. Anger began to rise in me. The next thing I knew, I found myself walking up to the teacher and sitting down beside him. I was much bigger and stronger now then I was as a boy. I sat down beside him and said, "Do you remember me?" He looked at me and claimed he didn't remember me. I said, "You were a teacher." He looked at me again, this time with something in his eye that told me he remembered who I was. That spark in his eye made me lose it. I totally lost control. I tore the newspaper from his hand. I started to punch and kick him. He was huddled up in the corner, and there I was releasing all of the pent-up anger that had been festering in me for all of those years. My judo instructor came along and dragged me off him. The emergency cord was pulled on the train and the train stopped. There was havoc everywhere. I was screaming that he had abused me. People thought that he had tried to abuse me on the train, so I said, "No, he abused me as a little boy." Then, all of a sudden, he was gone again. Even though he had disappeared, I had had my revenge and I felt much better for it. So now I really do believe in "what goes around, comes around." The bigger, stronger me finally got to speak up and act for myself.

Getting back to the comedy of my sexual abuse, when I was 15 years old, I had a job as a lounge boy, serving drinks to people at their table in a pub. I was really good at it. I used to make people laugh; I would tell jokes and keep them laughing. They would give me extra tips. Yes, as luck would have it, a barman who took a fancy to me, sexually abused me. As I said, it seems to have followed me in this lifetime, this karmic knot of being victimized by sexual abusers. I didn't understand this karmic consequence. I still don't understand it because I don't need to understand it. I've let it go now. Forgiveness is good and forgetting is better. I don't even think about it anymore, except when I think that someone might learn something from it or when I need a good laugh.

In my job as a lounge boy, I was a bit of a rebel. I was only 15 years old, but I was working and making decent money. The owner of the pub decided that she was going to drop our pay by 50 pence a night. I told her that was stupid; we were already underpaid. So she said she was going to let me go. In response, calling on all of my worldly wisdom of 15 years of life, I convinced all of the lounge boys to walk out of the pub that night with me. I caused a strike, believe it or not! We made up placards that said, "We are on Strike Because She Won't Pay Us Our Money." Some people turned away from the door and wouldn't go in. The police were called, and they came and tried to take our placards. I screamed at the police that we worked hard and this greedy woman, who made so much money from our labor, wouldn't give us our fair pay. The police, whatever they might have thought about it, said, "Disburse. Disburse." So we disbursed. As we were walking away, one of the head barmen called us back and said, "Come back tomorrow night. I'll talk to you tomorrow night." When we went back the next night, they gave us all our jobs back. I understand now that they had no choice because nobody else would have worked for them and they needed the staff.

One of the greatest stories of my life does not have to do with my sexual abuse, although it does involve sexual abuse. It is a story of destiny and karma, and it is the story of my brother Brian. When he was 7 or 8 years old, Brian was out playing with his mates when he saw a butcher's bike standing by the road. A butcher's bike is a bike with a large basket on the handlebars used for delivering meat from the butcher. Being a fun-loving lad, Brian decided to take a go on the bike and got on it to pedal around a bit. He wasn't trying to steal it; he only wanted to ride it for a second. As destiny would have it, just as he pedaled off, the butcher came out of the building and caught him. The police were called.

So off they went to the police station, the police and my brother. The police talked to Brian and decided to call our mother. When my mother arrived, the police had decided that Brian was on a path to ruin and thought that he needed a fright put in him. So they pulled my mother aside and convinced her that Brian was mixed in with a bad lot, that he would not end up well if he weren't brought to his senses. They told her that he needed a fright to straighten him out. The fright was three years in a child detention center run by Catholic monks. During those three years, Brian was systematically raped and sodomized by the brothers. At one point a brother was hitting Brian with a hurling bat, something like a baseball bat, while the brother sodomized Brian.

Brian escaped from the center and found his way home. My mother, not realizing what they were doing to him, handed him back to the police. As a result, Brian was sentenced to a more severe sentence in the children's detention system. As is not too surprising, when Brian got out of the children's facility, he turned to a life of petty crime, drug abuse, and alcoholism. This led him to spend quite some time in prison.

Brian was a very brainy fellow and spent a lot of his time in prison studying law, in particular. After reading a lot about laws and such, Brian decided to bring the Catholic Church to court to pay for the abuse he suffered when he was in the children's detention center. The case lasted for nine or ten years before he finally got his day in court.

The children's detention center and the long court case were not the only traumas that Brian had to overcome in his life. While he waited for his case to go to court, he had quite a few medical problems. Once he was hospitalized to have some tests on his heart. The doctors put him on medication while he was in the hospital, medication that made him hallucinate. One of the hallucinations that he had was that he was back in the children's detention center being sodomized by the priest who had beat him with the hurling bat. The hallucination seemed so real that he jumped out of his hospital room window and landed on the street below. The fall broke his back and he had to have an operation to repair his fractured spine. The doctors said that he was paralyzed and would never walk again. I told the doctors that he would walk again. I also believed in destiny or karma, and that there was someone more powerful than we were that would reward Brian for exposing the terrible abuses that he had to suffer. Having said that, almost a year later to the day, Brian was walking, to the amazement of his doctors. I believe that God had a purpose for Brian, and that Brian was allowed to walk again so that he could walk into the courtroom and expose the Catholic Church.

He was offered some compensation so as to save the Catholic Church the embarrassment of his accusations being made public. He decided that he wanted his day in court. When he arrived in court, the trial lasted for several days. There were witnesses, and counter-witnesses, who appeared and testified for and against Brian. The Judge summed up the evidence by saying that it was the most horrific case of sexual abuse he had ever heard in his career as a judge, and he awarded Brian a sum of money as compensation for what he had suffered.

Brian went directly home to his apartment from the courtroom. When he got to his apartment, he suffered a heart attack and died. This is how you know that your life has a destiny, karma, or a specific purpose. Brian was one of the first to come forward and accuse the Catholic Church of abusing young boys. As a result, investigations into organized religion and the terrible abuse that was going on took place. When he had fulfilled his purpose, his destiny, his karma, he went back to the light from whence he came.

CHAPTER 4

MY PERMANENT SCHOOL VACATION

My regular school days ended at age 16. My progress into second year, or comprehensive school as they call it, was like driving down a rocky road without tires. From the first day I walked into the school I seemed to have issues with the teachers, and they certainly had issues with me. One particular teacher, a physical education teacher, was a great bully. I was very fit from my martial arts training, and I used to compete with him with press-ups and sit-ups. I could do hundreds at a time, and I wouldn't let him win, ever. This competition and rivalry between us kept building until one day it just got out of hand. He was screaming at me about something, and I told him to back off me. He didn't, so I jumped up, picked up a chair, and hit him with it. He grabbed me and brought me up to the vice-principal's office. I was not expecting much sympathy from the vice-principal; his nickname was "Killer." While we were sitting there, the teacher tried to give me a dig, but he missed. When he missed, I picked up a chair in the office, and beat the teacher. Oh, my God, I'm not really this bad, but that's the way the events happened. So at age 16, I got an early and permanent vacation from school, because they expelled me.

First off, I got myself a job in a slaughterhouse, which was a skin and hide factory. I would take the cow skins and cover them with salt to prepare them to be made into leather. It was good work, hard work, and the money was good—far better money than my father had coming in. Little did I know that my father's pride would be hurt as I began to bring in more money than he did. This would cause him to deteriorate in his own being. I was on my own cloud, though, and I felt great. I was "the man with all of the money." I gave my mother most of the money I made and kept only as much as I needed for myself. I was always flush with money, and, of course, lots of so-called friends that come with that.

THE KARMIC SOLDIER

Next came a hugely important part of my life, what I call my "karmic soldier" phase. At the age of 17 I decided to join the Irish Army to follow two brothers who were in the Army at the same time. I was training for a spot on the Irish Olympic martial arts team at the time, and in my infinite wisdom, thought that going into the Army would help my fitness. I thought I would have lots of time to train and do exercises in the Army.

There I was at age 17, and I've joined the Army. Within a couple of weeks of joining, I woke up one morning at 5 a.m. by the sergeant screaming at us all and telling us to get into full battle order. In other words, we had to put on all of our battle gear—our webbing, backpack, and helmet with full combat headgear—as if we were going into war. We were to go on parade with all of our gear, which was very heavy. We got dressed, ran down to where our gear was stored, and put it all on. In typical military fashion, we were then told to go back up to our room, take our gear off, get changed, eat breakfast, and then be back at 8 a.m. with all of our battle gear on again for the parade. So we all went running over to the cookhouse. I grabbed a couple of sausages and other odd bits of food and start stuffing it all in my mouth. I noticed a sour taste while eating the sausages and thought that there must be something wrong with them. So I left the food on the table. Knowing that we might have to go the whole day without food, I grabbed a bowl and a big catering box of cornflakes. These boxes of cornflakes were huge and held between 200 and 300 bowls of cornflakes. I stuck my bowl in the box and shoveled out a bowlful of flakes and, without looking, poured milk over the whole lot. So I was stuffing my face trying to get something to eat before we went out on parade. As I was chewing and gulping it down, I heard a crunching sound in my mouth. I looked down and saw in my bowl what was left of a dead mouse that had somehow gotten into the box of flakes, died, and was decomposing. I realized what the crunch was and my stomach just heaved.

Just then, while I was looking around wildly for something to throw up in, the sergeant came in and screamed out orders for everyone to get out and get into full battle order or suffer the consequences. Even though my stomach was doing a good imitation of the spin cycle of a washing machine, I followed everyone out and got into my gear. I ran upstairs, got into battle order, and went downstairs. We lined up at attention in parade formation. We stood there for a long time. I remember it was August, and just my luck, one of the hottest August days on record in Ireland. When karma comes, it can come big and fast. So I stood there in full battle order with more than 75 pounds of gear on my back, on one of the hottest days ever in Ireland. The whole platoon stood there in formation at the back of the cookhouse at attention, and no one was to move. At that moment I began to feel very weak and I thought of the sausages and the mouse. I started to feel a bit sick, so I asked the sergeant, "Can I fall out, sir?" The sergeant told me to shut my trap and stand still. There was also a very young officer there, and I was getting weaker and my head was spinning, so I asked him, "Can I fall out?" The officer said the same thing the sergeant did, to shut up and stand at attention. So I stood there at perfect attention with the rest of the troops. Still, I felt really weak, so I asked the officer one more time if I could fall out. The officer screamed at me, "Stand still or I'll lock you up in the guardhouse, you waster!"

I was standing there and the world was spinning under me, around me and through me. I fainted and started to go down. The soldier behind me saw me falling forward and grabbed my webbing from the back to keep me from falling over. The officer screamed at the solder, "Let him go. He's malingering. He's wasting. He's a waster! Let him go, or I'll lock you in the guardhouse!" The soldier let go of me, I fell forward like a plank, and my jaw was the first thing to hit the pavement. There I was, lying on the ground, totally unconscious. As I lay there, the officer continued his inspection, ignoring me. Then he stood over me and said, "Get up, O'Neill!" When I didn't move, he kicked me in the side with his boot and fractured one of my ribs. Blood started gushing out of my mouth, but the officer walked away and continued his inspection. Right then an older officer came by—a general or the like, I am told—and saw me lying all bloody on the ground. He ordered that an ambulance be called right away and had a loud conversation with the young officer. For me, it was all black and lights out.

I regained consciousness while I was in the back of the ambulance. The orderlies held a kidney bowl under my chin, one of those tin, kidney-shaped bowls they have in hospitals. As I came to, I spat into the bowl and all I could hear was "click, click, click," which was the sound of my teeth falling out and hitting the metal of the kidney bowl. I was taken to the Army hospital to see the Army doctor on duty. He diagnosed me with food poisoning, cleaned me up a little, and sent me to get an X-ray. They took the X-ray and then sent me down to the dentist, so he could take a look at my mouth to get it cleaned up. They put me in the dentist chair and I saw the dentist, who was an old, old, old officer and a very angry man. I have no idea why he was so angry, but he didn't like me at all. He started to clean up my mouth and decided to start pulling teeth. I immediately felt a stabbing pain in my jaw, and I asked him to stop. He told me, "Shut up!" which seems to be part of the disciplinary code in the Irish Army. Officers know better than enlisted men, who aren't supposed to think for themselves, or so the mantra goes.

So this old officer had his knee on my chest and was pulling on one of my bottom teeth when I felt my whole face cave in; my jaw was giving way. He started to pull again and I started screaming, "Please sir. Please sir. I am in pain!!!"

The nurse then came running in and shouts, "Stop that! His jaw's broken!" It was too late, he had pulled my mandible, the lower jaw, completely away from my skull, and it had fallen down across my larynx. I was now bleeding inside my mouth, swallowing blood, and I couldn't breath. A big panic broke out and finally they got some oxygen for me. They rushed me back into the ambulance and took me to Dublin Dental Hospital, where I underwent emergency surgery. They had to reattach my jaw and wire my whole face back together. I was in the hospital for a period of eight to ten weeks with my jaw wired shut, and at one point my weight dropped below five stone (70 lbs.).

For years after I got out of the Dental Hospital I had pain in my jaw, so somebody suggested that I take the whole lot of them, the dentist, the officers, and the whole Irish Army to court for treating me like they did. Even though I was a soldier, they said I shouldn't have been ignored, beaten, and tortured. So I went to a solicitor, an Irish lawyer, and the solicitor was horrified at what he heard. He took the case, which ended up dragging along for four years before we ever got to trial. I ended up bringing Ireland and the Irish Attorney General to the High Court for what they did to me. My solicitor called 50-odd witnesses to say that my version of the story was absolute truth, that I had asked to be allowed to fall out, and that I was completely neglected while unconscious on the ground. The Army only produced three witnesses, the sergeant, the young officer, and the chief medical officer, who all denied how it happened.

During the trial, the Army's attorney asked to speak to the judge in his chambers with my lawyer. They all trundled back into the judge's office and the Army's attorney asked the judge if the Army could settle the case with my attorney. The evidence was just horrific and he said he would like to settle. In Irish courts the judge has to agree to a proposed settlement when the case gets to trial. The judge denied his request because the judge felt the public had the right to know what happens to young men in the Army, and since reporters were in the room, the public had the chance to exercise this right. The judge refused to let the Army settle the case and cover up the abuse. So the trial continued.

At the end of the case, the judge summed it up for the jury. It went something like, "Ladies and Gentlemen of the jury, as you all know, there is no doubt about the outcome of this case. It is your job now, ladies and gentlemen, to put a price on this man's pain." The jury was dismissed to reach a decision, and we waited for four to five hours until they came back into Court. As they filed back into the room, I turned to my mother, who was sitting beside me, and said, "We've lost." She said, "No, no, don't worry about that. We're fine." I knew differently because as I said before, I was able to read things about people that other people obviously weren't able to see. So the foreman stood up and was asked to announce their decision. He said that we had not proved that the Army or the doctors had done anything wrong. The expression on the Judge's face said it all; he was totally shocked. He looked down and summed up his thoughts by saying, "Son, you've stepped into what's known as poor man's law." I didn't understand what that meant. The jury was then dismissed. Everyone, my solicitor included, was in total shock. My solicitor said, "Look, just go home for a couple of days and we'll speak to you then." Two or three days later I contacted my solicitor. He told me that we could appeal to the Supreme Court, but that an appeal would cost a lot of money with little chance of overturning the jury's decision. So that was that.

I didn't get anything for all that I had gone through. Thank God I didn't get anything because that abuse was just one of the ways for me to pay back society for what I owed, just one of the ways to pay back my karmic debt. That experience was also part of my apprenticeship in learning the truth about life here on this planet. What you will hopefully start to understand as you read this book is that we are all in an apprenticeship that brings us to our destiny. We aren't going anywhere in this journey called life; we are simply being. We are not evolving into something new. We are already the something into which we want to evolve. When you start to understand this, the struggle of life stops

CHAPTER 5

LINDA

Not long after my military experience, I met Linda, the woman who would become my wife. As I had started this lifetime in a dancehall, I loved to dance and went to disco and dance every chance I got. I even worked as a professional ballroom dancer whenever I needed to get some coins to rub together. As with all of the important events in my life, the circumstances of meeting Linda were seemingly coincidental and definitely karmic in nature. So there I was at this dance. Like all dances, at the start the boys sat on one side and the girls sat on the other. As if on a prearranged signal, we began to mingle. I spotted this girl from across the room and I was immediately attracted to her. Finally, I got the nerve to go over and ask her to dance. She said yes; so we danced a few dances, slow dances. I bought her an orange, and when the dance was coming to an end, I asked her if I could see her again. She replied, "Next week."

There I was, completely entranced by this lovely girl. We all went off on our own ways, and I decided to get something to eat in a local chip shop. Just my luck, when I went into the chipper, that same girl was standing there. So, as we waited for our chips to be cooked, I started talking to her again. With that, she said to me, "Would you do me a favor?" I said, "Sure, anything for a few brownie points!" She said, "Would you walk this girl home?" and pointed at the person who was going to share the rest of her life with me and become my wife.

I walked Linda home. It was about 10:30-11:00 p.m., and we sat on the wall outside her mother's home and talked and talked and talked. Time seemed to stop. It wasn't until the sun started to come up that we realized we had been sitting there all night talking. We ended up becoming steady lovers, and I learned a valuable lesson—the difference between love and lust. I learned how lucky you can be to have a partner you are in love with and not just somebody you have some sort of contract with—"you look after me and I look after you" type of marriage.

We went together for a little while and it didn't take long for us to know that we wanted to get married. We made arrangements to talk to her mother about our getting married. Her father had already passed away. I went to her mother and asked, "Could I marry Linda?" Now, at this time I was wearing Doc Martens (heavy boots) and jeans and had a skinhead. I must have looked like a right gouger, not the kind of fellow mothers like to see their lovely daughters hanging around. Perhaps being a little judgmental, her mother said, "No!" Both Linda and I were devastated by her mother's position of not allowing us to get married.

We left her house and went for something to drink. We decided then and there that we would to try to live together at least. The next day we ended up going over to a place called Brae to find a place to live. We decided that we would try to have a child together because if Linda were to get pregnant, then her mother would have to allow us to get married. I like to joke around and say that, being an ex-military marksman, I hit the "bulls eye" with my first shot because soon after that my absolutely fabulous son Gavin was born. Gavin was to come teach me some things in his own right as a great soul in his own being.

As soon as we found out that Linda was pregnant, we went back to Linda's mother to ask if we could get married. At first her mother said, "No," but when we told her Linda was pregnant, the "no" changed to a "Yes!" and we got married. I was 19 years old and Linda a little older. We had an absolutely wonderful wedding with lots of friends. We did the catering ourselves. Linda's brother, who was a chef at the time, handled all of the food. It was the best food I've ever had at a wedding, even though it was done on the cheap and there was very little wasted. I've been to many weddings that were lush and plush but everything was wasted and nobody really ate the meal. Those weddings were mostly for show and a bit of a farce. Our day was not a show. It was a day when two beings became one being. We didn't know then that our journey together would be so eventful, but eventful it was indeed.

Our marriage allowed two beings to come together to support each other through thick and thin, through the real trials that marriage can bring. We came through all the trials and stood together as a little bit of a lesson on how marriages can really be. Our marriage was an example of how two people can look in the same direction and follow the same path without being so dependent on each other that they stifle each other's growth. In our marriage we allowed each other to be everything we could possibly be, free to do anything we wished to find our way home to the light from which we came. Linda was called back to the light on August 25, 2008. She is with me more now than ever before. When she was in physical form, I could at least have some time to myself from time to time. With her by my side now all of the time, I have a teacher much more demanding than any sergeant or officer ever was.

After a couple of years, we had our daughter Orla. We did everything that parents are supposed to do, like love their children. If you ever meet my two babies, they will be very happy to tell you, "My dad is a shithead!" If you sit down with them, you will get all of my secrets out of them because they have no problem telling you the truth. My daughter's favorite story is about the day she wouldn't eat her dinner. I said, "You are going to eat your dinner. There are children starving in the world." But she wouldn't. I took her face and rammed it into her dinner. I rubbed it into the potatoes.

Gavin, my son, found himself through his violent father who became love. As I have explained many times before, I learned about love, you see, from my mother who was an alcoholic and beat me up morning, noon, and night. But I loved her. As you all know, I would classify her as one of my better teachers. I carried that chain to my family, and it was no bother for me to give my son or daughter a good slap because I thought that was the way love was. The day came when I hit my son, and it was like this light just went on in my head. I realized I could not do that anymore.

I walked out of the house and decided to write letters to my children. The letters basically said, "I am sorry. I was doing to you what was done to me. I thought I was right but now I believe there is a better 'right.'" I asked them if they would help me. They were eight and nine years old at the time. I asked if they would help me stop being violent. I wrote those letters with tears flowing out of my eyes, and I can remember thinking analytically, "I am not going to give them these letters." I was in fear of rejection from my own children.

I took a walk and decided I would put the letters in a letterbox. So, I put them in the letterbox, and after I did, I just wanted to drag that thing out of the cement. I realized I would have to be at home to get those letters the next day because there was a twenty-four hour turnaround on the mail. I knew those letters would arrive the next morning. I sat up all night waiting for the letters, and at a certain point I said to myself, "Derek, you need to go." I got into my car and drove four or five hours away from my home. Doing this, I knew there was no way I could get back before those letters were delivered.

The letters arrived. When I returned home, there was a banner up that said, "We love you, daddy." I fell apart at the seams. Then I became the good teacher to the kiddies, and they became my teacher. What I see my kids do, I do. It is good for the ego to let your children teach you. It is really good. What can I say? I realized I was carrying out my parents' traditions. It was one of those spiritual "AHA" moments when I realized that I was more like my parents than I wanted to believe. I could then start to understand what they must have been thinking or feeling when they were dealing with a stubborn and willful child like me. I began to think of my parents more as humans than monsters.

CANCER

One day I went in to see the doctors because I had been coughing and not feeling well. They took X-rays and then came in and told me that I had lung cancer and had four weeks to live. That was the funniest thing I had ever heard. I had never smoked cigarettes and was a devoted martial artist. I turned to them and told them I didn't have time to die. It was hilarious.

I went home and Linda was sitting there, and she asked me, "What's the story?"

I told her that I had tuberculosis, TB.

She looked at me again and said, "So that is what it is?"

I said, "Yes." I knew that I would have to go into the hospital for a bit for the whole chemotherapy, so I just said I had TB.

Linda knew something didn't add up and she started to get suspicious. She asked if she could go with me to the hospital one day. I told her that she didn't need to go and sit in that stuffy place. She said that she had nothing else to do. I couldn't change her mind, so she came to the hospital with me.

I distracted her by sending her to get a bottle of water for me. It was just enough time to tell the doctors and nurses that if they told Linda I had cancer, I would sue them for every penny they could rub together. I knew that Linda loved me so much that if she became afraid, it would bring fear into my consciousness. I could not allow it in.

While we were sitting there, the nurse asked me if I had my X-rays. I didn't have them with me. The nurse said that they needed a new set of X-rays, so they sent me down to the X-ray room. I was handed the new X-rays and brought them back to the room where Linda was. I handed them to the nurse, who took them into another room to be examined by the doctors.

The doctors were in there for a long time, and then one of the doctors came out and asked me, "Can you hang on for a while?"

I said, "Yes."

He went back into the other room and then other doctors showed up. Doctors were coming in and out of that room like a bus station. Linda was looking at me, and I was just sitting there not saying a word. Then the doctors called me into the room. I told Linda that she was not allowed in there. Well, she would have none of that. She barged her way into the room to find out what all the commotion was about. By this time there were six doctors in the room and they were all looking at my X-rays.

One of the doctors turned to me and said, "Whoa! A miracle has happened." Imagine that, a doctor saying those words. He must have been an alternative healer. He held up an X-ray and showed it to me. He said, "Do you see that black spot there on your lung? That was the cancer on your lung. See this X-ray? That was taken a couple of months later. The black spot is bigger. Now do you see this one? This was taken today. Your cancer is gone." With that, Linda smacked me. I didn't even see it coming. I am a black belt in martial arts, and she nailed me. That was Linda expressing her love and shock about finding out about the cancer and its disappearance.

CHAPTER 6

I FIND A TEACHER

I had a variety of jobs after I left the military to support my family and myself. I was a professional dancer, a martial artist, and lots of other things. I ran a very successful martial arts school, which had a waiting list of almost one year for new students. As I started to grow spiritually and regain my spiritual talents, I became more and more interested in what was happening on the inside of people, much more than what was going on the outside. I finally decided to study psychology and perhaps start counseling. So I ended my permanent school vacation and went back to school to learn about psychology.

One bright and lovely Sunday afternoon, Linda, Orla, and I set off on a trip to a bookstore. I had completed my degree in psychoanalysis and was in training for a private practice. I was a psycho, but I didn't know about the analyst bit. I had to get this book called *The Psychopathology of Everyday Life* by a very brainy guy named Sigmund Freud. As I reached for Freud's book, another book shot off the shelf and hit me on the toe.

As I bent down to pick up this book, my daughter came over and said, "Daddy, I bought you these."

She handed me a package of Sai Baba incense sticks. I had never heard of this character. You know, the Jimi Hendrix look-a-like. As I picked up the book, I noticed that the title of the book was *Sai Baba, Man of Miracles*. Being an extra clever guy and knowing there was something to this, I decided to buy the book.

When I went to pay for it, I was told, "We don't sell that book." The clerk didn't know how it got on their shelf.

So I stood there like a fool and told him, "It came off your shelf and I want to buy it." Then it dawned on me, as I am not very quick.

I asked, "Can I have it for free?" Suddenly, the book was eleven quid. I bought the book and went home.

That evening I was getting ready in my office for the patients I would see the next day. I think I had about nine people booked in to give them the psycho bit. I started to read the Sai Baba book, and as I read this book, anger welled up in me. I thought, "These people are flippin' mad." In the book, it was basically saying this guy is God! I thought, "Hang on. There is only one God, and that is Jesus." I knew because I was dragged up in the Catholic tradition and I knew Jesus was God. Now, here was this anti-Christ who looked like Michael Jackson and pretended to be Him. I knew this because I knew the Bible. I took the book and literally threw it away. No way!

I woke up the next morning to my phone ringing in my home office. It was my first client apologizing because she couldn't make her appointment. No problem. She said she'd be there the next week. Great. I put down the phone, and ring, ring. Within an hour and some minutes, all my patients had canceled. I was now sitting there twiddling my thumbs. This was unusual: it had never happened before and hasn't happened since. I saw that book again. I had nothing better to do, so I picked the book out of the trash and started to read it. Again, up came this energy, but this time came the energy that I remembered I had felt from the healing I had done when I was five and when I saw my mother's bus crash and all of that.

A voice with an Indian accent was coming in parallel with that energy. It said, "What is this? Why are you sitting there like this? Why don't you write and ask me?"

I thought, "What? Write?" So, I got a notepad and wrote, "My name is Derek. If you are who they say you are, send me vibhutti and I will come."

Vibhutti is this sacred ash that he manifests. The book said that if he produces vibhutti and gives it to you, it is a huge blessing and you can become enlightened if that is your soul's purpose. I had no idea if this was true or not, but that energy that I was feeling from my early spiritual experiences guided me to ask for it.

Anyway, I put the letter in an envelope and addressed it to "Sai Baba, India," which is like addressing an envelope to "Paddy O'Brien, Ireland," and hoping that it would get to the right Paddy. Nevertheless, I posted it. I only told two people in the world about this. One was my wife Linda and the other was a colleague of mine. I told them, "You aren't going to believe me, but I am about to find God in India, and he has a big mop of hair and an orange robe. We are all going to see him soon." I said this in complete mockery, absolute mockery, and I posted the letter. I thought about ringing the college and booking me a big room in the mad house. About three months went by, and still I waited for the reply that never came. I forgot all about it.

I AM CALLED TO INDIA

My colleague and I decided to go to this Mind, Health, and Body Exposition. So we went, and I walked around and looked at other people's exhibits. I was thinking that spirituality had become a big business, hadn't it? It's great as long as some of the money goes to help others for good causes. After all, it is a lot easier to pay the mortgage with money than meditations. Can you imagine going into the bank manager's office to pay the mortgage, sitting on his desk and chanting "Om?" Even if you start to levitate, security will grab you and out you go! Money is a necessary part of life. You just have to remember to give some back to its source and share it with others. I hear that some shamans in third world countries will even pour some of their Coke and a few chips on the floor to thank the creator for their food. You don't have to go that far; the world is messy enough as it is.

My colleague and I were looking at these exhibits and the next thing I knew, I felt this tap on my shoulder. A guy wearing an orange shirt was standing behind me.

He said, "Are you Derek O'Neill?"

I looked at him and said, "I am. Do I know you?"

I thought maybe he was a client or something like that. If any of my brain had been working at the moment, I probably would have run for the door.

He then said, "You know of me. Can I speak to you for a few moments?"

I said, "Sure," and asked my colleague to come with me to talk with him.

I walked off to the side with this guy, and we sat down at a table with a couple of chairs. He just looked me straight in the eye. It frightened the crap out of me.

He said, "Your name is Derek O'Neill. You were born in 1964, your first spiritual experience was when you were five, and when you were around seven, your mother almost died...."

I said, "Jesus Christ, stop!"

Every emotion you could have came up in one gulp. I was in complete fear. I had had spiritual readings and psychic readings, but this was not a psychic reading, this was beyond anything like that.

I said, "Stop! Who are you?"

Then he said, "I have something for you," and reached into his leather satchel and took out a tin box. He said, "This is for you." He pushed the small tin across the table towards me. It was like all your fears in one go, in a tin. He slid this tin across the table and said, "You asked for vibhutti. Now you must come."

I knew what was in that tin and it frightened me. I just grabbed the tin totally unceremoniously, turned to my colleague, who was standing there listening to the conversation, and said, "Let's get out of here!"

She had the same reaction that I had to this man, except that she turned and walked into the wall, nearly knocking herself out. She, too, registered what was going on. I grabbed her and the tin and scampered out the door. As she drove, I was in a heap. We went and had a cup of coffee. Until that day, I didn't drink coffee, but after that day, I have been drinking it ever since. We went into this café and we were having coffee. I shook so much the coffee literally spilled all over the place. I was rattled, but it was more of an energetic rattle. It was "kundalini" (life force) all over the place, as if I had been plugged into an electric grid.

The café door opened and in walked an Indian woman wearing a green sari. At that time, Ireland was not as multi-cultural as it has become. If you saw an Indian, or a person from another nation, it was a huge event. Well, in this Indian woman walked.

She looked straight at me and came up to our table and said, "Excuse me for disturbing, but didn't I just see you sitting with Sai Baba at the Mind, Health, and Body Expo?"

Whew! It happened all over again, the "kundalini" energy started vibrating in my body and I was plugged into the electric grid again. This was too much for my brain to handle.

I got up, said to my colleague, "This isn't happening!" and ran out the door to the car. Thank God she was driving.

I got home as quickly as my colleague could get me there and went inside to my beloved wife Linda for moral support and grounding. I ran in the door and told her what had happened.

And as calm as you like, she said, "What? Isn't that what you asked for?" As usual, she was dead-on accurate. Be careful what you ask for, because you may get it.

MY FIRST TRIP TO INDIA & DISCOVERY OF MY MISSION

After my experience with Sai Baba at the Expo, I very quickly arranged plane tickets to India. Linda couldn't come at the time, but my colleague was not going to miss out on this for love or money. We landed in India, and a show was put on for us. You have to realize that I came from this little island of Ireland and the only time I had been off it was the time I fell into the Irish Sea. I now realize that my ego was so big, that I needed to see it all. There I was in India, a completely different universe than what I was used to. The first thing that struck me was that the odors were completely different. The second thing that struck me was the mass of humanity as I stepped out of the airport. It seemed as if there were millions of them, and they were just there, milling around, holding signs with names on them. Above them was a haze of heat, and above that was a haze of flies. It was extremely uncomfortable, and I wanted out of there so badly.

As I walked out of the airport terminal, I noticed children playing in the sand next to the taxi. I looked at them playing in the sand and I had this thought: "Now look again." I looked back and saw that they were actually half-children. Their legs were gone, their arms were gone, and they had elephantiasis. They were just lying there in the sand. My heart blew open. I realized why I had come to India. There was no need for a child to go through this. This was man's consciousness holding onto suffering, which God never intended

We went to a hotel for a few hours, as we still had to fly on to Bangalore. When we got to the hotel, it was unlike anything I had ever experienced, even in the military. The toilet was a hole in the floor and the shower was buckets and a tarp. The bugs, which we couldn't see, were eating us alive. We just laughed and laughed, otherwise we would have had to cry. We left the hotel and went back to the crowded airport to wait for our flight to Baba.

We finally arrived in Bangalore, with one more leg on to Puttaparti. We got in a taxi and went off to Puttaparti to see Sathya Sai Baba. We arrived at his ashram, stepped out of the taxi, and again were immediately immersed in a sea of humanity. Strangers pulled at our bags and said, "Sai Ram (Praise God), sir. We give you room. Sai Ram, sir. We give you room!" All I noticed was that everybody wore pajamas and that our bags had gone in every direction. Then the leader of a gang of people came up and said, "There is no room in the ashram. I will get you a room in the lodgings." My ego took a giant step forward and I declared, "Sai Baba has sent for me." I didn't notice the thousands of other people that had been called there too. Millions of people go to Puttaparti hoping to see Sai Baba just as I had.

I went into the ashram, and I got my first real spiritual lesson in Puttaparti. I thought that spiritual people would be nice. I had this illusion that spiritual people were helpful, but I quickly discovered that is not the case when they are going through their stuff. It seemed as if a lot of people were going through their stuff that day, including me. I asked a person if he could tell me where the accommodation office was. He screamed at me, "Sai Ram! Sai Ram!" and another did the same.

Baba's staff plants these guys called Seva Dals, or people in service, who are supposed to help you. I went to them and they told me where the office was. Off we went; I thought we were making progress. We were en route and now carried our own baggage, which we had rescued. I went into a room; ladies were to go to the left, and men to the right. You show them your passport to get accommodations in the ashram. I walked in, and there were these two old men sitting behind antique desks. I think the desks were younger than they were. The only thing holding these two up was Divine Spirit; they looked as if they were going to die at any minute.

I was about to address one of the gentlemen and the next thing I knew, he let out this roar, "Sai Ram! Sai Ram! Chapal, chapal!!" All my years of analysis went out the door as my mother issues, my father issues, my every issue from every lifetime, arrived right there in front of me, brought on by this old man held up by spirit, who looked very strong all of a sudden. He is shouting, "Chapal, chapal!" The only thing I knew about chapels was that is where you go for Mass. I thought, "Oh, God, I have just stepped into a sacred chapel. This is the wrong office or something." Then I realized he was telling me to take off my shoes. Chapal means sandal or shoes in India. I got it. It is disrespectful in many cultures to wear your shoes indoors. I walked back out, took off my shoes, and walked back in. Here was the same old guy who sat in front of me, this time saying very sweetly and gently, "Saaaai Raaaam." Talk about schizophrenic.

He then said, "Sai Ram, you have returned. You have come back."

I looked at him and said, "You must be mistaking me for somebody else. I have never been here before."

Then he said, "Derek. . . ."

At that point my brain started to freak out just as it had at the Mind, Body, Spirit Expo and the coffee café. How did a complete stranger know my name?

He said, "Derek, you have been here many times, and many lifetimes. Swami has been awaiting your return."

It started again; all of the "kundalini" energy was running through me as if I had been electrocuted. I was in shock again, in more ways than one! I was lucky; I was given a room that had between 20 and 25 other men crammed together. I felt fortunate. I dropped my bags and went to find my colleague to have a look around. I could not find her anywhere, so I decided to go investigate a large building near my room (I remembered to take off my shoes this time!).

I was looking at a large picture of Sai Baba when a commotion started up behind me. When I turned around, there was Sai Baba surrounded by his Seva Dals. I took a few steps towards him and put out my hand to say hello. Suddenly a big hand hit me in the chest, and I went flying backwards. Offering a hand is not how you meet a holy man in India, especially someone as important as Swami. When I picked myself up, all I could see was Swami smiling at me. He walked past me into the building and left me to piece together what had happened.

I AM INITIANTED IN INDIA

The next day I got up after not sleeping at all. I went and sat on the roof of the ashram to meditate.

When I opened my eyes, an old man was sitting in front of me and he said, "I am to make you a Reiki Master."

I looked at him and said, "I am already a Reiki Master."

He said, "No, no. You did Tera Mai. I am to do Karuna Reiki."

I didn't even know there are different brands of healing. I thought they were all One and that people just put different names on them. You know, like the flavors of ice cream. It is all ice cream. If you don't like rum raisin, we had better give you chocolate chip. He told me that the initiation would be done the next day after "darshan," a ceremony that Swami performs every day for the devotees in the ashram. Basically, Swami blesses the thousands of people who come to the ashram every day that he is in residence in Puttaparti by simply walking among the people who sit and wait for him to notice them.

I went up to the roof the next day, and as I sat there, the old man said, "Are you ready?"

I said, "I am."

He started and went, "Boof!"

I can't remember anything after that. Nothing. My colleague had to fill in the blanks. She was looking up at the roof where I was. When we started, the sky was blue over the roof that I was on. She said that a cloud then appeared and it trickled light rain. Then a rainbow formed that just incorporated the roof. She also said strong winds were blowing. I don't know if that is true or not. I can only tell you what my colleague told me.

Anyway, he initiated me and it was over. I opened my eyes and thanked him. He gave me a symbol drawn on a piece of paper, which I didn't understand. Back then, when I didn't understand something, I pretended I did. That was an old pattern that I had. I was terrified of letting anybody know that I was stupid. Now I just say, "I haven't a clue what you are talking about." The man left, and then I left. I didn't want to bother him again and ask him about the symbol.

Not knowing what the symbol meant was bothering me, so the next morning I got the courage to ask what the symbol meant. I went over to where the old man, who initiated me, was staying in the ashram. I knocked on the door and a Buddhist monk opened it.

I said, "How is it going? The old man that lives here, is he here?"

He looked at me and asked if I was the man that had been initiated on the roof.

I said, "I am."

With that, he got down on his knees and touched my feet, which was very embarrassing.

I sort of dragged him back up and he said, "I need to tell you something. He has gone home. He had a private one-on-one interview with Sathya Sai Baba seven years ago. Seven years ago, Sai Baba told him you were coming and that he was to initiate you and he couldn't leave the ashram until you arrived. He went home this morning."

I thought about how that man had served God and waited for me. Seven years this man was in surrender waiting for me, who could have gotten there earlier if I hadn't struggled so hard. The struggle was good. I enjoyed every bit of it. That is what you are supposed to do. You see, when you are struggling, you know you are in your body. That is why, people, if you really want to know truth, don't listen to an idiot like me. What do I know? Listen to your heart when the words come, when the music and the energy come through. Your body is your guide. Your greatest teacher lies within. Your greatest guru lies within. God lies within. He sends messengers to awaken you.

Several years ago, after thirty-five years of practicing martial arts, I officially gave it up and closed the clubs. The last time I gave up an aspect of the martial arts was when I went to visit Sathya Sai Baba. It was festival time and thousands of people were there. Baba gave me a front-row place. Crowds lined the red carpet. I looked up and down the red carpet and saw a grasshopper. I realized Sai Baba would see it as he walked by but maybe some of his helpers wouldn't. I was sitting in lotus position, and I reached out and gently brought the grasshopper toward me. I just kept it under my hand. When Sai Baba was walking by, he stopped and kept kicking my hand. I looked at him but I was not getting it. He kicked my hand a few more times and then walked away. The question was, "Could I give up martial arts? Was it time to take on this mission more than the martial arts?" His answer was kicking my hand. What started me in martial arts was a television program called *Kung Fu* with David Carradine. His character's name was Grasshopper. God knows your needs and wants. He only delivers what is best for you. You need to know that whatever is given is 100% correct for you because God doesn't make mistakes. Learn to accept it. Be still.

I have never asked anyone to do anything that I haven't done myself. At one time I had an issue with cleaning toilets. I was in India when I realized I had this issue. So what did I do? I got up at about 11 p.m. because the ashram toilets are a sight to behold. I knew a Yogi had visited the toilet at some stage because there was an imprint of one foot on one wall and the other foot on another wall. There was no way you would sit on that toilet bowl. I got up and personally washed the lavatories with my bare hands. You could have eaten your dinner off them. Just before the sun rose again, I came out of the toilet and just for a second, I got the message to put up a sign saying, "God uses these toilets, too. Please keep them clean." I actually thought that was ego, so I never did it. I went and greeted the sun, gave thanks and gratitude for that experience to manifest that helped me resolve my issue of cleaning toilets. That is me. That is the way I am. Do you know who you are?

Chapter 7

Healing and Workshops

After I got back from Puttaparti, I continued my day job as a psychologist. I became a student of Sai Baba, and I have learned everything I know from him. I became a "Sai-co-logist." I felt as if Sai Baba were helping and guiding me all the way from India. I must have been good at my work—the association of psychologists asked me to train and counsel other psychologists. I couldn't help but laugh about that. There I was, the craziest nut in the whole tree, and they wanted me to tell them how to be psychologists. Life is hilarious. If you don't think God has a sense of humor, think about that one! So there I was enjoying life like a kid who had broken into the candy store. Six or seven years ago, God decided it was time for me to take my little show on the road. I started holding some workshops called "More Truth Will Set You Free." I thought that I had truly blown a gasket with that one because the idea was that I would get up in front of a bunch of people for a few days, tell a few jokes, and have some conversations with people, and people were supposed to pay me a lot of money for this stuff. Well, God insisted, and since I surrendered to God long ago, I started holding these workshops.

At first I held workshops in Ireland, and they went pretty well, so I decided it was time to get my feet wet and go to the U.S.A. I packed up my kit and hit the road and went to the land of plenty. I have been teaching "More Truth Will Set You Free" workshops in Ireland and the U.S. for several years now. It simply amazes me what God can do: people come from all over the U.S. and the world to listen to me flap my lips. I get to spend a few days with some really great people and some good friends, and they pay me for it! The secret to abundance, which really is not a secret, is to find out what you really enjoy doing and figure out a way to make money at it.

God wanted to make sure that this was what I wanted to do. The U.S. Immigration people interviewed me for three days before they would let me come into the country. They said my workshops were illegal. I asked them in a very calm voice, "Why?" They said that I could not make money on a tourist visa. I agreed with them, but told them that I was soliciting money to give to orphans and the street people of India. The money goes to the charities, orphanages, and humanitarian relief projects that Sai Baba instructed me to create and support. The organization we have now formed is SQ Foundation, and information about this organization can be found at www.SQ-Worldwide.com. The Immigration officers asked me for documentation and proof, and I gave them the names of two charities that I worked with. When you ask God for something, God usually gives you more than you ask for. So they asked me for one, I gave them two. Then they let me into the country to do the workshops.

During these workshops, I talk a little bit and let the people know what God wants them to know about loving themselves and others, finding Heaven and peace, and some of the truth about what is actually happening on the planet. God also sends people up to a microphone we put in the middle of the room and has them ask questions or ask for a healing of some problem with their life. These problems may be problems that you are dealing with in your life. I have summarized the teachings that were received at the workshops in the rest of this book. Suffering is universal; you may notice some common themes running through the questions and answers. It is the energy of the answers that does the healing. I don't do the healing. The energy is there for you to take in if you wish. Share it with your mates if they are suffering from the same sort of problem. So off you go; enjoy the teachings, and if you apply them in your life I guarantee you that your life will change.

Here's one last story before you go. When we held a workshop in New York City in 2006, we set up the room with three handmade wicker crosses on the wall. We started talking about why people suffer, and then one of the crosses fell off the wall. During the workshop, I just turned and smiled as if

44

nothing had happened. I continued to talk about why people suffer, and the second cross fell off the wall. Shortly after the second cross fell, the last cross fell off the wall and I finally got the message. Jesus has come down off the Cross and the time for suffering is over. Our healing has begun. The message was so clear that day as many people healed and the self-suffering was over. May you find your message in the words that follow to find God, whatever path you have chosen to follow.

TEACHINGS

CHAPTER 8

ABUNDANCE

Give away what you have. The most valuable thing you have to give is your love. Worry not about abundance. Whatever you need will come to you. You think something like: "Money, money, money must be funny in a rich man's world. All the things I could do if I had a little money." So why don't you have all of the money that you want? When you were growing up, your parents either told you that anyone who had money was no good or anyone who didn't have money was no good. Hollywood always portrays people that have a lot of money as unhappy or defective in some way. This is a common problem for many people: they have been brainwashed into thinking that there is something wrong with money. Through love or intervention of God they find the light, and the true nature of money is revealed, which is that money is an illusion, often just a number on a computer screen or a piece of paper.

The problem is not money; it is people's attitude towards money. Look at all of the beautiful buildings, palaces, and works of art that have been created with money. Some people have money; some people don't have money. If the people who had a lot of money shared their money, then we would all be the same. Money builds beauty. Money causes pain. Money can be what you want it to be. It is all the bloody same. Love costs nothing and costs nothing to give. When you have nothing, there is a lot to go around.

Some people choose to come into this life as millionaires, and they are unhappy. Some people choose to come into this life as poor, and they are unhappy. Some people choose to come in as millionaires, and they are very happy. Some people choose to come in poor, and they are very happy. It is not the money that causes happiness; the cause is the awareness underneath the money. Money is simply energy. Otherwise, it is simply a number on a piece of paper. Some people think that banks are buildings that hold money. Banks control the flow of money as the banks of a river control the flow of water. Banks also control the floods, which are wonderful unless you are caught in one. Floods break down restrictions. If you were to take down the restrictions on the flow of money, then the wealth of the world would all be One.

Some people are hardwired for pain, while others are hardwired for bliss. Some people love pain; others love bliss. There are people who love pain; you only have to watch them to figure out who they are. Look at Michael Jackson. Look at Britney Spears. Why they wanted to make their life so difficult is hard to understand. They literally had everything. As fabulous singers and brilliant artists, they just threw everything away. Somewhere in their lineage, in their experiences, there apparently was a crack, a defect. Until you face your pain and get to the source of it—until you see the gift of your pain—you will never get through the challenges.

At the core of everyone is a question, "What do I want?" For most people, the answer is happiness. Happiness has nothing to do with money, stuff, people, or possessions. Happiness has everything to do with love. People who think that their happiness depends on what or whom they own are projecting an illusion onto an illusion. People who spend all their life waiting to win the lottery or to find their soul mate in order to be happy have simply wasted their lives. Even if they win the lottery or find their soul mate, they still will be unhappy and they will end up losing the money and the mate. So thinking that you need abundance in this lifetime to be happy is a huge illusion, a party game. It is a delusion that your ego creates in the game of life to distract you from love. The truth is that if you were full of love and nothing else, then there would be no need for the ego and you would merge with the Divine Creator.

Desire only pushes the object of your desire away. Thousands of books have been written on how to manifest the objects of your desire. How ironic! People would spend their last penny to buy a book that promises to teach them how to be rich and to get what they want. The more you want something, the more you push it away. So the hawkers sell their wares to people who not only don't need them, the wares make sure that you stay in a state of lack. The hawkers have convinced you that since you don't have the perfect mate or the perfect house or the perfect clothes or the perfect anything, you lack. Oh, fantasizing about all the humanitarian things you could do with the abundance you desire may make the object of your desire even more desirable. The reality is that this fantasy will never become reality because under all of the fancy talk is the belief that you are in a state of lack. If you believe that you are in a state of lack, then that is what God will continue to give you.

When you believe you are in a state of Grace, you start to eat at the big buffet line of abundance. When you focus your thoughts on the Teacher and realize all of the gifts that you possess, especially the gifts of poverty, pain, or struggle, you can start to reap all of the happiness in the world. Once you have received the gifts of happiness, all of the things that you desired in the first place are no longer important, and your heart begins to open up to receive them.

So many people have the illusion that once they get on the spiritual path they have jumped onto the Divine gravy train. They spend their last dime; they max out their credit cards going to spiritual workshops with the hope that their luck will change, that their teacher has some magic power to save them from the consequences of spending their last dime on a spiritual workshop. I have no problem with taking your money. I give it to the homeless orphans in India for food, clothing, and shelter. If you come to workshops thinking that miracles and money will start raining upon you, then you have a serious misunderstanding of how the universe works. Common sense is always worth more than spiritual sense. Many keep coming to workshops, even though they haven't applied any of the teachings they learned years ago.

If you expect any kind of reward or return for anything you do instead of doing it in service to God, this is called reaching for the fruits of your actions. This applies to work and relationships. God always gives you everything you need; you simply do not see it because you want something else. You quit the job that provides money for food, shelter, and comfort in order to do what you want. You see others who appear to be earning lots of money by teaching spiritual teachings, and you think that is what you want to do. So you take spiritual workshops to learn how to do that too. What you don't understand is that the spiritual path is not intended to make anyone wealthy. Any spiritual teacher who applies the teachings keeps enough for a bowl of rice and veggies to eat and gives the rest back to God. The teachers who hoard what God brings to them are not creating abundance; they are living in lack and will create consequences for their hoarding.

Being like someone else may not be what God has planned for you. You all have your own destinies based on the consequences of your past actions and life purpose. Being like someone else may not be in accordance with your destiny. Your destiny may be to labor in the fields, not sit in a cave. Your destiny may be to find enlightenment at your desk, not in a monastery. Some beings sit in a cave for 40 years or more meditating and seeking enlightenment. They finally achieve enlightenment and come out of the cave to find that the world has built a highway right in front of their cave. As they cross the highway, God sends a lorry to see whether they are aware. The lorry runs them over and the great enlightened being who spent 40 years sitting in a cave has to come back to Earth for another lifetime. It is the desire to be like someone else that will always block you from achieving what you want.

Yes, you have probably met people who have quit their high-paying jobs to go on a spiritual path. What you do not realize is that these people, either consciously or unconsciously, have the resources to do this. They do not quit their jobs with credit card debt and mortgages and no money. They also have been given the guidance to do this out of service to God, not because they want to be like someone else. You also do not understand the price that spiritual teachers have to pay for their service. By choosing that path, you may be ridiculed, crucified, and even sued for bringing more light to those that need it. I am in pain every day, but I do not see it. I have been called everything from a cult leader to a thief. That is great! You may lose your house, and ruin your credit and your health to chase this dream. It is all an illusion, and it is great if you choose to do this.

"Ignorance is bliss." This is an absolutely true statement. When you step up onto this path, it brings about certain tasks. One of the tasks is to clean out anything that is not love. So, when you "step up," you may have dreams of leaving your job and opening healing centers and all. That is your will and has nothing to do with God. God has you in the computer job so that He can utilize you as a light when He needs to get energy into that building. The truth that will set us free is that wherever we are is obviously where we are meant to be.

God is always sending us proof that we are in the right place. I'd like to share a story from a woman who attended one of my workshops. She drove from her home and used over half a tank of gas to get to the workshop. She always thought she had free will until then. See, I don't want you just to believe anything I say; but try it out. If it works, isn't that wonderful? And if not, isn't that wonderful? When she left the workshop, she left accepting the fact that she was being guided. She could call on guidance whenever she felt fear. She was driving home to a place she had driven millions of times and, of course, this one time decided to get lost and took a wrong turn. She ended up miles and miles out of her way in the dark and the electrical system in her car was not working. So there she was: it was dark and she was not able to see the gas gauge. She only knew how much gas she had when she arrived in L.A. She passed a gas station and then another gas station, then another one, and then there were five in a row. She still didn't stop. She got home, opened the car door, and the dome light came on. When she looked, she saw that she had as much gas in the car at that moment as she did when she left Los Angeles. God always lets us know when we are on the right path.

What is really going on in this drama that we call life is that God has trained you to do exactly what you are doing right now. If you are moping and being angry and pissed off, correct! Perfect! Well done and off you go. If you are all happy, blissful, and excited, great! Wonderful! You have been trained through experiences you have had in this lifetime and many lifetimes, to prepare you for every moment that happens. So, if God wants somebody to do charity work, He certainly isn't going to pick Hitler. If He wants somebody to program a computer, He might pick my webmaster because he knows about computers. He certainly won't pick me because I know nothing about that. Each of these things has been programmed in your hard drive. They have been programmed in there for a reason and that is you need to act in a certain way when an energy hits you so that God's plan on Earth can manifest. You have been well trained. You are all experts. "Ex" is in the past and "spurt" is a leaky faucet, which makes everyone a "drip."

You have been trained to be where you are now. Does that not give you permission to just be here? It gives you permission to be who you are. It is okay to be pissed off. The Man sent us down with no instruction book. It is okay to be "who" you are. It is okay to be "where" you are. You couldn't be anywhere else despite you. For those of you who work in corporations, sometimes God has you in a corporation as a "Wayshower," a light beacon. He doesn't have you fully tweaked yet, but he may tweak you at any moment. If you are still enough, he will tweak you and you will become a strong influence on morality in the corporate world. There is nothing wrong with the corporate world; people's greed for money is the only problem. Your difficulty lies in the fact that you don't see this great message. God created everything. He created Starbucks, didn't He? That's a huge corporation, isn't it?

Recently researchers took one hundred thousand children and showed them lots of pictures to identify. There were two pictures in particular, one was the McDonald's clown guy and the other was Jesus. More children knew who Ronald McDonald was than who Jesus is. So, if God wants to get into the corporate world, he sends you in. He gives you an analytical process to get in the door. In Ireland I am a psychotherapist. But I don't think I have ever done psychotherapy in my life. When people come to me, we have chats and their life changes forever. Society and duality told me I needed to have this piece of paper and sit in my chair to tag myself in this way so I could get people in to see me. Everybody is exactly where he or she needs to be.

Spiritual people are confused because they have read too many books. If anything, you need to un-learn, not learn more. UN-learn. You need to take yourself out of your head and into your heart and say, "How do I feel about this?" The first thing you have to understand is, you are not the Doer. You have the ability to change the corporate world forever, and you are the reluctant Messiah. You have to do something that is quite a big leap in order to step into yourself, in order to be more still where you are and just allow the signs and teachers to come. Whoever your company is, keep it holy and sacred. And be careful of the company that you keep because you will become it. Be still and the signs will come. One day in Ireland I was playing a song, "I AM WHAT I AM," and as I was driving home, a bus went by with a sign with those very words on it. From now on, this is your sign.

You can be a spiritual teacher at your workplace. If you can accept the circumstances of your job, apply the teachings, and become happy at your job, you are well on your way to enlightenment. Yes, there are spiritual beings that do nothing but meditate all day long in monasteries. Their souls' purpose is to hold space for the planet so that you do not blow yourselves up. They have nothing other than the clothes on their backs and one bowl each. Are you ready for that? Far better for you to stay in your job with the money for your house, family, food, and clothing and apply the teachings you have already learned there, than to lose it all by following me around and not applying the teachings. The world needs enlightened clerks, enlightened lawyers, enlightened doctors, and enlightened accountants just as much as it needs the monks who meditate and hold space for the world. If God wants to have the experience of you losing your job and becoming a spiritual teacher, there is nothing you can do to stop it.

By comparing yourself to others, you are only causing suffering. Are any of the galaxies any better than the others? You are wishing that your life were different. This is the ego at work. You got yourself into the circumstances in which you find yourself. It is time to start taking responsibility for the consequences of your actions. You may think of yourself as a victim. Well, you are not. Change your mind. When you change your mind you will change your life. When you understand that God is constantly giving you opportunities to be happy no matter what, then you understand that you have a choice. Have you ever noticed that happy people seem to have everything that they need? A lot of them have everything that they want. That is because they have learned a very high spiritual truth. The secret to happiness is to want what you have.

There is an old Middle Eastern story about two men who had lost everything they had. They decided to go to the King to ask for help. On the way they met a beggar who was on his way to see the King as well. When they arrived at the palace, they decided to camp by the palace walls and go in to request an audience the next day. That night the King was wandering around the city in disguise, and he heard the men talking. The King went to the men and asked them why they had come to the palace walls. One man replied that he had lost his business to a partner who had betrayed him and had lost everything. This man was going to ask the King for some money so that he could start a new business.

The second man said that he had lost his wife and was broken-hearted. He was coming to the King to ask for a woman to be his wife. He knew the King had many wives, and he was going to ask for one to heal his heart. The third man, the beggar, said that he did not want anything from the King; he simply wanted to see what the King looked like.

The disguised King asked the beggar, "Surely, there must be something that you desire?"

The beggar said, "No, God provides all I need. If I do not have something, God obviously does not want me to have it." The King then left and went into the palace.

The next day the King sent for the three men. The men were brought in his presence and the King asked each if there was anything that they wanted from the King. Each man repeated what he had said the night before. The King gave the man who needed money 1,000 gold coins. The King gave the man who wanted a wife one of the palace maids. As far as the beggar was concerned, he repeated that he needed nothing; he simply wanted to lay his eyes on the King in his lifetime. The King sent them home.

After they had left, the King became outraged because the beggar had refused his generosity, so the King sent a warrior to kill the man who had nothing. The warrior sped after the three men. As they were walking, the man with the gold coins had become tired and asked the beggar to carry the coins for a while. The beggar replied that he would. Just after the man gave the beggar the gold coins, the warrior appeared and without a word cut off the head of the man with nothing. The warrior took the head back to the King.

When the warrior returned the head to the King, the King realized that the warrior had killed the wrong man. Even more enraged, the King told the warrior to return and kill the man who had no wife. The warrior ran after the remaining two men. While they were walking, the man with the wife grew weary and told his wife to keep walking with the beggar while he rested. After the beggar and wife had walked out of sight, the warrior came upon the husband and without a word cut off his head. The warrior took the head back to the King.

Once he saw the head, the King realized that he had killed two men in error. He told the warrior to return with the beggar. When the beggar was before the King, the King asked the beggar if he wanted the woman and the gold. The beggar said that he had no need for them, and he would return them to the King. However, the beggar said that if the King wished to do penance for the men who had died, then the King should send large sums of money to the families of the deceased men. This was done. The moral of the story is that happiness has nothing to do with money or relationships. You should always be content with what you have.

You have to expand the word abundance. I believe the only abundance worth having is love. I have tried sitting on the desk in the bank manager's office chanting, "Om." He said, "Sorry, you will have to leave now." We didn't have money to pay the mortgage. At one stage, Linda and I lived on a bowl of corn flakes a day because that was part of our learning process. So abundance is yours. You can have billions if that is what you want. You can have it all. But if you become the camel, in other words, if abundance becomes a hump, now it is a problem. If you think you need more, now your ceiling on desires has gone. It is okay to wash in cold water. I can tell you that the people in India would give much for just that cold water.

You have to keep expanding into the bigger picture. If you are brushing your teeth while the water is flowing down the sink, shame on you for wasting that water. Why would you do that? That doesn't mean you become some sort of a miser and only use a tiny bit of water when you brush your teeth. It means just be conscious of your actions and see what your actions are manifesting as your future. Because what you sow is what you reap. Love is the answer. Now what is the question, right? As I say, when you are in a state of fear, don't talk to me about love.

You must always meet people on their level. That is why teachers contradict themselves all the time. When a question is asked, I answer on the level of the person who asked the question. This same question could come two hours later from someone else, and I would probably give a completely different answer. I have to meet you where you are. We have to become brother souls. It is no good if I come back in full Puna Avatar (Incarnate Divine Teacher) mode. You guys wouldn't get to see me. That is just the way it is.

It all is to bring you to the understanding of one thing that you will come back to time and time again: Grace falls upon you like the rain. When you need it, it is there. At times, you will be in the desert. When you need it, if it is God's Will, Grace will be there. That is true abundance.

Some people call me teacher. Some call me guru. Some call me Derek. Some call me "shithead." Some call me whatever. It is all perfectly fine. I don't accept any of those tags, because I am none of them. I am all of them, plus more, more than people can comprehend. That doesn't make me egotistical; that just makes me who I am. All these experiences I have had have brought me to where I am now with God's Grace. You see, it was God who raped me. I just never recognized Him. It wasn't until he showed me later on, and I said, "Oh, my God! That is it. That is great."

A young boy came to one of my workshops, and I took his cap. At the end of the workshop he said, "You are the man that has been in my dreams my whole life." I said to him, "That is correct. Welcome home." I hugged him and swung him around. He looked past "Derek" and saw what was sitting in front of him. He looked past the matter and went into Divinity. He did it as soon as I walked into the room. His energy was the first energy to connect with me that day. So I stole his hat and stuck it on my Crown Chakra (center of spiritual power on top of the head). There were people in the audience who would have given their left arm to have that happen. When I offered it back to him, he said, "No, that is fine." Non-attachment. That is the way of our journey.

There was a great, great guru on the planet. His name was Krishna Murti. Krishna Murti was looking at television one day. Imagine that, gurus look at television. So, he was looking at television and he saw these baby seals being clubbed to death. He turned off the television and that was it. He recognized it. He saw God's Will and he turned off the television. He was not going to allow that information into his body to pollute it. He just turned it off.

At the same moment, an actress in Hollywood called Bridget Bardot was looking at the same program. She was so moved by Divinity that she set up a charity that has raised millions of dollars. Here are the two reactions: if you are meant to be seeing that television program and you are moved by it, then do something about it. But if you can see that it is part of God's Will, you turn off the television. Both ways are correct because God works in the balance of duality.

If you are moved to do something, move! Otherwise you will suffer. This is how God will give you your mission. He will move you. He moved me by showing me the half-bodies of children in the sand in India, and look at me now. If I hadn't seen those half-children in the sand, I would be fishing. I didn't realize I was catching the salmon of knowledge.

That is the way the world works. It brings you to these great heights, like a bird that picks up a nut, and when he is up really high, drops it. Welcome to life. That is what life is about. That is just the way it is. Before you can have anything else, you have to have love. There is only one home worth going to and that is where God cleverly hid himself, in your heart. All other homes are transient, and they too will pass. Be willing to let them go and you will begin to grow; hold onto them and I don't know.

CHAPTER 9

ADDICTIONS

There are children on our planet now that you call junkies and drug addicts. That is their only mission on the planet. What they are doing is soaking up the pain of Mother Earth. And they don't even know it. Why would you judge, unless you don't know what you are doing? Maybe what you can do is to stop judging and criticizing others for following their destiny.

First, you have to know what an addiction is. Some people would say that an addiction is a way of masking emotions or issues. Others would say it is giving your power to a substance, allowing something to take control of your life. Some others might say that people can't stand life, so they want to numb themselves or distract themselves. Still others might say that people prefer to be high rather than deal with reality. A harsher way to describe addiction is to say that it is a coward's form of slow suicide.

All of these descriptions would not be wrong and they cover the basics of what an addiction is. The truth is that addiction is depression backwards. Depression is a decision by people, either consciously or unconsciously, to refuse to participate in life. Depression is anger without enthusiasm. The "backwards" part comes in when the enthusiasm is misplaced into drugs, sex, food, money, people, places, or things.

Addiction is also an attachment to something. When you are attached to something, you believe that you can't live without it. That belief creates a fear of losing it, which in turn forces you to want to control it. The more you try to control it, the more deeply ingrained the attachment becomes, and it becomes the habit from first-class hell.

In order to be free, we have to let go and change any and all addictions. Like all habits, addictions can be changed, but it takes discipline, concentration, and effort. The easiest way to let go of an addiction is to have it 100%. Most people who have addictions try to balance their life with their addiction, and they manage to keep the addiction going for years. They do not want to have the addiction 100%; they only want it enough to make themselves numb without suffering the consequences of the addiction.

It is not until people claim their addiction 100%, which is sometimes called "hitting bottom," that people are forced to decide whether to live or die. A 100% addiction will bring you to the dark night of your soul, which is the only place you are confronted with the question of whether to stay in this life or to go. The highest truth is that the ultimate addiction, the ultimate habit, is death. When we decide to stop being ruled by the fear of death and fully embrace life, we become fully empowered and begin to realize the concept of immortality. It may seem impossible, but there are actual beings who have been in the same physical body for over 1700 years. One documented saint is Babaji, who has been in the same body since 300 A.D. If you don't believe me, go research it. I don't want anyone to believe anything I say. You have to prove it to yourself. If you believe what I say and like me, great! If you don't believe what I say and don't like me, great!

When people enter the "dark night of the soul" and make the decision to live, life takes on a whole new depth, a whole new dimension. If you read the details of the life stories of many of the religious saints, they all were confronted with challenges we would now classify as addictions that they had to step out of. When you keep trying to rescue people who have addictions and keep them from reaching the dark night of their soul, you are interfering with their karmic destiny to pass through that dark night of their soul. If you know people who keep relapsing, let them fall into the bottomless pit and make their own decision to free themselves from the addiction cycle. Many people who have recovered from their addictions will tell you that it was not until they were faced with the possibility or reality of losing everything that they decided to change.

The reasons many people use drugs or alcohol is to get out of their mind. They have an overwhelming need to be closer to God, and the only way, they think, to accomplish that is to stop their minds with drugs and alcohol. Now, they may think that they are chasing a high or escaping pain, but the underlying cause is to get closer to God by stopping their minds. It works for a little while, but always the mind comes back and disconnects them from being closer to God. The lesson of alcohol and drugs is that they will stop the pain for only a short while, and then the pain comes back. When the pain comes back, it is always worse than before the alcohol and drugs. It is much easier to let go of the pain.

When you are ready to change an addiction or habit, the challenge is to stay focused long enough for a new habit to form. The new habit can be anything that creates a positive response or brings balance into your life. When people come into my presence, my energy and consciousness will not allow them to smoke, overeat, get drunk, or engage in their negative habits. My energy will not allow it. Many people come to my workshops and do not smoke a cigarette for days for the first time in years, even without meaning to stop. What is it that you allow in your life? Do you allow addictions into your life or do you let them go? People smoke or get drunk if that is their conscious decision. That decision is their free will.

I have had some success with helping my clients stop their addictions. It is very simple. I tell them to offer their addiction to God. I ask them to imagine God drinking that beer instead of them drinking the beer. I ask them to imagine God smoking the cigarette, not them smoking the cigarette. Then I ask them when they feel that God has had enough, to stop. I have had success with hundreds of alcoholics with this technique.

It takes the human body 21 days to form a habit. It takes 21 days to change a habit. You have to stay focused for 21 days to halt the addiction program running in your body. So, to stop any addiction, you have to concentrate on not using for at least 21 days. With smoking, this is how it works: if you can stop or stay off for 24 hours, you can stay off for 72 hours. If you stay off for 72 hours, you can stay off for 17 days. If you stay off for 17 days and then 21 days, the subconscious reasons for smoking have stopped running and are gone. That doesn't mean that new reasons for smoking won't come up and you may start again. If you are not through learning your lessons, you will repeat them until you are.

There is a very effective meditation that you can do to stop a craving. Close your eyes and imagine that you are sitting at a large table that is filled with what you crave. It could be alcohol, cocaine, little blue pills, little red pills, chocolate, food, or photos of pornography. Whatever your addiction is, it is sitting there in front of you. When you are ready, imagine eating everything on the table. Eat until your sides are bursting, your stomach hurts, and you start to gag. Imagine that you aren't through; you can eat some more. You eat and eat and eat. Finally, you start throwing up. Imagine the taste, the sound, the smell of your vomit as you vomit it all up into a big bucket on the floor. Imagine seeing bits of what you ate floating around in the bucket of vomit. You see the famous carrots floating around that you never ate. How did those orange bits get in there? Those are your stomach enzymes that you use to break down what you eat. Your craving is not done. You pick up the bucket and start eating the vomit. You are filling up again, this time with the vomit. You eat until you feel truly sick and will never eat that stuff again. You imagine that the vomit in your stomach turns into a beautiful golden light. It is love; it is the light of God. You begin to expand as more and more love pours into your body. The light is what you really wanted; you wanted love. If you do this meditation every time you have a craving, it will eventually go away and you will not want what you were addicted to again.

Many people have stopped an addiction, and let go of an attachment, but when faced with a stressful situation, they start the addiction all over again. This is not because the old reasons for their addiction have come back; it is a reaction to new reasons to "lose their mind." We all have a deep subconscious desire to go back to God that can be triggered by a stressful or traumatic situation. In that situation, the person is not through with the lessons surrounding artificial methods of escaping pain. There is no reason for shame or guilt; simply realize that those people are not through with the lesson. When they revisit the dark night of their soul, they will again be faced with the decision to live or die, and their decision will have its own new set of consequences. This is the game called life!

The closer you get to the truth, to knowing who you really are, the easier it is to drop your addictions. Addictions are created in the fear of being unlovable. You become addicted to the fear, the anger, the guilt, and the shame that build into addictions to substances, people, or things to try to numb that fear. Or worse, you become addicted to love and keep shoveling whatever substitutes you can find into your body to make yourself feel loved. When you find out that you are love and that you came into being to be love, then you start to let go of the fear of what you are not and merge with what you are. All you need to do is to get closer to the truth, the truth, the truth, and nothing but the truth. The closer you get to the truth, the more likely that all of your addiction just disappears. That is why all of the great teachers have come to make us "desireless." It's not to desire less, which is to still have attachments, but "desireless," which is totally without desire, nothing.

CHAPTER 10

ANGER AND DEPRESSION

Inside violence causes far more damage than outside violence ever will. The truth is that outside violence is merely a mirror of the inner suffering and violence of the persons participating in the outward violence. War will never stop until you stop the violence in your own hearts. The irony is that the inner battles create the outer battles, but the outer battles must cease before the inner battles can be healed. It is the classic "chicken or the egg" dilemma. You have to be still and focused and disciplined to bring peace to your heart. If you spend all of your time fighting your family, boss, co-workers, society, and God, you do not have time to deal with the inner battles. The battle on the inside is fought between the duality of nature, between the illusions of right and wrong, and good and evil.

Anger and depression are the same thing. Anger is energy projected outwards; depression is energy projected inwards. This energy is very simple: it is the consequence of the struggle between what you want and what God wants. It is the friction of you going in one direction and God tugging you in another direction. It is you resisting God's love for you because you think you are unlovable. Depending on how your parents taught you to handle this energy, you become either angry or depressed. If your parents were patient and forgiving, they probably let you throw temper tantrums and then sent you to your room to finish them. They tolerated your anger, so you learned to direct the energy outward. If your parents were not tolerant of your anger, they trained you to suppress it by "giving you something to cry about."

You deal with anger and depression by surrendering and realizing that everything is a lesson. You realize that you are not the Doer; you are only here to experience life. The fact that you are not getting what you want can be simply healed by wanting what you get. Success is getting what you want; happiness is wanting what you get. The bottom line is: what is underneath the anger? Is it fear that your parents or God don't love you? Are you angry or depressed because something happened in the past that you don't like? You have to understand that was God experiencing that experience, not just you. God was the person who did it to you, and God was the person who experienced it. When you understand that these events that make you so angry or depressed did not happen to you, that it was God doing it to God, then the energy of resistance fades away and all that is left is love.

If you take medication, you have to understand the purpose. Doctors have pills for every ill. Many people need medication so that they can hold onto themselves while they make a spiritual transition. You take the medication until you learn this concept and then you don't need it anymore. Some people take the medication to have something in common with all the other pill-takers, so they can feel like they fit in. I remember going to a doctor once. Luckily enough, I had a bit of enlightenment then, so when we sat down in his office, I pulled my chair around to his side of the desk. The doctor went into shock. It is in that space that you let go of depression and anger.

Many people think that they are angry and depressed because of their parents. Basically, you did not get the parents you wanted. Your parents abused you, criticized you, and taught you all sorts of bad lessons. So you are angry and depressed because you think you got a raw deal, that God made some kind of mistake. You think that life isn't fair, so you suffer. You suffer because you think you are some kind of mistake. Who wouldn't get angry if they thought their life was a mistake? You hurt, and that makes you angry. You don't know what to do about it, and that makes you angry. Here is the truth: you hurt because you love them and you think they don't care. This is true whether it is your parents, God, yourself, or someone else. What you have to do is admit to yourself that you really do love God, yourself, your parents, or that someone else and get over the fact that they aren't acting the way you want them to act.

When you have moments of frustration, you don't have to walk further down the path of frustration. You can stop for a moment and say, "Hang on.

Hang on a moment." That is why you have to stop when you are in pain, emotional or physical pain. You stop by going within and experiencing your Divine nature. If you choose to take on something that is painful, stop and ask yourself, "Why would I want to hurt myself?" If you believe that you are not hurting yourself, then why are you hurting? If you believe that someone else is hurting you, that is separation consciousness. One plus one equals two, which is separation. If you understand that it is you who are hurting you, then one plus one plus one plus one plus one plus one equals ONE. This is called Divine math. You let go of the anger and depression and become ONE with everything. But you go to your Divine Self and say, "Please make me whole, but not yet!" Why "not yet?" If you get to be too good, then you will leave the planet and go to the higher planes of existence.

Who would want to leave here and miss all of this beauty and fun? Who would want to come here and stay for just a minute as some babies do? These are highly advanced souls that only need to be in a human body for a very short while. That is why you do not need to be angry when a child leaves its body. It only came here to experience life for a short while. It experienced what it needed to experience and then went back to the light. For me, I want to experience it all. I want to eat the whole field of grass, not just one blade. It is all an illusion anyway. One plus one plus one plus one plus one equals ONE.

Life is a bit like a pendulum. One end of the arc of the pendulum is unhappiness, and the other end is happiness. Isn't that what life is like? Like a pendulum swinging back and forth? What happens basically is that if you start looking at the truth, it swings to unhappiness. You don't want to be unhappy, which makes the pendulum stick at the end of unhappiness. If you understand that pleasure is the space between two pains and pain is the space between two pleasures, you will understand that the pendulum swings back and forth depending on whether you are attached to where the pendulum is. If you trust that happiness always follows unhappiness, the pendulum does not stick on unhappiness. You can tell where you are on your journey depending on how long you stay unhappy.

When my wife Linda graduated to the higher planes, I processed my human emotions of grief and anger in about an hour. Then I let go of them. I was not attached to the feelings of loss or unhappiness. Many people take years to grieve the loss of a loved one, and some people stay angry for years. When you can understand that the soul is immortal and we never lose anyone, the pain does not come. If the pain does come, it does not stay long. The truth is that Linda is with me more than ever. I am in constant communication with her Higher Spiritual Being. She has not left at all. You can let go of anger and depression if you understand these are temporary states of mind. How long you hold on to these states depends on how attached you are to having life your way.

CHAPTER 11

ATTACHMENT

Most people who think that they are on a spiritual path learned the art of detachment before they learned anything about attachment. What people really ought to do is learn all they can about attachment before they get into detaching. My experience is that many people are simply numb, but they call it detachment. They never get to recognize attachment; they just avoid dealing with it. Detachment is when you can feel the pain of others without stepping into the melodrama surrounding or suppressing it.

Attachment is when you believe that you need something and you won't be able to live without it. At its core, attachment is simply a belief. You attach yourselves to ideas, beliefs, emotions, people, and material stuff. You attach yourselves to me sometimes, and you need to stop that. Don't become attached to me; I will let you down. Become attached to the Divine Being that lives inside this body and inside your body. Parents attach to children, children attach to parents, husbands attach to wives, and wives attach to husbands. You attach to your jobs, clothes, money, status, and religion. You attach to meditation, knowledge, and spirituality. You are attached to desires. One attachment that you have that you really can't do without is breathing. The number one cause of death is shortness of breath.

You are attached to your body. It is hard to live on this planet without one, after all. You are attached to your psyche, your personality. That is who you are; you don't want to lose that do you? If you want to feel safe, you have to find the truth, which is the part of you that is aware, that is immortal. You can never be hurt. The physical body can be hurt, your emotions can be hurt, but the part of you that is aware can never be hurt. The only way to learn detachment is to become 100% attached to something. Then you have something to offer back to God. It is the same as people wanting to manage their addictions. You have to experience your attachment until you recognize it is an attachment and then give it all to God.

Many times people feel that they need to forgive in order to become detached. Forgiving is good, forgetting is better. Go deeper. The truth is that if it is all God's will, there is nothing to forgive. There are only lessons. I have no fear. I don't know what fear is. Suppose you shoot me, then what? That is God's will, and I have been an instrument of God's will. I don't need to forgive you because we were playing out God's will. My workshops are play-shops, not work-shops. When you are at play, you feel safe. That is why most people go through life play-acting. They act out somebody else's life because they don't like their own life. They don't want to live their own life because someone mentioned the word perfection to them. They have not been able to be perfect, so they play being something else. They have not been able to live up to that standard, so they struggle.

You fear because you think that God has gotten it wrong, that you are a mistake. You feel that you will never get it right, making mistake after mistake after mistake. This is a program you were born with or were given by your parents. Do you really believe that God thinks that you aren't good enough? Events happen. Deeds are done. As with all actions, there are consequences. Your illusion is that you are doing it all. You are not, God is. You are not the Doer, only God. In order to petition God to remove your illusion, you can't come as a beggar anymore. You can't be polite. You may not always oblige, but you can always speak obligingly. You don't come with "dis-ease," you come with complete ease.

One of the best places I have found to petition God is in my bed. One of my prayers is, "God, if you want me to do your will, you better take this from me or screw off." You have to say your prayers with enough energy to get God's attention. I would lie in bed with my legs crossed and my hands behind my head. I would dare God to move me. I dared him to move me. Then I got a pain in my back and I moved. I got off the bed and made tea for my wife and me. Then it went from there. The one prayer that God must answer is the prayer for love. If you pray to God to love you, he must love you.

The struggle is an illusion. You have read all the books, you have taken all of the courses, and you take workshop after workshop. Still you struggle. Take all of the millions and zillions of your struggles, desires, pain, and broken dreams and imagine that they are all single gossamer threads of gold and weave them into a very strong rope. Then tie yourself to the feet of the Teacher, the Creator. There is a story about a fisherman who came to the river and threw out his net. There was one old fish that was very large and peaceful. He never got agitated when the fisherman appeared. One day the younger fish decided to ask him how it was that he had never been caught. The fish said it was very simple: "I knew when the fisherman stepped into the water, he would throw the net away from himself. I would always swim to his feet."

I was once ranked number 11 in the world in fly-fishing. I would often win competitions with a barb-less hook. One of the tricks that I learned was if you hooked a fish and it swam away from you, then you could always capture it. If it swam towards you, it would get away. This is your task, to swim as fast as you can with Grace to God, with all of the teachings you are accumulating on a higher level of being, as the lower levels are dropped away. One day my boat and rod were stolen. I went home and later found the book about Sathya Sai Baba, a story I mentioned before. I read it, and my journey began. I now have become a fisherman of souls.

CHAPTER 12

BLOCKS

I am often asked to remove this or that block because people think that they are stuck. No one is stuck. No one is ever stuck. People are always changing, whether they want to or not. People are always talking about being stuck or going backwards. There is only one direction, and that is forwards. We are here to experience life and to learn to have fun with the experiences. We continue to get experiences until we learn to have fun and to love. Everyone wants to have the same experiences all the time, the experiences that they want. They want to experience life the way they want. How boring is that?

People think that they have put blocks in their path and that they are doing something to keep them there. That is incorrect thinking. Everything comes from God. God gives us experiences so that we learn to love and to have fun. We are the ones that say, "I don't like that experience, so I am going to react in a negative way because I didn't get what I wanted." If you resist, if you struggle, then you keep getting bigger and bigger experiences until you learn to love and have fun.

Suffering comes from desiring life to be different. You don't have the mate, job, salary, toys, or feelings that you want, so you suffer. You criticize others, yourself, and God because you are not getting what you want. You criticize yourself because you think you are doing something wrong. Even worse, since you think that you are the one who must have done something wrong, you think you are being punished. This is the way people think, whether you didn't get the body you wanted, the money you wanted, the mate you wanted, or the life you wanted.

God puts experiences into our lives so that we learn what we need to learn before we go on to the next lesson. God set up the universe this way so that we don't get all of our lessons at once. God puts in these speed bumps so that you don't rush and go too fast. If you rush, you will get an experience that feels like a brick though a window. It would be like you storming the gates of Heaven. When you are in Divine timing, everything is wonderful. It is our ignorance and misunderstanding that makes us think that something is slow or fast. There is only Divine timing, there is no slow or fast. When you feel that you are stuck or not moving at a pace that suits you, then you have to look for the lesson. When you accept the fact that God created whatever block you think you have and that God created it for your own good, it makes you feel much better.

My mother placed a number of blocks into my life. She was quite psychic and terrified of her visions. When I started having visions early in life, she was terrified that I would be hurt as she had been hurt. She knew that those in fear would bring me to task. She tried to save me from experiencing what God wanted me to experience. So I blinded myself from these visions and became "normal" for a while. When I was ready, when I had learned the lessons from the experiences I had, God removed the blocks and I began to see again.

Many people are always running. They run from appointment to appointment. They run from relationship to relationship. They run from teacher to teacher. They are running from life. They need to experience being still. God is putting blocks in their life so that they will experience being still. People are always saying, "I want enlightenment and I want it now! Can you remove the blocks to my enlightenment?" The best gift I can give these people is to teach them that the blocks are there so that they will be still long enough to let enlightenment sink into them. When they realize that the blocks are for their benefit and they become still, the blocks will disappear. Then they get their next set of blocks. Isn't that great? Building blocks!

Learn to yield and be soft if you want to survive. Learn to bow, and you will stand in your own full height. Learn to empty yourself and be filled with light and love. The first concept of life is "You are not the Doer." That is the concept you have to understand to come from your heart. Otherwise, it will all come from your head. Imagine your moment has come and you decide you don't want to die. You are coming from your head. All this imaginary fear—there is darkness there, you are leaving your loved ones behind, and the ego of egos, and they won't be able to go on without you. Then Divine Grace comes and says, "Grasp as you will, you are coming with me." Divine Grace shows you the illusion of your thoughts, and your letting go then comes.

When you watch someone die, you see a pattern of death. I can usually tell two years before someone dies—the day, the time, and how. On a spiritual level, I see it in a moment. It is a journey to what we call death. Keep in mind, there is no death. So we learn to let things go. As you learn to let go of your family, as you learn to let go of your pets, you practice death. You practice death even by letting the next-door neighbor park in the space first. The main practice is for you to let go. If you can't, the Doer will do it for you. So surrender is what it is about. How do you do that? The next time you go into a shop and you see something you want, let it go. Offer it up. Now you are practicing dying, dying to the senses, to your emotions. You are being prepared.

You come into the world naked and you leave the same way. When Adam and Eve did their stuff in the Garden that was when God put skin on us. Before that, we were only balls of light. That skin has grown into reptile skin for some because they are so fearful. Feel the letting go through sacrifice. Then it will come in gently when it comes to that bigger letting go, and with it you actually start to rejoice about dropping that skin and taking on that light form again.

Let it all go. It has nothing to do with you. You are not the Doer—God is the Doer. You think people need you? They need God. You can be the instrument that you can be. In order to do that, you need to make yourself as clear an instrument as possible. Krishna blows through the flute. That is what you are, the flute. The more you unlearn what you thought was right, the sweeter the sound you will make as God sends the Divine wind through you. Unlearn the duality of right and wrong, good and evil, because it is all God. When you see God in everything, you will understand the beauty of the world.

CHAPTER 13

BREATHING

If you learn to breathe, you will be given everything. In other words, did you ever see a dead person do yoga? Your focus is on the physicality of the movements to get balanced, but the breath would give you the gift of the balance. When most people do a physical act, they tighten their muscles to do it. Masters loosen everything to do it. In the martial arts you have Tai Chi. Tai Chi is done with the smallest amount of movement to get the biggest effect. It is all done by lifting air into certain "nadies." Think of a meridian and a point on the meridian. In acupuncture, that point is called a nadie.

When you breathe, you not only breathe in air, you breathe in energy. This energy circulates through your body. This is why the number one cause of death is shortness of breath. When you do not take in enough energy, your body deteriorates. Only yogi masters can continue to live after they stop breathing. They have learned how to sustain their energy without breath. You are welcome to try not breathing, but I would not recommend it. It is important to realize that what you think about while you are breathing is just as important as the physical breathing. Gandhi would think "Sai Ram" with every breath, which means, "Praise God."

The best breath is called the "So Hum" breath. When you breathe in, say to yourself, "Soooooooooo," and when you exhale, think, "Hummmmmmmmmm." If you went back and were able to talk to the great Masters that have been on this planet and they were speaking the truth, they would say that without "So Hum" there is nothing. "So" means, "I am God." "Hum" means, "I am not separate from God." Get some technical people to come and stick a microphone in your face when you are breathing. You listen, and what you hear is "So" on the in breath and "Hum" on the out breath. "Sooooo Huu-ummm." There is the essence of the truth. You come into alignment, alignment, and alignment with the truth. One plus one plus one plus one equals ONE. So which one are you? Make your way back to that one if you have any sense of separation. You don't do it by going up. You do it by going forward.

Be aware of your breathing. Is it relaxed or hurried? Is it deep or shallow? When you don't get enough oxygen, your brain goes into survival mode, which is also called "Fight or Flight." Your body's physical reaction to lack of breath is fear. This fear will paralyze you or make you say and do things you would normally never consider. Taking deep and regular breaths will overcome the fear. When you feel threatened, you must be conscious of your breathing. When you are sick, you must be conscious of your breathing.

Proper breathing helps to balance and to produce calmness and happiness. If you are unhappy, perhaps you are not breathing properly. Fear, anger, depression, and negative emotions often are produced from improper breathing. Relaxing and breathing properly will eliminate the negative emotions. Deep and regular breathing allows your brain to function so that you can contemplate and focus on what needs to be done. Deep and regular breathing creates a space into which you can pour love and compassion.

Improper breathing also causes confusion and frustration. You have come to remember to forget what you forgot to remember. Now that you have forgotten to remember, you have remembered to forget. The clarity is all there, but now that the clarity is all there, you have forgotten what the question was, but now that the question is answered, you now know what the answer should have been before you put the question out there. Still confused? How many times did you breath while you were reading that statement? Keep breathing!

You do not have to get tired if you are breathing properly. You can give all of your energy to others and still be fully energized if you are breathing properly. When you are breathing properly, you fill yourself with Divine energy, which is capable of going on forever and ever. Some people will come to you for that energy with thimbles, and some with forty-foot containers. You can be the "Wayshower" and the Light, or you can try to hold onto it for yourself. If you do try to hold onto it for yourself, the Light will start to retract and go away. If someone is draining your energy, it is an emotional cord. We need to cut the ties that bind. Share the love. It doesn't mean the physical body doesn't get tired. There is so much energy running in my body in a day that I give thanks and gratitude that God has given me this really fit body that can hold this energy. That is why I say, "Look after the body." It is the tabernacle, the holder of the Divine, and the temple. The pinecone that releases the seed is as important a part of the picture as anything else. Look after it. Keep breathing!

CHAPTER 14

BUDDHA

Buddha came with one teaching, and there are millions of versions of it. I came with only one. Buddhists are tearing lumps out of one another because one tradition says it has the keys to enlightenment and the other one says it has the keys, and this is going on all over. It is the same with the Christians, the Muslims, and other religious followers. What Buddha said is that he came with one message, which is the same message that every other Spiritual Master came with. The message is that everybody dies of the same illness, lack of breath. You come here to breathe and go. Everything is in your breath. We just add theories onto that to keep ourselves amused while we are waiting for the breath to run out, and it will. The breath is the holder of consciousness. When the body dies, the consciousness lives on forever. It is all in the breath.

We must understand that the Buddha and all these Masters never asked for people to follow their path, ever. They said that they can show you how they did it, and there may be a time in your own experience when you will follow this path for a period of time, but even the Buddha can only bring you to the door. You have to open the door and you have to walk through it. That is the moment of abandonment. That was the moment when Jesus said, "Father, why have You forsaken me?" That is that moment when you find out: "Oh, You are here." Those are moments on our path.

There are two lineages of Buddhism. One is red and one is yellow. One follows the Dalai Lama and the other follows the Karmapa. There are two lineages because of EGO. It is the yin (female) and yang (male) coming together. If China didn't invade Tibet, we wouldn't all be sitting here now. Tibet had all the power and control over many mystical secrets and wasn't letting them out. So China went in, blew the place open, and now the secrets are coming out. Doesn't that put a different slant on "Free Tibet?" The karma is now working between the consciousnesses and the two countries. That is what you are going to see playing out. Follow your heart and your heart will lead you home.

No religion jumping. If you are a Catholic, be a better Catholic. If you are a Protestant, be a better Protestant. If you are Jewish, be a better Jew. You were born into a specific vibration in order to bring you home. If you deny your roots, you cannot grow. The church was built on the rock. That is what Jesus said to Peter: "You, Peter, are the rock on which I shall build my church." He knew Peter would be limited, and that is why the church is collapsing now. Perfect timing. Who denied Jesus three times? Peter did. There are little cracks that are causing the truth of the churches to crumble now. Churches are not built on buildings. The tabernacle is in you. The church is in you. Two people having a cup of coffee together, that is church.

Go to a building that is tagged as a church and instead of sitting in judgment, sit with all the people in that church and know that they are all there for the same thing. They are looking for God. They are looking for help. I brought two people to a church. One is Jewish, and I brought her up to receive Holy Communion of all things. Sacrilege! They both had an amazing experience because they felt the love of all the people there and they got what it was all about. The moment when she was going up to receive Holy Communion, her reconnection to her true Source, guess what the choir sang? The truth will set you free.

If you have a teacher or God, whatever you want to call it, get a picture of it and stick it in front of you. Stare into the spiritual center of your picture's forehead, and if your teacher is on the right wavelength, the teacher will know that you have set out to communicate, and he or she will immediately communicate to you. Teachers will even come in physical form sometimes to give you that little extra hello if you are ready. The Universe doesn't give you anything that you are not ready for. This is what causes great excitement in some and fear in others, because don't we all know it is impossible to manifest something from nothing? Or is that belief starting to fade as well? Good.

Now we are getting home. Now we are knocking, knocking, and the door shall be opened to you.

For most people in the practice of Buddhism, there is another name for it. It is called surviving. This is because the Buddha said the way is the middle path. The middle path is the way of the survivor, because if you are sitting on the fence, no decisions have to be made. You are just being, surviving, or meditating. The rule of the Universe is that wherever your mind rests, there is your God. As we know, the Buddha's mind rested on suffering and the releasing of suffering. What he had done was walk into one of the greatest traps of the spiritual journey, which is the trap of compassion without detachment.

Compassion without detachment is nearly as bad as no compassion, if there is indeed such a thing as bad, which I don't think there is. There just is. Truth is always and forever. True can change. Whatever is true in your life can now change to Truth. For that to change, all you have to do is understand the concept. So, here we have the Buddha, who is full of compassion because he sees people suffering. He goes out to help, and his mind is now focused on relieving that suffering. Basically, he is saying, "Hey, Big Buddha. You're getting it wrong." Isn't that what he is saying? As if God can get it wrong. Either this is all God's plan or it is not. You have to ask yourself these three very valuable questions:

Do you believe there is a God? If yes, then answer the next question.

Do you believe that God created the whole game? If yes, then answer the next question. If no, you probably think that you are God and are creating the game. In that case, you will go on the path of the Buddha and you will suffer.

Do you believe the Creator, in whatever form, got it wrong? If not, what are you doing trying to change it?

So, there are your concepts. The Buddha, in this wonderful compassionate being, went out and helped. Through the compassion of helping, Grace intervened. Grace is God.

Here is the truth that will set you free: you are not on a journey to find God; God is on a journey to find you. Compassionate acts that you carry out are like sending out a flare. You send out flares so that you can be rescued.

So, now the Buddha's compassion rose, but he had not detached from it. There came a moment where he had enough light quota to try, or attempt, the detachment process. He sat underneath the tree, looked up and said, "Big Buddha, here's the deal. If you exist and you are creating all of this, then I do not want to be here. So I'm just going to sit here now and wait for you to call me." And he sat underneath the tree. He sat there, starving himself to death, which was suffering again. Suffering, starving himself to death, non-nourishment, separation from Source, and putting it out that this is the way it was to be. While he was sitting there, compassion arose in the heart of the Creator and the Creator said, "What are you doing? Do you not get it? It is not about suffering. It is not about being in bliss all the time. It is the middle path." So, the Buddha rolled over onto his right side and attained. . . . nothing. Everybody thought he attained full enlightenment, but he didn't because he went out suffering.

In the Buddha's teachings it says your very last thought will bring you to your next incarnation. Compassion of Source said to Buddha, "I can see you're a good soul struggling. I can see there is no violence within you. I tell you what, wake up again." So under that same tree, Buddha sat up again and he opened his eyes and started to eat. He had this vision of a boat on a river, and the wind was blowing so harshly that they had to take down the sails. The next minute, there was no wind at all, so they tried to put up the sails to catch the wind. Buddha now thought he's nearly got it. Big Buddha looked down and said, "Nearly, but no cigar. Back again."

God is compassion again, and He will always put you back in your problems to make sure you deal with them before you come to Him.

Then, it happened. Buddha said these words, "Events happen. Deeds are done. There are consequences of the deeds (that is called karma). There are no Doers thereof." There are no Doers of the deeds. It is all God's Will.

If you keep applying this, you will start to realize that you can sit back and just enjoy life, because He's coming to collect you. It's that simple.

CHAPTER 15

CHAKRAS

Here's how the body system works. Do you know that you can tell anyone exactly what is happening in his or her life by just using the chakra
system? There are seven major chakras, starting at the bottom of the body
and extending up to right above the head. We call the bottom chakra the
Root Chakra. We call the top chakra the Crown Chakra. When a baby is
born, what chakra do you think the baby is born into? The baby's consciousness does not enter the physical form until the baby has grown for four
months in the womb. There is no growth until four months. This is because
the vehicle is being prepared for the higher self or soul. Within that period
of time, any beings of consciousness that are ready to take on their mission
can literally just come and touch human form and leave again. This is what
is known in earthly terms as a miscarriage. Miscarriages are not to be
grieved—simply to be understood that the soul who sat in that fetus only
needed to be there for a very short time to fulfill its life purpose. The mother
is very blessed to have carried that evolved soul for even a moment.

When the baby is born, it is born into manifestation. Mother Earth is
manifestation. It is born into the First Chakra. Let's understand what the First
Chakra is. What is the First Chakra called? The Root Chakra, which is what
holds you here. When you are in the First Chakra, you haven't got the tool
of creation. You get this tool when you come to the Second Chakra. You are

completely created by the Creator in the First Chakra, but you haven't got the ability to be a creator yet. You are just manifested. Here I am and here I am going to stay, the physical Derek. The physical is at three months, and its survival relies 150% on its mother. Love, nourishment, and security—if you are given those three things, you will never ever end up on an analyst's couch. This is life force. It is the plan of the soul to stay on Earth. If it's not the plan, the soul may just be born for the day. My twin was born for an hour and then left, though in truth he never really left because the two of us have great fun. The Root Chakra never opens if the soul is not going to be hanging around for long.

The first three months of a being's life set its Karmic retribution in place. The female baby is there sucking and notices a shadow in the background and starts to fall in love with that shadow but is too busy sucking. Who is that shadow? The father. What is it that we have come to do? "Go forth and multiply," say the teachers. Then she begins to rise into the Second Chakra, which is procreation. This is when she notices the Second Chakra and becomes aware of mommies and daddies, but mommy is not as important anymore. Daddy is the pro because he can make her grow. We are lifting up into the Second Chakra. That is why girls become "daddy's little girls."

Now switch the child. The male child is sucking, maybe a little more greedily than the female. After the three months, bang, here comes the shadow. Now, unlike the female child, he wants the shadow dead. The Alpha Male wants, and between a father and son, whether you believe it or not, the fact is that the two males want the other dead. That is why there is always this conflict going on between fathers and sons. This Oedipus Complex has not split properly, which causes a flaw in the personality of a person, otherwise known as neurosis. It has not split properly because nobody has been telling anybody about this information—nobody has been given it. Now, you have it, and you can do with it what you like. Okay, Alpha Male. So conflict sets up.

Now up to the next chakra, the Third Chakra. It is mainly associated with the Divine Will versus your will. It all happens here. When you look at your soul contract, you sort of go, "Ugh." You have to make some sort of unconscious higher decisions and conscious decisions.

That leads you to the Fourth Chakra, the Heart Chakra. As a child is growing into being, just watch its conscious and spiritual journeys run side by side in alignment. When it gets to the Heart Chakra, the child should be hitting around the age of twelve. Now, have you ever been twelve? That is when most people's emotional wounds come. If your contract is that you come into a family that is supportive and loving, you will bypass that Heart Chakra and you will enter into the girlfriend-boyfriend, boyfriend-boyfriend, and girlfriend-girlfriend relationship. The amount of love and support you got as a child, determines what kind of relationship you are going to have with the world. First, a hair appears on your head and out comes all the trouble with that.

You know that females have this thing you call a period. Well, let me tell you, I am a bit of a legend in my own town. A lot of women get headaches and become grumpy and all that. I have proven that that is just a program or belief. These women thought they were bleeding to death the first time because they never knew what was coming. They had not been shown all the right stuff, why it happens, how the body reacts, and all of that. If you know any women who have pain at that time, you can let them know they just need to go back and see whether they were prepared for it or not. It is amazing. There were two females living in my home, and no way would you be able to determine when that event was happening. No way. There was no pain, emotional or physical. If you went down to my sister's house you would see it is all based on "I can't go to work. I can't do this, etc." It is "excuse-itis." It is a deadly disease.

We have come up to twelve years and everything that comes from the heart and all that. By this age, certain programs have been put into your computer. Obviously, people look at your mom and dad, how they got on, or did not get on, and what you had or hadn't to do. All of these experiences relate to who you are now. In other words, you are now disconnected from the Divine Source. When you are three months old, you are running up into the Second Chakra. Look at any zero to four-month-old child. There are stories going around the planet that these children still talk to God. Of course, because the parents don't know what the children are saying, they say that there are no invisible friends, no invisible things, etc. Keep in mind that the lawyers, the legal people, are the ones you have to have words with. They are the ones that sat there and drew up your contract. Let's all blame them. If you want to be the Creator, then you have to understand that the lawyer is just a scribe who took the notes.

When you come to this planet, you have made up an agreement with the higher beings of the universe as to what you will learn and how you will learn it. Your contract may be that, "The two parents I pick are not chemically compatible. I am born deformed, with a leg bent around to show that love has nothing to do with shape and form. I would like to come back and help these two souls who are my parents because four lifetimes ago they helped me and I want to pay that back. Then, when I was a soldier, I hurt the kids. So I want to come back, and my being hurt as a child will pay back for that." Get this? These are your contracts. All that is in place before you go, "Oh no!" and, "Welcome to the world." With Divine Will, everything is perfect. If only you could see through Heaven's eyes.

By the time you are twelve you are programmed, which means all of your personality and beliefs are on your mental and emotional psyche. In computer terms, your hard drive has been programmed. In order to remember your Divine Self, you need to either press delete, if you are strong enough, or at least transfer these programs onto a disk that you can carry around in your pocket. There are degrees of doing this. The easiest reality is to take the program off the hard drive and put it onto a disk, because this is not as painful on the physical being. It takes great courage to press delete. Pressing delete is saying to your ego, "I don't believe in you anymore." The ego will fight tooth and nail. That is courage. The only courage that can move that finger to the delete button is the unconditional love from Source or the Divine or whatever you want to call it.

In order for this to take place, you have to have love enter the equation. In other words, the Divine Source comes and hits you, giving you the courage or the energy to start your "return home" program. There is your earthly journey. It is finished. It is actually over. Your fear of death is gone because you die at twelve.

In India, the experience of watching people is amazing because they have all this interaction with one another. They come up very beautifully and say, "Namaste." "Namaste" is a very spiritual greeting meaning, "my soul acknowledges your soul." Then they bleeding tear into one another because "You robbed one of my customers, etc." In other words, they identify the Divine spark, but then they identify the human part that may have got it wrong. And the word was made flesh.

The Fifth Chakra is the Throat Chakra. You must first say what your problem is out loud to God to help heal it. If you don't voice your wounds out loud, you will not be healed. Some people say, "I haven't got a drinking problem. I just have two bottles of bourbon a day." Anybody in AA will tell you if you don't first say you're an alcoholic, your journey doesn't start. You voice it. "I am a broken being, and I don't know it all." "I am not the Doer." You voice it. You enter the Fifth Chakra during ages sixteen to twenty, which we all know is the most difficult time to communicate with your parents. If you are blessed to have parents, then let me give you a couple of tools.

In our family home, when our children were coming up through the ages of twelve, sixteen, and twenty, we had this ritual that was called the Friday night ritual. We would sit at a table as a family and light a candle. When that candle was lit, we could say anything to another member of the family that we needed to say and we could get as angry as we liked. As soon as the candle was blown out, it was forgotten. In other words, there were no emotions left. The most amazing growth comes from that. When you first do it, it will piss you off because nobody wants to talk. Nobody wants to talk and there is frustration, which is the underlying cause of it all. Then they get into it and, by God, I will tell you, "out of the mouth of babes" comes. . . . The sorts of things we would have experienced as a family, for example, were, "Hey, Dad. You are someone to talk about the state of our bedrooms. Every time I walk into the shower after you, the towel is there and so is your underwear." So you empower your children to speak the truth.

Families break up over those sorts of things. Isn't that amazing? Relationships break up over these things because communication doesn't happen. Obviously, if you don't allow the communication there, you end up with all the tripe we call life. It's also very important for children not to smoke or drink or hang onto a cough, particularly a cough due to smoking because it (the Throat Chakra) just isn't working.

This is the point of existence, the Fifth Chakra, the Throat Chakra. That is why the whole of creation began with a word and the word became man. The vibration of the throat and what we say is very important because it is manifesting our belief systems. So if you say something positive, you get a positive return, and if you say something negative, you get a negative return.

The next chakra is the Third Eye, the Sixth Chakra, which is located in the forehead. The Third Eye is intuition and everything that comes with intuition. Most people on this planet have left their body by this stage. They are not in their bodies to know what intuition is. If you are not in your body, you can't feel who you are. You see, the way everything is stacking on everything else, all of your experiences pile up on one another. We all have these experiences, and we have gone up into our intuition part, and this is where Jesus said, "Unless the eye be made single, you should not enter the Kingdom of God." Don't tell the Catholics that this statement comes from Hinduism and Buddhism. Don't do that. It is a bit like the bee. Scientifically, the bee can't fly with its weight and mass. If the bee takes on the consciousness that it can't fly, that is the end of bees. Thank God they don't believe that. So, a belief system is running through all the cords.

When you get up to the Third Eye, L.I.F.E. happens, which means "Look Inside For Everything." This is where most people retreat into themselves with fear, or with love. It is the path. It is the crossing of the roads. It is the elimination of the karma. It is where you become crucified. Every one of us will have to face crucifixion, not being nailed, but a crucifixion like when your best friend throws you to the lions. That is the crucifixion. Everyone has it and will go through the process. The little I (ego) is eliminated. Cross out the I.

That only leaves the last chakra, connection to Source, the Seventh Chakra, the Crown Chakra. There is only one sin, and that is disconnection from Source. You disconnect by thinking that you are the "Doer," that you are separate from God. You disconnect by blaming yourselves for your problems, by thinking that you are defective in some way. When you start believing that you are not perfect, you close your Crown Chakra. When you believe that God has abandoned you or is punishing you, you close your Crown Chakra. The Crown Chakra is also known as the "Suicide Chakra." People who have ever committed suicide or attempted suicide did so because they had completely disconnected themselves from God. They felt so unworthy and disconnected that they turned everything off. They have to come back and relive their life over again.

If you are struggling and afraid, your Crown Chakra is shutting down. When it is completely closed, you think about taking your own life. That is total disconnection. In order to open it back up, you have to be of service to others. When you are feeling alone and depressed, that is your body's way of telling you that you are not thinking of others and God. You are becoming self-possessed. The best way to open your Crown Chakra is to help another person without that person's knowing it. Get your ego completely out of it; don't reach for the fruit of your actions by seeking recognition or reward. When you are in service to others, you are in service to God. You will open your Crown Chakra.

CHAPTER 16

COMPASSION

Compassion is absolutely brilliant. Compassion is walking in someone else's shoes and becoming aware of what is happening with another person. It is absolutely necessary to develop compassion, but compassion without detachment is useless. Compassion with attachment is suffering. This is why it is very hard to understand God's plan. You buy into the illusion that suffering is real. This is especially true when you see young children appearing to suffer. In war-torn countries, children often appear to be the innocent victims. This is the big test: Can you see past that? You think that you are seeing their innocence being torn away. The truth is that the child is mirroring the innocence that was taken away from you. That is why you feel the pain, the hurt. You identify with the child and step into the melodrama. They are simply little Masters who are showing you what you are really about. If you buy into the illusion of suffering, what do you think you will create more of? If you think that someone needs to be punished, you are punishing yourself. You have to learn the art of detachment with the compassion. Then you have a powerful tool.

Whether people like me or don't like me, I love them. You have come to me and hugged me, touched my feet, robbed my money, and called me a thief. That is wonderful! When you are down, I will be there with you. I won't leave you. When you think you are cursing me, you are not. You are cursing yourself. I am only a mirror. That is all I am at times, a very shiny mirror. I am just an ordinary guy. There is nothing extraordinary about me. Perhaps one thing that is different between you and me is that I love you. I do not need anything from you, so I can love you without attachment. Ordinary love is all that I have. You think it is extraordinary because you have never experienced ordinary love. You have experienced love with contracts and conditions: "If you love me, then I will love you back. If you don't love me, I will stop loving you." Most of you have had lots of this kind of love. Very few of you have had ordinary love that has no attachments whatsoever, whether you received it or threw it back. This is really what our journey is, to come to the realization of the beauty of life on this planet we are on.

The problem with most spiritual people is that they can't mind their own business. They see another being who is sick or suffering and immediately give healings or send energy to end that person's suffering. That person is sick or suffering for a reason. Until that person learns life's lessons, that discomfort is necessary to get that person's attention. Ram Dass is a well-known spiritual teacher who wrote lots of books on his stroke and paralysis. He calls it "God's Grace." He needed his experience to balance the events of his earlier life. If someone had interfered with that, they would have interfered with his path.

Many healers get sick themselves because they are attached to the fruits of their action. They do healings with the expectation that their clients will heal. When the client heals, then they are great healers. When the client doesn't heal, then they aren't great healers. This is attachment to the results. This is the trap that healers fall into, and it is very hard to come out of it. Healers continuously forget that they are not the Doers. If it is God's will that the client heals, there is nothing that the healer can do to stop that. If it is God's will that the client continues to learn the lesson from the illness, there is nothing that the healer can do to change that either.

Whatever you are doing that brings you sadness, change it now. Whatever you are doing that brings you love, give it away. Whatever you are doing that you are conscious of, quit lying to yourself. Whatever God is doing through you, may you have eyes to see, ears to hear, and a tongue to taste its sweetness. Be happy!

CHAPTER 17

CREATION AND MANIFESTATION

Your manifestation is from your mind. That is the path of manifestation until you become Divine, and then you manifest from the heart. How I know that my ego has gone on vacation is when the words come from the heart up, not from the mind down. How I know my ego is back from vacation is when it goes from the mind down again. The reason that gift was given to me was to give people the gift of the truth that will set them free. Your thoughts are manifesting your world. Any crap that is manifesting in front of you, you are doing. Any law that is manifesting in front of you, you are doing. The you that I am writing to is the God that you are, but you just don't know it yet. You just don't believe it yet. As your journey progresses one way or another, you will be brought to the belief that you are God. There is a journey from yourself to yourself. And it is the longest journey you will ever take.

Your last thought is going to create your next manifestation. That is why it is good to go around chanting and singing. You don't need anybody, but it's nice to have company on your path. It's nice to have many trees in the forest; otherwise you're just a single tree. Everyone wants to manifest a companion, money, and material possessions. This is an illusion. People are creating an illusion to create an illusion. Perhaps this will explain for you why this kind of manifestation never works.

If you are coming from a space that you want something and you can manifest it, then you are coming from the space that you are the Doer. It is okay to come from the space of being the Doer if you actually believe it. Belief creates good and bad. I have seen people create stuff only to find out that is not what they wanted. A prime example of this is the great, super Hollywood stars, and I have had the pleasure of meeting some of them. I can tell you from experience, with working with some of these famous people, that you may be much happier and content with less pressure in your life than they. That is the truth. Because they thought they wanted big houses, cars, and fame.

It's a bit like Ratzinger, who is the Pope. His life is over. No more going to the cinema or strolling in and waving to the public as he did before he was made Pope. That is over. Are you ready for that? If not, stay humble. Walk behind. I always open the door for people. I always let everyone go in before me. Because I know God when I see God, and I wouldn't dare put myself in front of God, ever. That is not a phony humbleness. That is not, "Oh, someone will not see me being humble." That is who I am. That is why it takes no energy or thought. It just comes naturally. That is what manifestation is. It is you setting the goal, focusing, and then saying, "I actually don't know what I want."

People are taught that humility is a weakness, but humility is a very, very powerful place to be. The usual place is, "You better give it to me." That is why humility is a powerful place. That is why, when I find myself in a slightly uncomfortable situation, I make it slightly more uncomfortable. If you are comfortable, you've stopped. We have to get to this stage. Be careful what you ask for, you might get it. And if you get it, are you grounded enough to handle it? If you find yourself scraping through life in regard to being able to pay for things, please don't make that a huge disadvantage. You are just having the same lesson that Michael Jackson had with all his money. If you think you want to be a billionaire, you can make it happen using positive thoughts and actions. But you must take responsibility for that. I am telling you now; you won't be able to take that responsibility. It will send you into such a spin that you will become so depressed. It is about balancing. It is about understanding that this Spirit, God, Divine Presence, Life gives you what you need, not what you want. Ask yourself this question, "What do I really need?" Are your needs being fulfilled? If so, be happy.

It is much easier to manifest for someone else. Ask or demand that God help those less fortunate than yourself. I personally now don't manifest anything except for other people, because I am not in need anymore and I don't want anymore. So my manifestation period for myself has ended. If you're a fireman and you have to get to the top of the building, are you going to get there in one step? No. You are going to have to take many steps. It is the same with manifesting. They are called steps, and you keep stepping, stepping, stepping until you outgrow the old. I assume you are not wearing diapers anymore. That is a good start. That is called step one. We only manifest what we are ready for.

If you look at it from that perspective, you have the brilliance of wisdom there. That means if you go home today and there's a letter saying that your landlord is evicting you from your home, you manifested that. You must be ready for that lesson. If you were not ready for the lesson, the love of the "I AM" would not allow it to come out of love for you. That's where this free will thing gets all jangled and mixed up. You have no free will. If you think you have free will, you are at one level, and when you get to the next level, you understand. It's like the donkey with a rope around his neck that's tied to a pole as he walks in a circle. Now, as you get closer to the pole, you are going to get strangled, and a marriage with the "I AM" occurs in the center. If you are a really clever donkey, you can turn and twist and loosen the rope instead of getting caught. That is what this is about, steps of a journey. There is a big picture, you are a part of it, but you don't believe it. Those steps will bring experiences that will help you to believe. When you believe, then you and your Father become One, and you are there.

People ask what they can give. You can give your love because God needs your love. The truth that will set you free is that you manifest God. You manifest everything that is going on in your life. If the right ears hear this vibration, the manifestation will speed up rapidly until such a time when Babaji will take it from the air and show the scientists that they are wrong, by being right. Scientists are starting to come into alignment and seeing that everything is in unison. You don't need a train or a car to get where you need to go. You need "I AM."

CHAPTER 18

DESIRE

Desires don't have to be given up; you simply must let go of your attachment to them. This is based on a particular theory that "God separated Himself from Himself so that He could love Himself more." The basis of that theory is duality. If this wall behind me were one plain, simple, white wall and you had to do nothing in life except look at it, you would never sit in duality because it just is. Now, if you get a troublemaker like me who comes to your lovely white wall and makes a dot, now I have created duality. So, in other words, if your focus comes off the white wall to the dot, that is a personal desire. If you stay looking at the white wall, then that is the Divine Plan. Desire is based on anything you hold onto that is an illusion. Anything that will pass out of existence is a personal desire.

Linda and I were married in a church called the Priory. Not long after we were married, the statue there of Our Lady was seen to move by a group of people. Thousands of people came to watch this moving statue. They were there morning, noon, and night, praying to the statue. So let's all pray to cement. That is the personal desire. You think it has to be in form, it has to be materialistic to be real. You think the truth will always stand behind the cement. It was the Spirit moving, not the cement. That is an example of personal desire versus higher desire. When you are sitting still, everything that happens is the play that a director put together. The director is the Puppet Master, and in our lives the director is God. If you believe the play to be real, you are going to have an emotional connection to it. It's like when you look at a film and find you have tears rolling down your face because you have left your body and entered into the movie. You entered into the film, the drama, and the desire.

You only enter into desire to look for bliss. It is solely by the Grace of God that this desire can ever be eliminated again. It is by the Grace of God that desire gets eliminated, not by something you do. Even if you have been sitting there meditating for forty years, you can't move it. It is the Grace of God that eliminates it. Your desire to be liberated will keep you here because all desire must be gone for full enlightenment. In other words, you become the bigger picture. I have come to make you desire-less. Take away your home. Take away your animals. Take away your family. Take away your money. Take away and take away until you finally get on your knees and say, "Am I happy? It is I. I am sitting here under the Buddha tree, and if you don't show me enlightenment, then I am just going to die." That is probably one of the most enlightened statements because it takes the "dark night of the soul" to sit under that tree to die. Everything that you can see is not real.

If you want to let go of your desires, when you are drawn to do it, go and do it. I will tell you that if you don't do it, you will come into the next lifetime to do it, and the next lifetime if you refuse to do it then, and the next time after that. So there you go, gentlemen, if you ever felt like kissing a man, you better go and do it. Ladies, if you ever felt like kissing a woman, you better go and do it. Because anything that rises as a desire must be let go. The best way to let desire go is to have had it. Of course, there may be consequences to your actions. Don't be kissing people without discretion.

All suffering comes from the desire for life to be different. You should have more of this or that. You should not be married, or you should be married. If you are using the word "should," then you are stuck in the illusion of suffering. If you believe that God makes no mistakes, then you are free from criticism. If you believe that God has no favorites, then you are free from jealousy. If you know from what you were created, you are free from pride. The path of desire is laid with the presumption that God has screwed it all up. That is quite arrogant. You will always get what you need in perfect timing. Desire what you have and your life will be perfect!

Desire is the seed of a thought that is ready to manifest. Many times this thought is simply a habit. You think in certain ways out of habit, which was programmed into you at an early age. You are trained to think habitually about all the things you don't have. You think about how ugly you are and want to look like someone else. I am constantly laughing about all of the models that I talk to that think they are ugly. In order to break these habits, you have to look at who taught you the habit, how they taught you the habit, and then look at the habit through Heaven's eyes.

A desire gives you the opportunity to be acted upon by a higher Source that created the opportunity in the first place. Life is a distraction, because life is what happens when you had something else planned. If you beat yourself up because you are not getting what you want, life becomes an even bigger distraction. One way to deal with desire and the suffering that it causes is to focus upon service to God. You can pray that your actions be pleasing to God. When a desire surfaces, simply repeat the prayer, that your actions be pleasing to God. In this way you shift the focus of the desire from what you want to what God wants. This is a powerful way of shifting pain to happiness. When you stop desiring for yourself, and with discipline desire for God, then the proper application of desire is realized. When you focus your desire on God, you will manifest that desire. When you call on God to love you, God must obey.

CHAPTER 19

DISEASE

People do not heal because they blame themselves for being ill instead of looking at the illness as a Divine Gift that is given to them to get their attention because they are not listening. If you are not listening, you get ill. God speaks in volumes, starting at less than a whisper, and then each time getting louder and louder saying, "It is only because you feel separate. It is only because you feel separate." Until finally, you hear a car crash or the roof falls in on your home. You don't want Him to speak to you like that. People have been fooled into thinking they have free will. It is very difficult and very frightening to hear that they haven't. If you realize that you have no free will, then you have to be in a state of surrender. That is difficult. Who wants to surrender? You think, "I come to a workshop. Listen to music. Have some cries and laughs. But don't ask me to do any more than that, like surrender, and know actually who it is that is here. Don't ask me that." That is all illness really is. It is an instrument to get your attention to show you that you are not sitting in as much light as you could be.

You don't bring illnesses onto yourself. See, that is one of the great tricks. Does that mean we have to get rid of all the self-help books? No. It just means there are many steps on the ladder. You should not get rid of a disease until you get its message. If you don't get the message and don't change whatever the message tells you, you will simply get sick again. All you have to do is to understand that it is all God's will. If you reverse illness for a moment and put it into its true light, an amazing thing happens. It is in the acceptance of your disease that you let it go. It is in the acceptance. God does not make mistakes. God sends messengers, and we flippin' crucify them. It is because nobody has ever told us the truth. Nobody has told us the truth. You have to know what pain is. Pain is a messenger that tells you something is wrong. Once it has delivered its message, it should disappear, unless you didn't get the message. Pain is your pain of not accepting you.

Many illnesses are caused by emotions. Not just emotions, but emotions that are trapped. Release your emotions, and you will release your illness. Many of you were not allowed to show your emotions as children. You were told, "I will give you something to cry about!" Being the powerful beings that you are, you trapped the emotions inside of your bodies. This is not where they belong. If you feel like crying, you need to cry. If you feel like shouting, go to an appropriate place and shout yourself hoarse. Everyone is different, so you have to find out for yourself how to release your trapped emotions. Go for a walk in the woods or park and swear at the trees at the top of your lungs. People will think you have lost your mind. Good for you!

ADD/ADHD

People with attention deficit disorders are blocking their ability to focus. There is a simple technique to help focus. Close your eyes and imagine a light bulb shining in the middle of your forehead. Focus on it as long as you can. Then imagine that the light bulb moves over to the left side of your forehead and focus on that as long as you can. Then imagine the light bulb moving over to the right side of your forehead and focus on that as long as you can. You may not be able to focus on it for very long at first, but after 21 days you will be able to focus longer.

God gives illness to awaken you to the truth. You just need to ask the illness, "What are you providing for me? What is the message that I am not hearing?" Then be quiet. In comes this little voice; usually it sounds like your own voice, so never doubt your own guidance. If you think you are not psychic, you are wrong. Every one of you is psychic. You have not listened carefully enough to yourself. You are the wise ones, getting wiser by the second. You, wise guys!

ALZHEIMERS

I joke about the fact that the pharmaceutical companies have made a cure for Alzheimer's. The pill is 100% effective. The problem is that the people who need to take it keep forgetting to take it. The companies need to train the children of the Alzheimer's patient to make sure that the patient takes the medication.

The truth is that people with Alzheimer's don't want to be on the planet anymore, so they go out of their minds. Alzheimer's also affects people who can't handle their past, so they shut down their minds so they don't have to remember. So let them forget. Why do you want to rescue them? Is it so that your life will be easier? Losing their mind is their path and that is how they are supposed to be. Your job is to love them. You can love them and let them go on according to God's plan. God is shutting them down, getting them ready for their next transition. Don't interfere.

CANCER

Most of the high, high vibrational Yogis and Masters use cancer to leave their body. What they are doing is taking on the cancer of the Universe. So people who have cancer here today are actually taking it on for the Universe, yet they are still blaming themselves. So, what do you fear? You fear leaving here? What you need to do is go to a psychiatrist, a "Sai-chiatrist." You need to go and say, "I am rubbish at your feet." Then your teacher can say, "Yes, I know." And your ego finally departs and illness cannot get in. Start off with that and all that is lesser than that will drop away. That doesn't mean you get angry with God and stay angry with Him. People will just go and say their piece, and say their piece, and then leave again and slam the door. If you slam the door, you have to go back. If you gently close the door, there is no going back. As long as you are slamming the door when you are leaving, you have not dealt with your anger.

Many people get cancer as a warning that they are not dealing with anger caused by events in their past. You want to heal from cancer? Let go of your past. Erase it from your being. God does not cause cancer; you cause the cancer because you do not want your past. Then give it away, give it to God who put you through it to teach you something, whether it was that you are not your body or that love is not what you think. Cancer comes from the belief that you are defective, wounded, or imperfect. If you think that, you are causing the cancer to prove that you are right. So stop thinking that! Understand that you are perfect and thank your cancer for bringing your negative thinking to your attention so that you can correct it.

EYESIGHT

Poor vision has to do with not being able to accept the truth. It is associated with that thing on this planet called Alzheimer's. It's the same thing. People with vision problems don't want to see the truth. People who forget don't want to hear and remember the truth. That is what disease is about. It is really just about understanding the world that we live in now. Some Russians have actually taught blind children how to see by using their Third Eye. These kids are blind and they can read your nametag and everything. Obviously, sight has nothing to do with anything unless you are in the physical realm and you are using that sight.

When I sit in front of people, I am blind as a bat. I just see this incredible light, and I see past all the blocks that you people try to put up. Then I know which people need a good vacuuming and which are softer and I just have to dust you off. The two best communication power points are sex and talking. Look at the business world. They will either bed you or talk you into giving them your money. Our journey is to squash our chakras into the one chakra. If your Heart Chakra is open, there is no need to go to schools of philosophy, schools of mystery or non-mystery, schools of religion or non-religion, or anything else. You don't need any more protection. An open heart is the ultimate protection.

Don't take offense when I say that a ritual is usually done for the glorification of the person doing it. Whether it is a magic trick or a religious ceremony, it is more about the person than God. God doesn't need ritual. Ritual is necessary because that is what the performer needs to do. You teach that which you most need to learn. So I am an awful liar. Whenever you are ready to see the truth, your eyesight improves. I wore glasses and I stammered. I used to hate it when people finished my sentences. It was very frustrating. I needed to learn that what was causing the stammer was the frustration. As soon as the frustration stopped, the stammer stopped. I seldom spoke until the age of sixteen. I was so quiet; I was brought to all the different doctors because they thought I didn't speak at all. Of course, I was just being quiet. Now I am just a mouthpiece. I can play any role if that is what you need.

FRUSTRATION

When you are having some moments of frustration, you don't have to walk further down that frustrating path. You can stop for a moment and say, "Hang on. Hang on a moment." I have seen Sai Baba build hospitals that were a better standard than anything I have seen in America. I have seen his colleges where people can be trained as heart surgeons and not be charged a rupee. I had this experience. How can I deny that because he didn't look at me today? How can you let all of that go for that one moment of frustration? That is why you have to stop when you are in pain. You don't go through pain. You stop pain. You stop pain by bringing in the experiences of the "I AM." If Sai Baba is not who he is, that is Sai Baba's problem, not yours. He has to deal with his crap if he is fooling you. What you do is you take all the good bits that are there and go back and collect them. Then look, you are back in alignment again. Then all of a sudden Sai Baba might take on a different form. He might be John of God in Brazil or Mother Amma. He doesn't care. He doesn't care what form you go to because the Divine takes all forms.

HEARING LOSS

The reason for hearing loss is that you don't want to hear something. Generally, what you don't want to hear is that you can't have everything at once. You can't let go of everything at once. You are not ready for that. You are pushing the envelope. You need to let go of little pieces at a time. Gentle, gentle. See, you have to love yourself first. You do that by showing self-compassion. That doesn't mean you eat all the sweets in the candy jar. When you show self-compassion, it expands outwards.

The unfortunate thing for people who can see the bigger picture is that they want everything all at once. It is the wanting that is holding them stuck and lost. You need to let it go again, then slowly release your little attachments that are going on. I guarantee two things will happen. One, your hearing will return, guaranteed. Be slow and gentle and let it go. Here is a golden rule from God: "I will never ever take anything from you that you have earned honestly with truth, ever." If ever you have been conned out of money, you haven't; it is just God taking away karmic debt. How would insurance companies survive if everyone lost their fear of death? If everyone realized that illness is an illusion, where would the pharmaceutical people go? Who is holding them in place and who can cut them free? You.

PAIN

Pain is a signal that something is either changing or needs to change. The place where you hold onto the pain is the place that has to change. There are lots of books about what the message is based upon where the pain is in the body. Be sure to understand what you need to change before you let go of the pain or it will return. Many people make the mistake of not going to doctors. Doctors are God, too, and have been sent by God to help us hold space until we heal. Whether that means taking medication or having surgery, doctors are not the enemy.

If I cut my finger off, I am not going to go to a spiritual healer. I will run like the wind to the nearest surgeon, who is God, to sew the bleeding thing back on. I know when to use doctors and when to go get a massage. Most people don't, and that is why they have so much trouble with pain. It is time for spiritual people to start using common sense before spiritual sense.

STRESS

Stress is a chemical process that happens in matter. When it doesn't matter, there is no stress. In other words, when you are not concerned about being the Doer and being responsible, then stress doesn't manifest. When it isn't matter, it doesn't matter. When it does matter, it shows up in a chemical reaction. Now scientists are starting to see.

National Geographic published an article on love. Love causes a chemical reaction in matter. It is a matter of fact. So does anger. It is a matter of fact. When anger arises, it arises through a thought. You see, everyone says that what you think about when you are angry comes from the inside, but talk comes from the outside when it is negative. Positive comes from the inside. You have a thought. You don't even get angry. You don't know what is true or false because it is just a thought. Then you have a chemical reaction to that thought. If you know how to meditate, that anger might pass. If you're good at being a loving person, it will pass fast. If you're not good at being a loving person, then there's a chance you will feel anger for a good while, and those chemical reactions will grab on to you.

You draw to you that which you are. Anger draws anger. When there are enough little cells of anger, they change their name to hide. They then call themselves cancer. Cancer eats away. Their own anger eats away at them until somebody injects them with love. Science, which used to be the enemy of spirituality, and spirituality, which used to be the enemy of science, are now drawing together because of God's will. Now we have words to describe love. If you want to let go of stress, use your ears. Give three pulls on your ear. That is it. Instant stress reliever! You don't expect it to go, you just let it go. If you expect it, you will find that other things happen.

TRAUMA

Most people who have been hurt protect their heart from the front and completely expose their back. When a Master is walking away from you that is when you get the most Grace, not when He is walking toward you. The Master sucks love in and sends it down. He uses the front to suck it in.

When you experience trauma, you are separated into three aspects. There is the "I," the "me," and the "experience." There are three separate consciousnesses coming out of you. Let's call these consciousnesses male, female, and Divine. In other words, if you can eliminate the "I" and eliminate the "me," you are in your heart forever. As long as "I" and "me" are still hanging around, you will visit them on occasion. Everybody does. Visits are good. It is only if you want to stay there that it is not so good. Visits are good and vacations are great. It is very boring being nice all the time. All that is, is the concept I mentioned of the white wall with the dot.

People get attached to the melodrama surrounding the event that they perceive as bad. The event just is. There is no good or bad, or right or wrong. There is only the gift of life, the Grace of the event. There is no difference between a miracle and a disaster. Enlightenment comes when you discover that there is no difference between pleasure and pain. There are only your preferences that are based solely on your programming. If you can let go of the melodrama, you will let go of the trauma.

TUMORS

There are no weak, stupid, or silly questions. All questions are asked in order for clarity to come. Just ask the question, and the clarity will come. Tumors are capsulated anger that you refuse to release. When you hold onto anger, you are playing God. Look at what you are angry about and you will find that you are resisting God's plan. Whether it is you suffering or someone you identify with suffering, it is all an illusion. If you don't like it, you are fighting God, and I wouldn't want to be in that fight.

Many people have a Savior Complex and want to save the world. The world does not need saving. You get angry and sad, and that is the separateness from "I AM." That is your dichotomy. Who is it that looks after all children on this planet? God. You are an instrument of God. Why do you feel unworthy to be the instrument of God? Because you enjoy some of the praise you get from your work? It is okay. We need praise sometimes to keep us going. You don't need to feel guilty about it. Simply be aware that if you are serving God for the praise, you are reaching for the fruits of your actions, and that will lead to suffering.

Tumors are your body's way of telling you that you are angry. It is only a message. When you get the message and let go of your anger, the tumor will probably go away. What you are conscious of always changes. What you are not conscious of stays stuck. The tumor will not go away until you get the message. So go deep into your thoughts and find the one that is angry. Sai Baba says, "Be happy, very happy. Anger no good." Only good can motivate you. If it was the anger that motivated you, the tumor is telling you to stop. If you feel unworthy, the tumor is telling you to stop. Why are these seals being killed? Why are these children suffering? What sort of God would do this? He is trying to get all his children home, and He will use whatever tool is necessary. So don't interfere with the Plan. Go with the Plan and be like water, flow.

CHAPTER 20

EGO

S ervice to man is service to God. If you want to get through this ego that is negative, then do it through service. I love laughing at the messages that are given to me. This is for all the people who are caught up in materialistic stuff: "Ego is like when you have moved from a house or town that you have liked for years. You are sad to be leaving your friends and house, etc. Then it takes two trucks to bring all your valuables with you. These valuables are your ego that you have been carrying from lifetime to lifetime."

There are a lot of teachers and books teaching about killing the ego, erasing the ego, and getting rid of the ego. The ego is what keeps us here on this planet, so killing it would not be a very good idea. For all of you computer experts, the ego is like the operating system of a computer, a sort of Divine Golden Apple program. In computer lingo, the Ego program gets corrupted by programming we come into the world with, and by parents, teachers, friends, Hollywood, etc., etc. So when you hear people making silly comments like "Derek has no ego" or "so and so has no ego," you can be absolutely assured that they are not telling the truth.

The ego has a slightly lower energy field than your Divine Self, or soul if you want to call it that. There are different levels of ego depending on how low the energy vibration is. There is the lower ego, or base desires, and there is the higher ego, or higher virtues of truth, love, peace, non-violence, and right action. As your vibration gets higher, you begin to separate into the Light, atoms, electrons, and ether until you merge into the Divine Ego, which said "I separated myself from myself so that I could love myself more." This is called ascension.

You have come to this planet to have experiences, so you had to separate yourself from the OM, the ultimate being that contains everything. The problem is that you won't allow yourself to have the very experiences you came here to have. You came here to experience the positive and negative ego in their entirety and to fear or to accept either or neither as reality. The ego is the opposite player on the chessboard that we call life. For every move that we make as a Divine Being, the ego makes a countermove as a physical being or vice-versa. This duality, the ego, and God playing a game of chess, manifests when we make judgments such as good and bad, right and wrong about events in our lives, or the players. When we get caught in this duality, we create the capacity to feel pain that is the very thing that most people don't want to feel.

There is no good/bad or right/wrong; there are only consequences of your actions, and as long as you are willing to accept the consequences of your actions, you are enlightened. I know a lot of people who pray every day for enlightenment. What they don't realize is that total enlightenment may come in the form of a lorry crashing through your living room window and landing you in a wheelchair like Stephen Hawkins. If that happens, then you have the choice to be grateful for the experience or to throw away the experience and feel sorry for yourself. For enlightenment to happen and for you to merge back into Source, you have to eliminate good/bad and right/wrong from your consciousness. There just is. So when somebody is born, someone dies. When someone wins the lotto, a lot more people lose the lotto. Someone may get married while someone gets divorced. The game will continue as long as the Divine Source wants the game to continue.

You are not the Doer until you are ready to understand that you are the Doer. It may sound contradictory, but think about this: if you did realize that you are the creator of your world, you would probably sit back and enjoy this blissful experience so much that people would think that you are whacked, off the head, touched, or just plain crazy. You wouldn't be a little touched or crazy, you would be a lot crazy, thank God!!

Many people worry about making decisions and stress out about making a decision that would result in a consequence for which they would not want to take responsibility. They get all analytical about it. The truth is that you don't have to worry about which decision to make, just make one. For example, you are out walking and see a piece of trash on the sidewalk. You don't know whether to walk by or pick it up. God doesn't care what you do. Your ego will tell you one thing, your Divine Self may tell you something else. Whatever you do, there will be consequences. If you want to pick it up, that is great. If you don't want to pick it up, great!

If your destiny is to pick it up, then bigger and bigger pieces of trash will be placed in your path until you get the message to pick it up. Eventually you may live in a house full of tinsel and trash, such as yachts, limousines, Rolex watches, and servants. Everything is a symbol to the ego and is a message from your higher self to your ego. God doesn't care whether you pick up the trash or not, God is only love. How you live is up to you. You have to take the consequences of every action that you do. If you are picking up the trash in order to look good, to be seen picking up the trash, or you pick up the trash in judgment of the person that threw the trash down, you might as well leave it sitting on the ground. To do something hoping that you will be seen is the ego. To sit in judgment of those who gave you the opportunity to have an experience is ego.

The proper way to make a decision is to first be still. You can't make a decision while an emotion is rising. You have to allow the emotion to wash over you and you have to calm yourself. Then still your mind as much as possible and ask your higher self, or God, which choice is in your best and highest good. You have to understand that your best and highest good may not be what you expect. It may produce a consequence and experience that may be very challenging. Your best and highest good often is not the easy path. Remember that you are here to have experiences and to love life. You are here looking for ways back to your Divine Source. That path may not be smooth or downhill; it may be bumpy and a rollercoaster ride. Aren't rollercoaster rides fun? You pay a great deal of money to enjoy a rollercoaster. So being on one may be evidence that you are on the right path to God, or not. It is all the same, as long as you understand that you are simply having an experience. Your ego will try to convince you that either your life is terrible and you are a loser, or your life is perfect and you are a winner. It is all an illusion. You are who you are, and your experiences are your experiences, and nothing more. God loves you, I love you, and if you love you, then you have found the secret to life.

Ego causes confidence. The negative ego I am talking about is ego that is not "I AM." The healthy ego is good. The healthy ego lets you stand in your power of "I AM." You know when you have a healthy ego because it comes from experience. Unhealthy ego comes from somebody else's experience. For example, "The world is flat. If you go to the end, you fall off." Everybody in the world believed that. Whose belief system was that? It's somebody else's. Then they discovered the world was round. Who discovered the world was round? Galileo. What did they do when he told them the world was round? They imprisoned him for life. We have a pattern: shoot the messenger.

You have to identify what your experience is, and then it becomes healthy ego. I can tell you stories that would blow your socks off, and if they start to resonate with some stuff within you, then it brings you to an experience. For example, one day we were walking through Ireland's Powerscourt Gardens and smelling incense. Powerscourt Gardens was owned by the Irish government and is a large estate with a beautiful palace and gardens, but the Irish government is a bit stuffy and would never allow incense to be burned there. So we were experiencing an odor that was not there. The odor was from another dimension that was encroaching on our dimension. If you have these types of experiences from other dimensions, the people in this world will try to take them away from you. In other words, as soon as you share that experience with others, they will say, "That didn't happen. You are whacked, mad as a brush, and should be locked up." Isn't that the way the world works?

That is why they say, "Don't be too eager to share your experiences unless you can share the experience and not be rattled." When people call me this and that and say "You are mad as a brush," I say, "I AM!" When people call me "Whacked," I say, "I AM!" When people call me a womanizer and claim I only do workshops to hypnotize women so I can have sex with them, I say, "I AM!" When people say their children are not safe with me, I say, "I AM!" When they say that I am here to take your money and run, I say, "I AM!" Whatever you throw at me, "I AM." Now what? That was part of my journey. Now, I have a lot of Grace. All the realms and all the Archangels and all the Lads (Masters) take care of all that for me now while I just stand here. I don't have to think about these comments anymore. There is a whole big battle going on, and I am just drinking Guinness saying, "Whoever told them drinking was bad?"

It is important to hold onto the ego. There is a thing called positive ego. If you kill the ego, you kill the Creator because the Creator created everything, including the ego. What I would call the positive ego is what gets me to do what I do. Without it, I would be petrified. That ego can also be called the confidence of fate or the confidence of conviction. In the duality world, you will know when the ego is in alignment with love and out of alignment with love. Any part of the ego that is out of alignment with love needs to be looked at, but not eliminated. You have been doing this eliminating out of fear, thinking that anything out of alignment must be destroyed. Does this sound like some religious beliefs? If it doesn't agree with us, it must be destroyed?

When Jesus said, "I have come with the new covenant," what He was saying, if you had ears to listen, was that you were basically getting it wrong. Otherwise, why would He want to be coming with this new one? Instead of embracing it, we were getting rid of our shadow side. You don't run from your shadow side. You embrace it. You can embrace all of it in. Some religions call it the devil, maya, or whatever; embrace it in and have no fear. If you are coming from integrity, then mind, body, and actions are in alignment, and you cannot be vexed by anger. Your shadow side can be a good thing, and most people are getting it because if you start to throw it away, that is when fear can get in. There are teachers who say, "If you don't do the initiation that I have to offer, your children are going to die." The only reason that they can get in is because you are thinking you have something to get rid of, and fear has crept in. We want to start taking the fear element out of the journey.

If you really did get the experience, you'll know why all of these Saints are just praying to come back onto this Earth: because this is the party, boys and girls. This is where it is all happening. If you want to go onto a different dimension, that is fine. You just go there and "be" this light bulb. You will sit there like a light bulb, fully enlightened, or full wattage. That is great if you are a "Wayshower" for the angelic realms. But it is far better to be a "Wayshower" within the mix that we call human existence. Your journey is much quicker and more effective if you hold your wattage here.

When Sai Baba first spoke to me in my head, it was okay because I already knew I was schizophrenic. It was fine. When I heard (in an Indian accent), "What is that? Why aren't you writing me?" I knew. Hey, I didn't even know how to do an Indian accent then. This is what I am saying about the whole compassionate bit. Psychology has become very detached, in a way, because you have to be detached to give a diagnostic reading. If the problem is a chemical thing, which is a matter thing, then it can be helped with chemicals introduced to create balance. You have to keep in mind that God is in the medicine. Nothing cracks me up more than spiritual people who say, "I will just suffer through this and heal myself." Have you tried a pill? You will find it cuts through all the suffering—just one pill. Take it and there's a chemical reaction. Now we know if it is matter suffering, or Divinity that doesn't suffer. That is only a messenger. "I have headaches." "Take a pill." "I still have headaches." "Take another pill." "I still have headaches." "I suggest you go to a doctor."

The doctor will give you a pill. Unless you tell him or her that you have already taken that pill. "Well, today I have a special pill because the pharmaceutical company gave this to me." Try this pill before they send you for a CAT scan to tell you that you have a tumor. That is life, and doesn't it happen all the time? We need processing. Everything is God now. Are you starting to get this message? It is all God's Will. If you need to take Prozac until it is hanging out of your nose, then Prozac it will be until you are brought to a space where you don't need these things anymore. Until you are there, you better take the pill.

The mind is just threads of desires. Consciousness is the way to balance yourself. Doubts are good because they make people look deeper at the situation in themselves and others. Diamond energy comes in as coded energy: "Die Mind." I think everybody at every moment is dying to their lower selves and awakening to their higher selves. The whole process is to look at nature. If you look at nature now, you will see it is returning to sleep. In the winter, the trees are not dying. To someone who doesn't know, they look like they are dying because they are dropping their leaves. They will be back again in all their glory. You know what is great about trees? They don't worry about it. It is the mind that causes worry. Die mind/diamond.

When the mind dies, you realize that you never had a mind. All you ever had was consciousness. You had disempowered yourself to a bunch of spongy stuff that very quickly goes into mush. You then do what you do best, give food to the worms, and they in turn oxygenize the clay, which brings up the tree again. The cycle continues. Death. Schizophrenia. I know many an enlightened soul that the doctors labeled as crazy, and they answered, "Of course I am, because you said so." Take your power back. Only you can see who and what you are. Only you.

You need to get real about your beliefs. If you don't believe in God, it's best to say so because then God can come. You need to be truthful; that is why it is said, "More Truth Will Set You Free." You are not meant to understand it all. You are here for cheesecake and sex. This is it. It is all happening here. Everybody is trying to get to the other dimensions. You would be bored out of your tree over there. It is all light and stuff. You want to be here where it is all happening. We want to feel. Let's feel something. Either you believe it or you do not. Believing it will lead to an opening of energy whereby you can then keep your mind in place until such a time when you lose it. A lot of people say they are in their heads doing all sorts of analytical processing. Here is the truth that will set you free, that is basic: you have no free will, end of story, full stop. But act as if you do or you will not survive. That is it. If you can get that, you have it. If you feel what I just said, you have no free will. So does that mean your thinking mind has to come in at some stage? Because it does, right? Does that mean you can lie in your bed at home and do nothing? Yes, if it is God's will. If it is not, then you will not be able to lie in the bed. Try it. I dare you. I dare you all to lie in bed and see how long it takes before your back starts to hurt or you have to go to the bathroom.

Life is about going out of your mind. Here is the story about it all: If you are in your mind, it is you. If you are out of your mind, it is God. The Universe is made up of atoms and anti-matter, which I know nothing about, thank God. What usually happens is that, in order for enlightenment to happen, you are brought to what some people tag as being "the dark night of the soul." The Tibetans call this the "demons" that you go through when you are leaving your physical body. You go through different "bardos" and you meet all your different demons. That happens because you haven't met them in physical form in this lifetime. Usually, just before the dawn it is the darkest. That is what is "going out of your mind."

We live in a world of duality, and you have people writing books about being in the "Now." It's wonderful. "Well, how do I get there?" "You are there now." That is no good. It is all mind games. We will be lost forever and then some. You are going out of your mind and it is wonderful. This is why people write these books about being in the "Now," but nobody tells us how to get there.

In Ireland we have many signposts because our roads are very narrow. We have signposts saying, "Dublin this way" and "Limerick that way." One day I found myself going to Cork. I was trying to find a place called Clonnity, but someone turned the sign. I ended up in this town where there were only a handful of people. You know, the kind of town where when you are driving through and you blink, the whole town is gone. There were seven churches and one pub. The Lads kept doing this to me; I kept getting lost. Then I realized that no, you are not lost. You were brought to where you were needed most. You thought you were driving? Watch. Take your hands off the steering wheel. I did and went over a cliff and crashed. Then I realized that it's better to live in duality and hold onto the steering wheel. That is what they do in Ireland. They teach you how to be in the now by turning the signs.

What people usually do is stand there for ages at the crossroads looking at the signs, and then they suffer. They are analyzing the signs instead of just going in the direction that they are pointing. It is easier to follow the direction because it is impossible to be lost. If you think you are lost, then you don't believe in God, end of story, capital letter, full stop. You can't be lost. This is where the power of "BE" is. Forget "NOW" because that was then, and we are 'HERE" right now. But that moment also is gone and we are "HERE" again, but we were "THERE." How deep down the rabbit hole do you want to go into—a warren of mind clutter? Not too deep, I hope.

Some people, because of their programming and up-to-date conditioning, decide to go on the path of suffering. "Just stop the bus and let me off!" Switch paths. That is all you have to do. Just watch it happen. Look at it and say, "I am on the wrong track." And switch tracks. What was the cause of your being on this track? Trace it back and you will find the event that caused you to go down that path of suffering. But now you know you can just switch tracks.

Picasso said that he used to draw like Michelangelo when he was young and that it took him years to draw like a child. What he was saying to you is this: every being on this planet has two minds. One is a thinking mind. The other is a functioning mind, or a consciousness. The thinking mind is the one that drives your car; and then you go from the thinking mind to the functioning mind. For example, imagine that you are a surgeon who is the best surgeon on the planet. You go into work and you have made this particular cut thousands of times in this particular operation. That is because you were trained to do the operation. That is the thinking mind, the "anal-ytical," going to the functioning mind.

So, imagine you are a surgeon, and you go into work one morning. The nurse slaps on your gloves and you are just about to make this incision you have done thousands of times and the nurse says, "Do you know who that is on the table this morning? He is one of the most important men in the world. If you get this wrong, your career is over." All of the sudden you stop and begin to think about where to make the incision. That is the analytical mind. You could have done it blindfolded (functioning mind or consciousness). That is what people are doing all the time; they switch to the analytical mind, and it causes confusion.

Sai Baba says very clearly, "I am God," and everybody runs. They don't hear the next part, which is, "And so are you. But you just don't know it yet." The most important part of that whole thing is "yet." That means it has to take place. That means it is going to take place. So why worry? Why do you keep putting yourselves through this drama and saga? Is it to get attention? Did you learn as a child that to get your mother's attention, you must get sick, so have you continued to carry it through? You are programmed by everybody else. You are not even living your own life. You are living everybody else's. The day you start living your own life, it is just flippin' wondrous. You have nothing to do and all day to do it. You will end up taking full responsibility for nothing.

Sometimes we turn to God when our foundations have been shaken, only to find that it was He that was shaking them. Every day can be like this. You are not the Doer. Even when events labeled disasters are going on, come back to this room, if that is what it takes, to remember how every day can be like this. That is why God gave you memory, so you could remember those places where you can hide right inside yourself. See, God was a very clever Guy. He hid Himself right in the place that He knew we would never look, in our hearts.

CHAPTER 21

ENLIGHTENMENT

The simplest definition of enlightenment is that it is the state of mind where there is no difference between pleasure and pain. In other words, there is no attachment to either pleasure or pain. You recognize both for what they are, which is simply steps on the path. Pleasure is the space between two pains, and pain is the space between two pleasures. If you push, The Divine laughs. If you pull, The Divine laughs. And if you sit, The Divine says, "Another one ready for enlightenment." It is about being still and patient, and waiting to be guided. Most spiritual people say they are looking for enlightenment. But when enlightenment happens, life becomes a mess because all of a sudden you realize that you are totally and utterly responsible for everything that has happened to you. You are responsible for your house being robbed, your good looks, your bad looks, etc. Enlightenment is just a glitch on the journey. When it happens, everything continues to happen. It is just that your reaction to it has changed. Like when you go outside and find that your car has been stolen, you don't get angry. You just say, "Thank God for insurance."

Remember when you were a baby and your mother fed you? Remember the day when you picked up the spoon and brought it to your face and stuck it in your eye to feed yourself? Remember that moment? Well, your first moment of enlightenment came at the moment when you put that spoon in your mouth. You are such a Master at it now that you can have a conversation and have a million thoughts and judgments about other people and still not stick that spoon in your eye. Do you understand? You are fully enlightened. Enlightenment doesn't have anything to do with the end of a journey. Enlightenment has to do with the beginning of a new journey and the letting go and integration of the old.

If you have a program that says, "If I am enlightened, I am always happy, and I know everything, and I can levitate," you have to change that. Enlightenment is the moment when you decide that something in your life is not love and you change it. Sathya Sai Baba always opens his discourse with the statement, "Prema Swarupa" which means "Embodiments of Love." At some point he will say, "I am God." It is at that stage, as I said before, that most people become deaf. They don't get to hear the second part, which is, "So are you. The only difference is that you don't know it yet." This gives great hope for the world. He has an expectation that we are going to make it. Your job is to become accident-prone because enlightenment happens by accident. Workshops and events in your life make you accident-prone. If you want to feel immortal, live fully every single day. You are already immortal.

In life I have had the challenge of many people challenging me. I say, "I accept the challenge." Other times, I just laugh. When I want to amuse myself, I say that I accept the challenge. What I say is, "I need you to go and do something for me. If you can do this, I will guarantee you that I will give you absolutely everything that you think that I own. I guarantee 100% enlightenment. I will give you Shakti Bhakti (devotional worship of the Divine Creator)." I give that offer to everybody on this planet. All you have to do to come and receive this from the "I AM" is one little thing. For the next year, at six o'clock every evening you have to take in one deep breath. Nothing else. Just one deep breath at six o'clock every evening wherever you are in the world, and I will give you 100% "Shakti Path Enlightenment." I will be very impressed if you even go past a month.

You need to understand that you are perfect as you are. You are meant to be exactly where you are. All you have to do is surrender to the fact that you are not the Doer. The journey that you are on now is not your journey; it is the destination.

Surrender means I offer to God anything that is done. I will not reach for the fruits of my actions. I am willing to accept those fruits, whether they are nice, fresh green apples or rotten fruit. It is all reward. There is no such thing as punishment. God does not punish. We do, but God doesn't. God is just love and that is it. What I hope you understand today is that your biggest fear—listen carefully to what I am about to say—your biggest, biggest, darkest fear is of being loved. You cannot hack it. You cannot handle it. When somebody comes into your life that is a very loving being, it is very difficult for you. Hopefully, with surrender it will be easier to allow these people to cross your path.

When you are a "Wayshower" and in a state of surrender, the strangest events happen. I was in New York City and a friend and I had a cup of coffee. We met at the Virgin Music Store and we were just standing there. I told him to follow me and not say anything, just follow. He was awake enough to just follow. I said, "We are to go down to the New World music section." So down the elevator we went. The sign said go left, so I went left and around this bend. It said go right, so I went right, then left, and "Boof" the New World music section. We were just standing there, and my friend was going on about all the millions of CDs and how did I know where those CDs were. I just glanced at him and said, "I didn't come here for the CDs. We are just waiting for a soul to come." He didn't hear me and I knew he didn't hear me.

So here comes a guy, and he just walks right up and stands beside the two of us and goes, "Oh, my God. This place has really changed. I am out only four years and this place has changed."

I started talking to him and said, "Change is good. It is okay to change. Nobody has to wear the tags that they were given. It is over."

He said, "Yeah, man. That is heavy."

Then he headed off with his Irish lesson.

My friend just stood there looking at me trying to figure it out and he said, "Why would a stranger...?" That was his first mistake because nobody is a stranger to me.

"Why would a stranger come up to you from across the room and say he had just come out after four years? And he didn't even look gay."

I said, "I think he was talking about prison." That is how my life is every day. You can see why I laugh so much.

A teacher or guru comes into your life to bring you on a section of your journey. They already know exactly what it is you need to work on. What they might do is grease you up with a load of love at the start. Get you all happy and excited: "I am so special. My guru gave me a flower." Then the very next day, "He didn't even look at me. I am going to kill myself." India has lakes full of dead people because their guru forgot to look at them that morning. It is true. People are mad. When you find a teacher, the first thing you have to do is to physically ask, "Will you be my teacher?" At that stage, either yes or no is said. For example, if you need the type of teacher who is going to sexually abuse you, well, guess what? You have just called in the perfect teacher. And if you call in the one who is going to bring you to enlightenment, guess what? You have just called in the right teacher.

There are grades of teachers. That doesn't mean that some are better, it just means that some are a little bit more awake. The greatest teachers on the planet at the moment are children. When you say to children, "Why did you do that?" They come out with this wisdom and say, "Because." Be cause. That is correct. My mother used to have this saying, "If you fall off and break your two legs, don't come running to me." That was usually followed by, "I will give you something to cry about."

Teachers come in all shapes and forms. Yes, when you get to a certain level on your path, you get a teacher who can bring you across the Samsara bit (cycle of birth, life, death, and rebirth), the real mile materialized. People touch their teacher's feet, get tea for them, make sure their water is filled, and do all sorts of things. The true teacher doesn't care whether you make the tea or not. You don't surrender to the teacher. You surrender to what the teacher may or may not be representing at that point. May or may not be. If you need, for example, a teacher to steal your house or whatever, guess what?

The true teachers just sit back and are unaffected by whether you love or hate them. It is all the same to a true teacher. I got an email from a man whom I allowed to come to Ireland and study for a week, and I paid all his fees. He came in October and he wanted to come again in June. I asked him, "Why don't you have any money?" He got angry and sent a scathing email. I don't allow people who don't have the money to come to the workshop anymore. If you don't have the money, it means you were not meant to be here. It is that simple. It cuts out all that nonsense. I love all the emails. I love them. That guy knows that he has decided he doesn't want love. So, if you find a teacher who can read your angry email with a smile on his face when you are giving him big verbal abuse, hold tight.

There was a great teacher, Neem Karoli Baba, who gave this wonderful piece of advice. He said, "Look at all your desires like threads of gold coming from your heart. Now take all those desires and twist those desires into a rope and tie them to my feet and never let go of them." There is great wisdom in that. That is what you are supposed to do with a teacher if you find one.

When I would go to India to be with Sai Baba, he would come up to me in physical form every day and say, "Where are you from?"

I would say, "Ireland, Swami."

He would say, "Huh, Iceland?"

"No. Ireland, Swami."

"Huh, Holland?"

Then he would laugh and walk away. This went on for years. My ego held tight because I knew he wanted me to say, "I am from you." No way was I going there because I didn't believe it then. He helped me to grow. Then came the day, and I remember the exact moment, when I attained full enlightenment. I was walking down the street and I stopped for a second. That was it. No bells, no whistles, nothing. I was so disappointed, but then I got over it. I declared Sathya Sai Baba my teacher. I am happy with that arrangement until it changes. That is what is great about life; it is full of change and wisdom grows. Character comes and grows. For wisdom and pearls, sometimes you have to dig deep. Your teacher will scold you when you need to be scolded and give you a flower when you need to be loved.

CHAPTER 22

FEAR

Fear is false evidence appearing real. It is appearing real because it is real to you. Again, if you are in your body, you will know the difference between genuine fear and imaginary fear. Most people die of imaginary fears; very few die of real fear. People fear they are going to lose something or that they are going to get hurt or sick. The thing about fear is this: fear, too, is a warning system. It is warning you that you are not in love. If you fear losing your partner, you are not in love. Somewhere along the way you have disempowered yourself to that partner. If you give people permission to make you happy, what have you done at the other end? You have given them permission to make you sad. In this, you have to be very careful. This is the one trap we walk into most of all.

The only way to eliminate this is to be in this famous thing that upsets everyone: being in the "now." Some ask, "Isn't that difficult?" It is only difficult if you try to do it with your head. Be in the now. Now is when it is happening. Now is your time. Now, now, now! So be gentle and just be in the now. When you are in the now, you have the ability to enjoy the experience, whether it is wonderful in your perception or not. But you have the ability to enjoy it by being in the now. Most people fear the truth. The truth will set you free after it upsets you. Know that what you fear most will come upon you. Your fears come to you so that you can embrace them with love. Then you will be healed.

A lot of people come up to me and say, "You frighten me."
I just say, "Do I?"
What we think we fear is the darkness, but what we fear most is the light. "Don't you dare ever love me that much. You frighten me."

If you are one of those people who gets frightened by that idiot Derek, don't be, unless you get into a physical scrap with him. Then you can be frightened. See, he still has ego, thank God. So, of course, when the light is manifesting through Derek's body, you are going to be frightened. You will be attracted to the love, but you will have those moments of fear. It isn't Derek that pushes people into the real pain. "No, I couldn't take that. It would be too much!" The fact is, even though you might battle it, you signed up for it. It wouldn't be given to you unless you were ready for it. It just means you are going to have to stop and do a little push.

It is true that most people are terrified of love and actually prefer fear. Yes. Fear we live with all the time. We have become friends with it. When love comes, it can be very frightening. Let's say it was God's will that somebody got pregnant. It was God's will because this baby was one of the higher beings who just needed to touch physicality in this physical dimension and then go straight back out again. You might be required to be a vessel for that, and the length of time would be unimportant. You could actually go have an abortion, and that, too, has to be God's will, as crazy as it may seem. You might decide to have the baby and give the baby up for adoption. Sometimes you might have to be the carrier of a baby that comes in through you to get to its real mother. It uses you as a vessel. You give up the baby for adoption, and it arrives at its mother. Isn't God clever? Once it is Divine that they come, they come in. If they don't, that is okay, as well.

There are all these guys, St. Francis of Assisi and other Divine Beings, who would love to be in human form right now. What they would give, because they still have desires by the way, to be in physical form right now. There are lines of entities up there who would give anything to be back on this Earth at this time while there are so many spiritual masters on the planet in physical form. Let me tell you a new thought: You are beautiful. You are a child of God. You can be whatever you want to be. You have to stop making up fear. You have nothing to fear. You have nothing to fear but fear itself, which is false evidence appearing real.

CHAPTER 23

FOOD

I used to bless my food like a good Catholic. That was until I knew what I know now, which is that food is love. I am love! People consume me every day. I don't bless my food anymore. Why should I? I would only be blessing myself. When people bless their food, they are acknowledging that they are not what they are trying to put into the food. It is far better for you to realize that food already contains God's entire blessing for us. When you think that you can put something into food that God has not already put into it, you are saying that Divinity is not in you and that God is somewhere else. As it is said, God made us in God's image, which means that God is in us. When you perpetuate the illusion that you are not Divine, you separate yourself from God and condemn yourself to suffering.

When people overeat and abuse food, they have the illusion that they are not loved or are unlovable. They are trying to feel loved by stuffing food into their mouth and stomach. They confuse the feeling they feel when their bellies are full with love. They think they are filling up the holes inside their heart. It feels comforting, so you have the illusion that if you eat more of it, then you will feel more comfortable. The truth is that the opposite happens; when you eat more, you become uncomfortable again. People will abuse anything to prove others wrong. They want to show people that they are right and the world is wrong, and they are willing to make themselves sick to prove their point.

Many times overeating is caused by parents forcing a child to eat more than the child wants to eat. Never force a child to eat. A child is born with a preprogrammed sense of how much food is healthy to eat. The parents will force the child to eat more than the child wants because the parent thinks that the child needs to eat a certain amount of food to be healthy. The child wants the parent's love, so the child eats more than the child wants. This is the start of overeating. The child is reprogrammed to think that if it eats more than it wants, then the parents will love the child. So the child is programmed to overeat to feel loved.

There are good teachers and bad teachers. The bad teachers are great teachers for the people who need bad lessons. The good teachers are great teachers for the people who need good lessons. When you take judgment out of it, they are all great teachers. Good teachers will tell you to eat quietly and be conscious of why you are eating, to nourish your body. The bad teachers will tell you to talk with your mouth full, to shove the food in while you are on the run. They will teach you to be unconscious while you eat. Where is God in that?

The other day I shared a mantra for people to use when they are eating. When you eat, start the meal in silence. Sit in silence, offer the first mouthful of food to God, and chew well. Offer the second mouthful of food to you as God, and chew well. Offer the third mouthful of food to all of the people in the world that are hungry, and chew well. That is it. Then you can start talking, have your business luncheon, and chat away. If you do not sit still as you begin to eat in silence, you will have a physical reaction to the food and get indigestion.

People are always asking me, "Should I be a vegetarian?" I don't have a clue. My favorite thing to eat is an animal because people keep killing them. I eat them so that I do not let their existence go to waste. Even though I eat animals, I am a vegetarian. I have the ability to change the vibration of any food to the vibration of any food that I require. I do this by saying a little prayer that I learned from the Masters: "I give thanks and gratitude to the animal that gave up its life to sustain this body, which is the tabernacle where Christ lives." Then I send the prayer out into the Universe. Sooner or later that consciousness will join with other consciousnesses like it and we will stop hurting our animals. I don't kill animals; I honor them. Animals will actually give up their life to sustain the tabernacle.

When I was in the Army, I was sent out on an exercise where you had to find your own food. We were to eat whatever we could find, nuts, berries, and all of that. At that time I was a corporal, and my men led me further than I led them. We had to go seven days on this exercise, and we all suffered from hunger. One of the men got quite ill from starvation. So I sat down away from them and prayed. When I opened my eyes, there was a pheasant that had died at my feet. So I picked it up, cleaned it, and gave it to my men. We didn't have to kill anything. If you have a need, God will provide whatever you need.

For the vegetarians who are in judgment of meat eaters, God is the giver and receiver of all food. Are the Eskimos bad for eating meat, which is the only food God has provided for them? Are they going to go to hell for eating meat when it is impossible to grow vegetables on the ice? What about the hunters who provide food for their families? God is the hunter as well as the hunted. God is the prey and the predator. When God wants you to be a vegetarian, it just happens. I was talking with God one time, and I told him that I was struggling with not eating meat. God told me not to worry, that he would let me know when it was time for me to die. Then I could eat a piece of lettuce and declare myself to be a vegetarian, and I could die without a desire for meat. That God sure has a sense of humor.

People don't understand that God created McDonald's and "Quarter-pounders." God also created Pizza Hut and the Meat Lover's Special pizza. God created the whole game, and when you start to understand this, you will understand that God created variety for us. There is no right and wrong; there is only God experiencing life through us. It is flavors of ice cream. Some people like rum raisin, some people like strawberry, and others like vanilla. Here is the big secret to life: it is all ice cream and we can have whatever flavor we want. We have to start with ourselves.

I know someone who ate only raw food for a few months. What you have to understand is that you can eat whatever you want to eat, as long as you understand that it is all God. Of course, whatever food choices you make have consequences. If all you eat is ice cream and cake, your body will look one way. If you eat love and energy, "prana," your body will look another way. We eat whatever is God's will. Whatever happens through you is God's will. Whenever we think we are in control, we suffer. Let go of that and experience God.

Here is a great story: Shirdi Sai Baba, a very famous holy man in India who lived in the early 1900's, was invited to a student's home many times to eat meats, papaya, and rice. In India that is quite a feast. Shirdi finally agreed to come one evening at 7:00 p.m. The student and his family worked all day preparing the feast in honor of this holy man. Everything was ready by 5:30 p.m. While the family was preparing the house, a mangy dog came in, jumped up on the banquet table, and started eating all of the wonderful food that the family had prepared. The wife came in, saw the dog eating the food, beat the dog with a brush, and chased him out of the house. The family hurriedly put the banquet back together and waited for Shirdi. Well, 7:00 p.m. came and went and Shirdi didn't show up. The next day the family traveled to Shirdi's home and asked the great teacher why he didn't come. Shirdi replied, "Of course I showed up, and you beat me with a brush."

I often challenge my students to go live on leftovers from McDonald's for a while. I have them imagine asking people for their uneaten food and going into trashcans to get food to eat. I don't really want them to literally do that; I want them to have the consciousness of that experience so they don't have to physically experience it to learn to appreciate food. People waste so much food. When you go to restaurants or to friends' houses, be aware of how much food you are throwing out. When you go to a potluck dinner, see how much food is left over. Here is the truth; food is God. You will acquire the consequences of wasting so much food. So be gentle. Eat only when you are hungry and drink when you are thirsty. You don't have to eat or drink just because other people are. If you go out to eat, share meals; not everyone has to order a meal. When you waste food, your life will begin to starve in all sorts of ways: love, money, or health. God is the food, God is the cook, God is the waiter, and God is the dog waiting for scraps by the back door. God is you. Be conscious of what you eat and what you waste.

CHAPTER 24

FREE WILL

God is playing his "bored game." For all you people who believe you have free will, well done. For you people who know that you have no free will and act as if you do or you won't survive, well done. You are not the Doer. You never have been the Doer. All you are is up-to-date programming, programmed into you by the Divine to play the role that you are now playing. You have been trained for your role. People always say, "What is my mission? What is my mission?" I want to say, "Just shut up for a minute and you will find out." I act a little bit more loving than that though because I have been trained. The Oscar should be given to me.

I will tell you what your mission is, and it is very simple. It is to offer everything to yourself, through yourself, by yourself, and to know yourself for who you are. What I have repeatedly said is, "You are God. You just don't believe it." You don't believe it because you have been trained not to believe it. It took great courage for you to read this. Your higher self went through battles and went though its things to read this. Some of you read this just to sit in judgment of me. What a waste of time. It is very easy. I am guilty! There. Go.

You have no free will. The fact that you think you have free will is causing all the suffering. This is because we live in this fabulous dimension of duality. Without duality, you could not be here. If you cross over from duality, you leave here and become one with the Source. Duality is what keeps you here.

You have about as much free will as a donkey tied to a post, walking in circles. One day it will merge with the post. That's the easy way out for people who are not ready to hear. You're not even the donkey on the post. We are living in duality, and this is for people who get caught up thinking that they have free will. Duality works on this basis: there cannot be light without the dark. There cannot be love without hate. Nothing can exist without its mirror image opposite to show it where it is. God created this great board game called Earth. We are just the pawns being shifted around. He created the illusion of free will just to make sure we didn't leave His game too early, because then He would get bored. That is why He calls it a "Bored" Game.

Once an event happens, it is God's will. As soon as an event happens, duality sets in, since there is no happening when you are just being. There is only happening when you are out of being. An event happens and the deed is done. You have read this today. There is the deed. The deeds are done. There are consequences of the deeds. Here is where free will is. You can either walk this path, which is the path of love and surrender—or you can walk this other path, which is the path of anger and suffering. There are only two paths in the world of duality. That is why they didn't call it "triality." There is no Doer of the deeds. In other words, if you are meant to be suffering right now, it is God's will. Don't try to work out God in your head; you will either get a migraine or a tumor. Don't try to fathom the unfathomable. If you are suffering, you are meant to be, because the suffering, in its own way, is your forward journey to God. When you are not suffering, you are not going anywhere. You are at rest. You are just being. Very few people on the planet stay there for very long. Even the great Masters couldn't stay there forever. Once you are in this dimension, it is impossible to stay there because you need darkness to show your light.

Consider the events in your life. You might have had to steal or whatever to show you and let you feel what it was like to be out of alignment and to show you what path you are on. A beautiful child comes into the world suffering. Why does God do that? Isn't that the question that keeps catching us all the time? Why does God have me, the little leprechaun, flying all over the place to feed the street children in India? Why doesn't He just feed them Himself? He is playing His game. Suffering is "our" way home. Rest is God's Grace whilst you are on your way home. We'll have many teachers to help us on both of those paths, especially our family saying things like, "Are you going to that cult meeting again? You are a bunch of 'weirdos' and 'wackos.'" Yes. . . . Sai Ram.

This is the journey, and I did say I would show you how to collapse into yourself. In other words, I will show you how to go back into your heart. God was very clever. God hid Himself in the part He knew you would never look, your heart. He knew you would look everywhere else, even under the bed, but never in your heart. How do we get there? How do we get from where we are to our hearts? We do it with one simple word. Acceptance. I accept that I asked for all these events. I now choose a blank record, and I will be the writer of the rest of the play. If you are ready, if you don't worry about it, it will happen.

Divine Will versus your will is in the Solar Plexus, the chakra below the Heart Chakra. When the fight between the Divine Will and your will is over, you are back in your heart. What is the one above the Heart Chakra? It is the Throat Chakra, and when you ask for something, it must be given. It is the Divine Creed. If you come from the Throat Chakra, you ask. And if you come from the Heart Chakra, it happens. The will collapses into the Divine Plan.

This is you, you think. And that is them, you think. It is all in the mind. It is an illusion, and I like to play illusion games. At some point it gets a bit painful. It is a bit like those electric fences they use for cattle. The cattle hit the fence, and they go, "Uh-oh!" and jump back. When you go so far, you will hit that fence until someone guides you in. There is a really good metaphor in that. This means "hurt" can bring you closer to God. Think about it. When you are getting really close, this is the dangerous part. As I like to put it, the closer you are to enlightenment, the easier it is to have your wings burned. Ignorance is bliss in that if you are ignorant, it doesn't hurt you. But if you know you are doing something wrong, don't come crying to me. Mothers are great for saying things like that.

What is happening, of course—this is it, this is your moment—it's the "dark night of the soul" because you are flying to the flame. There is the flame, people. You have to go into it. No fighting; just go into it. You merge with the flame. That is your moment and that is the moment where this happens— Shhh. I prayed for all the world because you become all the world. There is no more "me."

How do you do God's will without it breaking your heart? He gave us the answer Himself when He said, "Do not reach for the fruits of your actions." You see, as I have said time and time again on this journey, "If you like me, that is wonderful. If you don't like me, that is wonderful." Priests have often attacked me, but I have a defense. Sometimes, when we have conversations, I say things like, "I don't know what you do, but I usually go to bed at three o'clock a.m. after sending love to the world. Then I usually rise from the bed at four o'clock a.m. to begin to send love to the world." My actions are that I get on planes that are stuffy and cramped, and fly around the world as an instrument to be played through. Sometimes the tune is very sweet, and sometimes it is raggedy at the edges. The children are the motive, and I take full responsibility for nothing. It is not my will. If it was my will, I would be stretched out on the bed.

I go and encourage people to give back to God what belongs to God, the means to feed the children. He needs to send a message to the children that are in the separation. It is Grace. See, God uses me to display Grace. So, I go to these children who have leprosy and I pick them up, kiss and hug them, and I say, "God has not forgotten you. He has sent me, His messenger, to remind you." That is what life consists of, being of service. It makes me feel good. I also offer that to God. He catches me now and again though. When I was in India, I saw a baby, six or seven weeks old, being thrown onto a pile of garbage. That got me. It just hit hard and I said, "Please use me more. Don't let me lie on the bed anymore."

That is what your mission is too. In order to do it, you have to drop the old consciousness of hiding in a cave. The day of "OMMMM" is over. Now it is "om." You are not the Doer. It is being done through you. The days of sitting in the cave are finished. You have to be in the world, but not of it. You will return home like the rest of us. When you do, your heart that you lost will be returned, buried here in your chest. Through your heart, make a new start. "I AM" me. Who are you? I can feel your energy. These people here who are in any way feeling, they can feel it too. Just be who you are, and when the tune is not so sweet, that too is okay.

There are people going to psychologists every day saying they are Jesus come back to earth. Here is how you know the difference: if it is not true, you will be suffering. If it is true, suffering will be absent. People in the body can only register suffering. That is why you are given the radio station called the body or the tabernacle. When you are in your body, all the great teachers have said this same thing, "Be still and know that you are God." They didn't say you should keep chattering and know that you are God. They said, "Be still and know that you are God."

Within that stillness, you actually discover the most amazing piece of wisdom on the planet. It is that you are human. You discover that and you remember that you have a physical body, but you remember it on all levels. It is very interesting that as I was going through my own particular journey from nowhere to nowhere, when I would sit in my office, being extraordinarily quiet and lying to people by telling people I was a psychologist, instead of a "Sai-chologist," the most amazing events would start to occur. I knew what their trouble was before they thought about it. Imagine that. That is a handy tool to have. The tool came about like this: when somebody held a lot of anger or a moment of anger, in the past, present, and future, because it all happens in the now, my finger would twitch. It was actually that simple. That finger twitching meant anger. Another finger twitching was anxiety. The little finger on my left hand was depression. The toe moving meant suicidal tendencies, at that moment. When my hands would drop to my lower body, there it was, sexual abuse. And another movement was love. I learned all these signals by being still.

As you get closer to God, it is easier for your wings to get burned. This is why when you become a teacher, the most tests come your way. As I've told you, you get diamond rings, and you have to throw them in the middle of the lake. People will want to give you millions of dollars, and you have to say, "Thanks very much," and you chuck it in the trash. It is all fine. It is grand. "Oh, you are giving me land? Don't forget your legal team. There you go. Thanks very much. Now, those gifts will be utilized to help humanity, not me. I don't need it." As you get closer and closer, all the tests become more and more because the world will try to buy you back.

I had a great experience in Los Angeles. You know, that lovely, lovely place, Los Angeles. It was one of those crazy situations where I went to a party with people who knew everything. Let's just say, it wasn't my type of party. There were people there with egos that were so big they were in need of squashing, actors and whatnots.

This guy came over to me and said, "I have to work with you! I can see you. I have to work with you!" He said, "I worked with one of your colleagues in Ireland."

He mentioned my colleague's name, and I said, "Ooohh. Yes."

Then he said, "I have just closed a deal for seventy million, you know."

I told him I had to leave and I left the party.

This guy followed me to the door, saying, "I will give you anything. Whatever it will cost."

I said, "I don't have the time."

As a matter of fact, I was royally angry. I was brought to an ego session, not a party. In Ireland, we love parties. When we party, we party. We don't swap cards. That is business. This gathering wasn't a party; it was a big business conference or something, a waste of my time and the children's time.

I had to give him what is called "the stare." If you have experienced "the stare," then you know what I am talking about. I gave this guy "the stare." I went back to my hotel and lo and behold, at 8 a.m. the phone rang in my hotel room. It was the guy. I would love to know how he traced me there because if he knew where I was staying, something good must have happened.

I picked up the phone and said, "Hello."

"Before you slap down the phone..." he said.

Now I knew we had a door open. Then he closed it again.

And said, "Look, I think you might've picked up the wrong idea about me. I can give to whatever charities you have. Millions!"

I said, "Piss off."

That was it. Then the phone rang again and I picked it up. It was a woman and she wanted to meet me.

So I said, "Sure. What do you want, a cup of coffee? Starbucks? Yeah, I will meet you."

I didn't even know where in L.A. it was, but I found the place and the woman. We had this most delectable cup of coffee. I call it the Irish therapy. If I sit with you and have a cup of coffee, you are in trouble. When I was finished, this being sitting in front of me wrote me a check for four million dollars. I took it, tore it up, handed it back to her and said, "You cannot buy your way into Heaven with guilt." She hasn't spoken to me since.

Your tests will come. Your family is going to attack you. That is what families are there for. You may understand why they do this because you are now a member of a cult. This is a cult here. You see, the dictionary's definition of the word cult is, "a group of people coming together with like minds." So, the Catholic Church is a big cult. What is wrong with the word cult? Yes, I am sorry, you are a member of a cult for as long as you want to remain a member, because this cult doesn't have doors, it only has arches here and there. In and out you go. One minute, I am this teacher all very loving and the next minute I am the anti-Christ on legs. It is all fine.

It is good to ask for God's help if it arises spontaneously in you. It is not possible to eradicate evil from the world entirely because the world would not exist without it. Light cannot exist without dark. This is the duality that holds our planet in space. So, hello, come on people. Come in and let's have good and evil, good and evil. You know it is evil when you wake up the next morning with a hangover. Prepare yourself for it—it is coming.

When it comes, you are going to smile and say, "This is exactly what he was talking about."

That awakening will happen, and you will say that this, too, is part of the plan. Then you will find it is easier to let it go. You will say that it is okay.

You say to your mommy, "Do you really love me? Well, if you love me, will you let me grow? Can you stop smothering me please?"

"It is my job to protect you," she says.

"Who told you that?" See, the wise child teaches the parent:

"Who taught you that?" And we have a whole healing change going on now. If it were any simpler, it would be A B C and C B A.

Listen to your thoughts. You say to yourself "I" and "me." There are two of you standing there. We live in a world of duality. We just need to accept that. It is not possible to eradicate evil out of the world completely. How can light identify itself if it doesn't have something to shine off itself? That is where our duality comes in. As soon as you have pleasure, a bit later comes some pain. That is the duality of the world. The difference between the Master and the student is very simple. There is none except for this: when an emotion spontaneously happens though Divine Will through a mind/body mechanism, which is me, it comes up and leaves. A Master's anger and frustration still rise because he is living in part of duality. So it still arises, but the difference is that he doesn't hold onto it. He accepts the gift. It arises and goes.

I will give you an example. You see, I didn't get it when it was originally given to me because I was too busy processing. I told you the story. It was God who was there the first time I walked into the accommodations office at the ashram in India. He was a Master because he screamed at me, "Sai Ram!!" This amazing amount of anger passed through him to get my attention. As soon as I turned around seconds later, there was no anger. He said calmly, "Saiiii Raaaam." That is a Master. The student allows anger to arise, but instead of allowing it to go vertically though the chakra system, they make it go horizontally, usually at the Heart Chakra. Then they hold onto it for forever and then some.

The first thing you have to do is eliminate everything that you think God is. Gone! Let it go. Whatever your concept of God is, it is wrong because you can't conceptualize the Divine. You can try, but you'll cause some pain and suffering along the way. God is a loving God. He loves you enough to be angry with you. He loves you enough to give you cancer. That is our God. That might be a bit of a struggle for some people, but that is the truth that will set you free. God is the creator of everything, the Divine Director. Here is your script. Go play your script. And if you get an Academy Award, you are doing really well. Go play. Here is your part in this lifetime. I want you to be depressed, manic, psychotic, blah, blah, blah. Do a good job and I will bring you home. Fight it, and I will leave you there while I drink Pina Coladas on the beach. This is what it is.

We have to un-learn what we know for the truth to come in. The majority of the people in this world are living everybody else's life, not their own. They are living their parents' lives and concepts. There is nothing new on the planet. I haven't come to teach anything. You already know it, my friend. What is my label at this moment? The Divine Awakener, that's how I'm tagged. The truth is that you need to be who you are. Only you know who you are. There is nobody who knows you, only you. You know how much energy it takes every day when you try to be nice to people when they come in shouting and roaring. Only you know how much energy that takes.

There is a great story, a true story. In England there is a footballer. Now, he and his wife have money dripping out of their ear lobes, and they think they are important. Fools. They were at the airport and went to check-in for their flight, but their airplane was delayed. The wife was screaming at the poor woman behind the counter, "Where is the plane? I have to be in New York at such and such a time. Do you know who I am?" The woman at the counter sat back really calmly and pressed the button on the intercom system and said, "Ladies and gentlemen. We have a lady here at the British Airways desk who doesn't know who she is. If anyone can identify her, please come." The woman lost her job, wrote a book about important people, and now is rolling in money.

This story is about the self-importance that people put on themselves. How important are you on your deathbed? What difference are you making then? What difference are you making now? None, I hope. Because you are perfect exactly as you are. What are you doing trying to change this perfect vessel? God made you and trained you up to this very moment. What are you trying to change? All you need to do is accept. Then you might see change. You have to accept yourself first. The only way to do that is to know you are in duality. And now what? Just be, and see what happens.

It is time you get rid of this wrong image you have of God. The idea of the donkey and the carrot should have given it away. Does God give a child an illness so He can bring the child home early? What was his carrot? Cancer? Sure. Suffering comes from how we want to continue to look at right and wrong, and good and bad. There is no right and wrong. There just IS. If you can accept your enemy like your friend, then you are home. Enemies come. It is part of the game. Men have been shot for just speaking the truth. Others have come along and been crucified. What is the game? Nothing happens unless it is the Divine Will. If you can get that now, feel the truth of three questions I'm going to ask you. Do you believe in a God? Do you believe God makes mistakes? Do you believe that God is the director of the whole play going on here? The Creator? The problem for people is that they would like to give God their opinion and tell Him how His plan is not good.

The truth is that your ideas are not yours. All ideas are God's. God wrote all the books. He wrote all the prescriptions. He wrote all of the plays. All you have to do is take YOU out of the equation. They are not your ideas; they are God's ideas. All these ideas and concepts—that is all they are, only ideas and concepts. They are all His. I blame Him for everything. It is great! If something goes wrong, I blame Him. If something goes right, I blame Him. If He decides He doesn't want any more "More Truth Will Set You Free" workshops, how wonderful! That way, I wouldn't have to sit in flying cigars for hours and hours and hours when I could be sitting in Ireland looking at the fairies and the leprechauns. I do workshops because I tried to lie on the bed and He wouldn't let me. I even gave myself cancer to try to get to lie on the bed. He got me out of the bed. Whose ideas are they really?

Life is God having a conversation with Himself based on, "I separated Myself from Myself so I could love Myself more." As long as you think you are the Doer, you will suffer, and suffering will be part of who you are. When you finally release the doing, suffering continues to happen, but it will move through the chakras and it's gone, gone. What happens now is that the suffering goes horizontally. You hold onto it because you think you are the Doer. When you know you are not the Doer, it rises through the chakras, so it is just a happening. If you happen to be standing at the right spot for a car to hit you, then you happen to step back as the car goes by, it is a happening. It is not something that you do. Nobody knows how the Creator is going to call you home. When you are in a state of surrender, you're like a feather on the wind. You don't know where you are going to end up. You don't know where your next meal is going to come from, or if it is going to come. And if it doesn't come, you just die. That is the physical body. Spirit never goes anywhere. I'll bet everybody here, and I can feel your silence now, is as confused as the belly is about its next meal. There is a nice silence. That is all. It is that simple. You are not the Doer. It might take a few days to sink in, but you will get it.

All tightness and tension leaves, and illness is no more. Once you start to grasp the concept in your head, you have not got it. When you feel it in your heart, it's a release. Then you have got it. And Grace falls down like rain on all that is broken. God doesn't make broken toys. He doesn't make mistakes. Everything is perfect. Sai Baba says, "Miracles are my calling cards." He makes diamond rings and trinkets appear. One was valued at forty million dollars. He makes these little trinkets and just gives them out. What he is telling people is, "Mind die. Die-mind." Those people are going around flashing their diamonds from Sai Baba, thinking how great they are. They completely missed the message. But that is okay. Maybe they will get the message their next time around. If Sai Baba gives you a chain, you are chained to something. The subtler the sign you get, the more aware you have become.

So, your free will is just you making the choice of acting as if you have free will. You will be happier, that I can guarantee. Events will happen. You know, the Buddha never attained enlightenment. But don't tell the Buddhists. I told this to the Dalai Lama. He thought it was hilarious. The Buddha never attained enlightenment when he was sitting under the tree because he was too focused on suffering. He still had recognition of suffering. So he died. Very quickly he came back. When he came back, he made a statue of himself and on the statue he wrote, "I got it wrong." Then enlightenment fell. These are the words that came with enlightenment: "Events happen. Deeds are done. There are consequences of the deeds. And there is no Doer of the deeds." There is great enlightenment in that statement to meditate on.

Everything is Divinely guided. You didn't come here; you were brought here. Now comes the ultimate statement of truth: You never set out to find God. God set out to find you. You are not the Doer. All action is His. You are not the Doer. You could never find God. God finds you. When the student is ready, the teacher does come. The readiness comes from being still and knowing that you are God. The problem is, you bleeding well got the gift before He delivered it. Be still. Know you are God. Who is making you breathe right now? If God wanted you to stop breathing, do you know how simple that would be? Do you? You never know when He is going to call you home.

Always have His name on your lips and in your heart, for the moment He may call, then you go first class. That is why you are not asked to be anything but what you are. You are not asked to act like God. You are asked to act from God. God needs ill people. God needs teachers. God needs students and wars and crises and love and bliss and poverty, and for light and dark to exist. God cannot exist without you. That is the contract. You are not the Doer. Sit back and enjoy the ride. Now the laugh is on me. It is true. You think you surrendered by letting go of the rope. But what happens is, down comes the barrel to crack you on the head and make sure you have, in fact, let go of the rope.

God did not give you free will. That is the illusion. That is the tool He uses to keep you. God said this great statement: "I separated Myself from Myself so I could love Myself more." God was sitting there one day, bored out of His tree, and He created a board game called Earth. He was going to call it Monopoly, but someone copyrighted that name before Him. So He called it Earth. He sat there and it was wonderful and nice. The water wasn't polluted. The air wasn't polluted. People were going around naked and happy.

Then, someone said, "Look at me. I have five pounds."

Someone else said, "I have six. I have more than you."

That is when you thought you had free will. So, God is sitting there and it's a good game, but you know that game Chutes and Ladders? What happens is, you roll the dice and you climb the ladder. Then you roll the dice again and down the chute you go. God created that game Chutes and Ladders. Now, He's sitting there watching and He says, "I think I will get this person to play the laugher. And I think this person over here can play 'Who does he think he is "slagging" my God?'" He gave everyone parts. You all have been given your part. Now, here's the problem. You all can't get Oscars. You get something else. You get Love.

The difference between a Master and student is simple. They both pull down their trousers to go to the toilet. Isn't that wonderful! But the Master does this if he can: when anger arises he just watches the anger leave. A Master screams, "Don't do that anymore." Then he turns around and gently gives the person a flower. See, that's the lesson I got in Puttaparthi. The man screamed at me because he was an instrument. You will always experience anger and sadness in your life, and grief and love and happiness. It is a "happening." It is not a "doing." It spontaneously arises and when it does, the Master lets it go. He is not attached. He is not inflated by pride or dejected by depression. It is just a happening. Everything arises and goes to Source. You poor people keep doing this: anger arises and it hits the control box, the heart. Then it goes outwards and you hold onto it. It remains with you until some idiot from Ireland arrives and draws it back in, into alignment, and lets it flow again.

The consequence is the duality that was given to you at birth. Duality means when an event happens you either go down this road, which is the road of love and peace, or you go down this road, which is the road of anger and upset. That is your free will. It is just duality. You can, believe it or not, petition to walk down the road of love and peace more often. How do you do that? By doing nothing. Just watch what is going on in your life now. Watch as you sit there and say, "I am not getting this." Watch it. It is not that you are not getting it. It is anger arising because everybody else is floating in the sky with angels with wings and all sorts of fireworks going on. You say to yourself, "I see 'piss off,' so there must be something wrong with me." You all are spiritual people, and yet you don't have jealousy issues? Please stop buying into everybody else's life and start living your own. First you, then two. One plus one plus one plus one plus one equals ONE. First YOU, then two.

When you become a watcher, then you know that you are not the Doer. There is a simple way of becoming the watcher. Start with yourself and work outwards. Watch yourself. Watch every emotion rise and say, "Isn't that interesting?" Then let it go. Just acknowledge it, and then let it go. Don't say, "Look at that! What's that?" If you do, you will probably be brought into some place you don't particularly want to go. Just "watch" is what you are supposed to do.

CHAPTER 25

HEALINGS

I teach several healing methods, which are known as Prema Agni, Rising Star, and Prema Birthing. Go to www.SQ-Wellness.com for more information.

PREMA AGNI

This symbol is called Prema Agni, and it came back to reawaken the Heart Chakra of the world. Basically, what God said was, "Hey, Derek, this is what is happening. People are bypassing their Heart Chakra and that is why there are so many bypass operations going on in our hospitals." He said that they are either bringing the energy down, and it is going down, down, down, and stopping—these people are becoming scientists because they are all in their head—or it is coming up, up, up, and these people are becoming sexual deviants. So He said, "I am giving this symbol back to the world because it is time that love poured forth, back to all the places where love was locked out." He gave that symbol back.

Within the Prema Agni symbol is represented every major religion in the world. They are all in there. That symbol incorporates everything. You have all the numbers. The nine-pointed zigzag lightning bolt represents completion. Nine is the number of completion, and when that lightening bolt hits your heart, it is opened. If I had a single thought to manifest out in the world, it would be to have the Prema Agni drawn on all the children when they're born. Better than a slap on the butt. If it is drawn on the dying, their transition will go smoothly and easily.

RISING STAR

This symbol is the Rising Star. The top of the star represents the Crown Chakra. The heart shape represents the Heart Chakra. The bottom, center of the triangle is the Root Chakra. So, within the symbol, you have your seven chakras. Now, right from the bottom of the star there are five strokes coming out. Then on each side you have three strokes coming out of the star. What is five and three? Eight. And what is eight and three? Eleven. The number eleven is Christ Consciousness. So these three strokes on each side of the star are wings. The five strokes below are a tail. Together they represent the peacock. That is because if you ever look at a picture of a highly evolved being called an Avatar, you will see that he always has a peacock beside him. The peacock represents the ego, and the Avatar always travels on the ego's back.

When you start doing a Rising Star healing, what happens as soon as you set down this grid on the Crown Chakra is that the Rising Star symbol sits right on top of the person. You could actually tell people to get off your healing table at that stage, but that probably won't give you any more business. People like a process, so you better give them the whole process. The truth is though that as soon as you put your hands in that position, it happens and the healing is done right then.

When you start to use the spiritual energy for yourself, what begins to happen is you let the world be. You don't even use the words, "I am a healer." That is not really what you are. You are greater than that, particularly when you use a system like the Rising Star that is on the planet at the moment. It incorporates any tag that is otherwise labeled as healing. It incorporates it right into itself and is of the highest vibration. It gives anyone who is attuned to it the opportunity to feel what it is like to not be the Doer. I say, "Hey, stop trying to add to perfection." We don't need it. People ask me questions like, "Is it okay to wave my hand behind my head six times before I start?" The Rising Star is so simple, outrageously simple, because you are not the Doer. I tell all practitioners of the Rising Star how they will know they are a real practitioner of the Rising Star—it is when they walk into a room and cancer is gone. Now for those of you who are a practitioner of the Rising Star: If you are really channeling to its full strength, nothing can stand in its way. The only thing standing in its way is you. You can only do what you do, which is nothing. But you must live your life as if you were the Doer because if you don't, you won't survive. During the Rising Star treatment, not only are you getting paid for meditating on God, but you also have the opportunity to sit with God and be paid.

PREMA BIRTHING

Prema Birthing does not have a symbol at this time. It is not necessary. Prema Birthing gives clients the opportunity to reprogram their minds and bodies to the original program they had when they were conceived. It allows clients to experience how it feels to be without all of the lies and negative programming they pick up after they are conceived. Then clients have the choice of whether to live without all of that programming or to take it all back in. It is extremely powerful.

If all you do is chat, chat, and chat all day and then think, "God doesn't listen to me," that is because He is popping pills for migraines caused by your ignorance. The path of healing is the path of silence. That doesn't mean you can't be in a traffic jam, hearing horns bellow. It just means that you honor where you are and drop into your space. When you do so, all the clutter and the clatter goes where it goes, and you can then just sit there in the rhythm of God. If you are in the rhythm of God, it creates health and well-being. If you aren't, you go into a different rhythm.

PROTECTION

Some people are on ring number one. Some are on ring number two, and some are on number six. You have to take people where they are and leave them where they are. It is not your job to change people in any way. If they choose to come into your company and they hear something that changes their life, that is wonderful! If not, that is wonderful!

I was five when I first felt healing energy coming through this human form. I was acutely aware that this was something elevating inside and outside of myself at the same time. I began to build a ritual around that, consciously and unconsciously. One of the rituals I built got me into so much trouble. It was the ritual of skipping school. Instead of going to school, I went to the local river or forest and sat there all day. That was a ritual in a sense. I was trying to ritualize that healing back to myself because I felt I had been a part of it somewhere. So, whatever ritual you have that makes you feel good is a good ritual. There is no need to create a ritual to protect yourself. God does that automatically. Remember that you are not the healer, God is. The best protection against any negative energy is laughter. That includes any illness or disease going on around you. It also includes any negative energy some people call magic.

MONEY

I have never charged a dime for healing work. I have charged a lot of money to train people. That is because my overhead is very expensive. So I don't believe any healers charge for healing work. What I believe they are doing is making their living, which is a fair enough thing to do. It is really interesting that nobody cares about the fact that one of your baseball players is getting one hundred million dollars a month to play in a baseball game. When healers want one hundred dollars to bring God back to your experience, they get criticized. Does that say something about the psyche of this world?

The Rising Star Healing System is tackling that issue. When it came down, it came down into a workshop with two or three hundred people. I was talking, and I stopped, and down came this brand new system. I offered to show the people at the workshop because I felt it was the energy of the people in the room that brought it there, not me. Lots of people wanted to see. We asked for a volunteer, and a lady put her hand up. We took an ordinary table, put her on it, and did the Rising Star Healing on her. Once I started to channel this system down, people in the audience were completely silent. We heard, "Crack, crack, crack." It turned out this woman suffered from scoliosis, and her spine was straightening there on the table.

I just channeled it down and then said, "I will have to leave now, go to my room, and take down the intimate details that came down with it." I was actually expecting it to go for nothing, for no charge. I had seen other modalities become money-oriented, and the healing art had become tainted. I thought this was going to come down as a balance to that. It came with very specific instructions. One of the instructions I received was that if some person cannot afford to have this healing modality done, the healing should not be given. The reason is that the majority of people are in victim-hood and are being held there by those who haven't dealt with their own issues of abundance. These people who haven't dealt with their abundance issues are called healers and therapists. You are not doing anyone any favors by not having an exchange of energy for what is going on.

The victim/abundance issue was brought up in a workshop in New York. A woman said, "I don't agree with that." You could catch the energy where that was coming from. "My friend is a junkie, and I am going to give her healings. I give her healings every week." I sat and absorbed it all. The first thing I said was, "It is very unpleasant for anyone to be called a junkie. I don't think you are much of a friend to address anyone as a junkie. If you wish to use the word 'drug-addicted,' that is a neutral word. You give this friend a treatment every week for nothing? So, where does she get the money to buy the drugs? Does her drug supplier give them to her for free? Is it not better that she gives that money to the Creator, 'I AM,' and drops to her knees and says, 'I am sorry,' and lets the healing take place? The facilitation you would be giving is facilitation where everybody gets what he or she needs. If you haven't dealt with your own abundance issues, you are going to be calling everyone 'junkies' and 'sick.' I have never seen a sick person or an ill person, not even a diseased person, actually. I only see God. I transfer this system back to them. So I bring God-to-God, Source-to-Source. That is also God."

CHAPTER 26

JESUS THE CHRIST

Jesus was a highly evolved spiritual teacher, and He was human. He was a handful when He was a child. He gave His mother an awful time. I think if Jesus were alive now as a child, He would be diagnosed with ADHD or something similar because He was hyper. He was hyper because physicality meant nothing to Him. He went to all the places of interest and workshops because He was looking for answers. He knew there was something else. He ended up sitting with the wisest of the wise and then disappeared off this planet. He had His poor mother worried to death because He went missing so many times for His growth.

He learned and came to the understanding of His purpose. He said, "I understand now that I have to be conditioned by God, through the experience of humanity, in order to be of service and return to God." So off He went. He went to India and learned about Buddhism and Hinduism and "this-ism" and "Derek-ism" and "isms" everywhere. He took this, this, and this, which are the essences of all of them, and put them in his heart. He then came back and said to people, "Your way is not the way." He started to show His given powers through the Grace of "I AM" by always saying, "My father, who art in heaven." He was telling you that above Him was brilliance and perfection. He always said it. When He said, "I and my Father are one," that was the moment when there was no above. He had become enlightened. So He came along and showed people the way. "'I AM' the Light and the Divine."

He went into the den of thieves that used to be His sacred temple and confronted the thieves who were masquerading as moneychangers. He ripped them apart, tossed their table up, scattered their money, and let out their pigeons. Anyone looking at Him would think He was a raving lunatic full of anger. Correct? What was He showing you? How to let the emotions arise within you and when you are the instrument of Him who is my Father in Heaven of Whom I sit on the right hand side. He gave us all the teachings as best He could until the church got Him. It was all part of His plan, as well.

By the way, do you know why He took Peter? What did He call Peter? The rock. Who denied Him three times? Peter. So He had a weakness. He built the church, and the church would have to fall around a given time, around 2012 (the end of the Mayan Calendar, thought to be the completion of the current era and the beginning of a new era of Enlightenment). The rock was limited to a period of time that we are watching now, are we not? "On you I will build my church." He never meant for huge cathedrals and buildings to be built. "Wherever two or more are gathered in my name, there I shall be." He went through the same human experience that we are going through. That is what is great. We can all be like Jesus. We only have to believe. There can be miracles when you believe. Though hope is gone, because we are told so, it's hard to kill because it is deeper than that.

When Jesus said, "Turn the other cheek," people got it a bit confused. They thought He meant that when someone slapped you on this side, you turned to the other side and let them slap you there too. He didn't mean that at all. There is an old martial arts concept that says when something is coming at you, as a target, make yourself a smaller target. That is what He meant. He meant bring yourself into rhythm with it, and when you do, you become a smaller target. When you become a smaller target, he who has used force against you will now miss the target, and with the smallest piece of that force, you will see him topple. If you break anything down to its essence, you will find it comes from God.

Jesus met this character called Lazarus. That was the great thing about Jesus that many people don't recognize. Okay, He cured the sick and He helped the poor, but He slept in beds at Lazarus' five-star hotel. Just read your Bible stories. Whose house does he go to? Lazarus was one of the richest guys on the planet. Jesus' physical body needed Lazarus' house to carry out the work and to bring that much energy down. It's like traveling in a Lear Jet which is easier than having to be cooped up for many, many hours in a crowded plane. Another thing is, Jesus didn't hang around with the sick. He just healed them. He hung around with the rich because He used their abundance to heal the sick.

Lazarus was thinking, "I will buy this guy. I will give Him all the best food." And of course, Jesus ate all of the best food, and why would He do anything else? Now you can see where your abundance issues have to be dealt with. So, Jesus was at Lazarus' house, eating. They were merry and everything was fine and dandy. Then, next came the big one.

Lazarus says, "I want to follow you, Jesus," because he recognized who Jesus was.

Jesus said to Lazarus, "Sure. Just give away everything that you own."

Lazarus' sister intervened and said; "You know, my brother gives a big stash of money, ten percent of all he has."

Jesus said, "I know of a better one. I know of a woman who once gave two pence."

Lazarus' sister said; "What is two pence compared to what my brother gives? He gives millions away."

Jesus answered, "It was all that she had." When you let go of your attachment to money, you will detach from your misery surrounding that attachment; I am here to take all that misery away from the lot of you. That's a lot of misery.

Then Jesus said that where your heart is, here is your God. "It is easier, if money is your God, to at least admit that it is your God and go to it. It might turn you at any stage." Then Jesus left, and because of Lazarus' attachment to his money, Lazarus could not follow.

Lazarus sat there contemplating. We call it a meditation, but he was contemplating on the Karma that had just taken place. He sat there and thought, "What did Jesus mean when He said, 'It is easier for a camel to pass through the eye of a needle, than for a rich man to get into heaven.' What did Jesus mean?" That statement has held so many people in poverty because it has been so misunderstood. "It is easier to pass a camel through the eye of a needle than for a rich man to get into heaven." People interpret this to mean that you should not have money or you should not get rich. That is what it means to most people. That is what we were told, anyways, growing up in Ireland. Then, of course, they really did us a big favor with films like Scrooge for instance. Look at him. He had money. Money always equals unhappiness. It's always the same in films.

What Jesus meant was this: you are the camel, and to get through the eye of the needle, you need to take off your hump. The hump is the attachment you have to anything you think that you own. That is your hump. You can't serve two gods: money and God. Money comes and goes. Love comes and grows. If you are out there making lots of money, fine. Be happy. Don't beat yourself up for being rich. If you are not making lots of money, fine. Be happy. Don't beat yourself up for not being rich. The truth is that being rich or poor is simply the paths that people choose to find God. Both rich and poor have an equal chance for full enlightenment, like Jesus. However, if you have an attachment to being rich or an attachment to not being rich, you will not pass through the eye of the needle.

When Jesus was sitting under the bridge, one of the lads had his cloak stolen. He was cold and angry with this thief that had stolen his cloak. Jesus gave him this teaching, "Find the thief and give him your trousers and anything else you have. Your attachment is anything that can be stolen."

Jesus was sitting around the campfire, and a messenger came and said, "Lord, Lord, come quickly. Lazarus is dying." Jesus told the messenger that this illness had not come for Lazarus, but for the "glorification of My Father." He ignored the message. A couple days later, He decided to go to Lazarus. He wanted to teach His followers a lesson. They were all sitting there, wondering, "Maybe He is a fake. Maybe He is a great talker, but...."

Jesus got up and they followed Him like sheep. It is good to be sheep when you are following the Lamb of God.

When they arrived at Lazarus' house, Lazarus's sister ran to Him saying, "Why did you not come? Why did you not come for your friend who gave you everything?"

She was very angry and thumped Jesus on the chest. He just watched her.

Then the other sister came and said, "Why were you not here?"

Jesus says, "Do you know who I am? Do you not see the truth in me, Marta?"

Then she said the truth that would set her free. In her anger and with her anger in place she said these words, "I know if You had been here, my brother would not be dead." Do you hear the truth in that?

She knew who was standing there, and she said it in her absolute humanity because you have to engage humanity with spirituality. In her humanity, she said the words that were the most truthful: "I know if you had been here, my brother would not be dead." In other words, in code, she was saying, "I know you are the Christ." A single tear rose from His eye. He went to the cave where Lazarus was buried, and He said, "I call on the four winds. Lazarus, arise and come home." If a Master says it must happen, it must happen. Then out walked the dead man.

Lazarus served Jesus for the rest of his life, and that is when Jesus taught him that the camel goes through the eye of the needle if you take the hump off its back. The hump is just all the materialistic stuff that you think you need to be happy. As the story goes, Lazarus had another couple of years on the Earth, and then he died again, which only goes to show that immortality has nothing to do with physicality. It doesn't matter. It just doesn't matter.

Jesus said, "Blessed are those who soften and become ripe." He didn't say meek. See, the Aramaic words he used came from seasons, astrology, and nature. Jesus would always speak from nature when teaching. There is a season for everything. That is why if you want to be really healthy, don't eat vegetables out of season. Eat them in season. That is when they are offering themselves. That is when a carrot is being a carrot. Do you understand? This is the truth that is starting to come through now.

When Jesus turned water into wine, He never looked at the problem. He looked to the Source of everything. He was attending a wedding and the party ran out of wine. He said, "Bring me water." If you are looking for something, know you have it already. If you hold onto the fear of lack, like the wedding party who was partying hardy and didn't have enough wine, instead of looking at the source of non-fear, God, you will not manifest anything. So, Jesus did not see the water. He looked at God and saw wine. He also did this in front of everybody with the loaves and the fish. If you look at the problem, the problem stays in this dimension. He said, "Father, out of your hands." Then He said to the apostles, "Go and feed them." As we all know, the multitude was fed with just a few baskets of bread and fish. What is the greatest form of protection? Love, which manifests as an open heart. By seeing only God's love and not seeing any lack or fear, Jesus was able to perform these manifestations.

There He was, and then comes His finality. He knew it. He had been shown the picture. "Those that I have sent You to awaken will kill You now." And He goes, fully knowing, and still He goes. He was very brave about it all until that moment when He was in the garden and His humanity flooded back to Him. He said, "Take this cup from me." That was His human self. He was not Christ-ed at that stage. He was a Master-in-training, like you. God sent Him two angels. What He sent was the Prema Agni symbol. The symbol that would rise above the Prema Agni symbol is that of the Rising

Star. He had to wait for that moment to give it. So, "For this task, I have come to this world."

Then He was arrested. He was flogged and He was tortured. He stood it with as much Grace as He possibly could with someone lashing his skin. Then, they hung His body high. It was vitally important that they hung Him high because He needed to see everybody. They waited to see Him, so there would be no misconception.

He said, "Father, can I be of one more service before I leave this world?" You didn't hear that. This was His moment.

He knew it and He said, "Is there anything?" Now, He was suffering and yet He still asked if there was one more service He could do for you before His physical form dropped.

The Father said, "This service, the world will hear." And He put crosses on the side of Him, two thieves.

One who said, "If you are God, why not save yourself?"

"Non-believer you will suffer," He said.

The other thief said, "This man did no wrong."

Jesus said to him, "Today, you will sit with Me in My Father's home." Jesus came to show how to live in physical form. He didn't have all the guidance, all the answers, and He suffered. I don't have to go into what happened when they finally decided to stick Him up on the cross and all the symbology of the good thief on this side and the bad thief on that side. There are no thieves. Ice cream is one treat, yet flavors are many.

One thief said to Jesus, "Why don't you show us who you are and do one of your magic tricks and get us down off the cross."

Jesus turned to him and said, "You will be in Heaven with me and you will come back to Earth." That is what He was saying. That is what that scenario was set up for.

Then He felt that abandonment again at that last moment when He said, "Abba, Abba." He is calling His Father, "Abba, Abba, why have you forsaken Me?" The Father arrived and collected His son.

That was His message to humanity that humanity could understand. Even through the suffering, he worked. Then at that given moment in time He said the Almighty words, "Father, Abba, Abba… Father, Father, why have you forsaken Me?" He was back into His humanity. The Prema Agni won and He was there and He was pleading, "Why have you forsaken Me?" That was the separateness. Then came the Divine Fire in all its glory riding the ego as it does, in the form of the peacock. It rested upon Him. The Holy Spirit rested upon

Him. The symbol is the symbol of the Holy Spirit in all its aspects. It rested and then He said the words of liberation, which are, "Father forgive them."

The people must hear Him because it has to happen on a "matter" level so people can hear. He had suffered and suffered and suffered and He still said, "Love, love, love!" He said, "Father forgive them, for they know not what they do." He was pleading for the people who had been battering him! There is love, love, love. Then He said, "Into your hands I commend My spirit." Then He came back just to show people that death is a habit. It is one of our greatest habits. You don't have to do it (die), you know. You can just switch bodies, and that is it.

So Jesus was trained, as you are trained. He came back to share his discovery and to teach. Not that He wanted to come back, because He knew what was going to happen when He came to teach. He learned this while He was being trained. He said, "I am going back for the glorification of My Father who is in Heaven and they will crucify Me for it."

The God for most people at that time was the shekel. The priests charged money before you went into the temple because you had to have a bath to make yourself clean. And who owned all the bathhouses? The priests who fulfilled God's purpose for Jesus. So, Jesus came back and taught us about the illusion of death and who God really was. However, He still had to deal with His humanity. He said, "Father, why have you forsaken Me?" Those are not the words of a Master or Savior. Those are the words of the human being. The Holy Spirit, or angel, descended upon him, otherwise known as Kundalini Awakening. He received the strength and the courage to say to this world, "You are," and "This is why I came."

Jesus came in as a man amongst men, and came back to give the world's greatest lesson: that death is an illusion. He showed people that when people are born they come in with the mustard seed missing, but it is only a mustard seed. Did He not say, "If you only have the faith of a mustard seed, you shall move mountains?" It is only a mustard seed that is missing. All human beings, whether they are priests or prostitutes, those in the bars and those pumping chemicals into their bodies, they all have a chance at enlightenment, as you do. That cuts out judgment, doesn't it? That is all the faith that you need.

He came back to show you that you have to have a human crucifixion before you rise to the Father. Every person reading this, and on this planet, will be crucified. It might just be that the love of your life walks out. That is a crucifixion. Your best friend could betray you. That is a crucifixion. Here is an interesting turn of events on Judas. Judas loved Jesus with all he had, and he knew, more than anyone, who Jesus was. The reason that Judas did what he did was that Judas was convinced that his God was going to annihilate evil. So Judas brought evil to Jesus. Judas knew Jesus was capable of destroying the evil he brought to the Garden of Gethsemane. Judas loved Jesus, and he was His greatest disciple. He knew who Jesus was, he knew He was God, and he knew who he was. Judas really and truly was trained in mantras (sacred sounds or words capable of creating transformation) and mudras (sacred hand positions that guide energy flow), and all of this by Jesus, to give him the courage and strength to do what he had to do: deliver the son of man to the Son of God so that His glorification could be sung throughout the world.

Judas was the mustard seed taken out of place because that mustard seed was the only difference between Judas and Jesus. He took it out, and Judas walked the soldiers to Jesus so that Judas' God could go and wipe out evil. Judas never, ever thought, even for a second, that Jesus was just going to go. It is very simple. You are questioning God's will, and if you do you will suffer. There are two paths, the path of love and the path of fear. It's duality, and once we are here, we are in duality. Events happen; how you react to them is more important. Prove your fabulous relatives wrong and just don't die, just for the fun, for joy and laughter.

CHAPTER 27

JUDGMENT

Judgment stops when Truth is present. Put your baseball bat down and stop beating yourself. It is important that you acknowledge that your judgment is there, because if you don't acknowledge it, you hold onto it forever. The awakened ones look at a situation not in judgment, but in silence, and watch the manifestation afterwards. It is important to stay still and quiet at all times, particularly if you are out of your comfort zone. That is the opportunity to bring the silence into the uncomfortable zone so that the uncomfortable zone becomes comfortable as well.

The awakening factor is this: Send me, oh, Lord, all that is mine. Next, people come, and events happen, and items appear. Isn't that our prayer? Give us what we need. You contracted to arrive here. That is the Divine contract that was written from your Higher Self to your Higher Self. People can be awake in their body and be walking toward the light, then something happens. But those moments pass. Remember the pendulum I was talking about? Those moments pass extremely quickly. That is the lesson of who you are. Don't be anxious for tomorrow. It is already waiting. You just have to make the choice. Do you want to get to tomorrow this way, or would you like to get to tomorrow that way? Either way, you are going to get there, because you are getting there. You will make that choice consciously or unconsciously.

Everyone struggles between awareness and judgment. Awareness just is. Judgment is not. Awareness and judgment are a double-edged sword with an extraordinarily sharp blade. The way to know the difference between the two is to feel it in your body. The discernment of awareness has no fear. It just is. The discernment of judgment cuts hard, and when you find out you judged wrong, it creates pain. If you want to know the difference between the two, it is a feeling. Awareness is sent down the tube of easy reality. Judgment is sent down the tube of your will. The most important awareness is to be aware that you are not aware of anything.

What is causing most of the pain is judgment. Judgment comes from information from others, gleaned from others in this lifetime and past. Judgment causes a lot of pain. Judgment comes from comparing yourself to others. If we take the word judgment and transfer it to conditioning, well, then you know why you are here. You have come here to have your conditioning updated to Truth. Judgment stops when Truth is present. You have to know the difference between Truth and judgment. We all know there is a fine line between judgment and discernment. Sometimes we don't know which side of that line we are walking on. It is very simple. When you are in discernment, there is no suffering. When you are in judgment, suffering will always be present.

Here is an example: You know that the north of Ireland and the south of Ireland are now in peace, and it is actually from the example of the north and south of Ireland that the wars will stop in Iran, Iraq, and all those places. We were so close to peace in the Middle East last year, with the peace process, but humanity wasn't ready, and it blew back out again. The peace process will remain out until humanity's readiness comes back in. Ireland is the blueprint for all wars. That is why America played such a big part in coming to Ireland, learning and being involved in the process that was happening in Northern Ireland. The sectarian killings are felt quite deep. So, if you can have peace here in Ireland, then you have the blueprint for all upcoming wars. We are actually quite close to having peace as a human race, perhaps in five years. Always keep in mind that you are limited, because if you do, then you know it is not possible to have the full picture in front of you. If you haven't got the full picture, then there's a good chance that you are in judgment. If you sit quietly there's a good chance that discernment will enter. It will come from a Source that has a bigger picture than you.

In Buddhism, connecting with this Source is called, calling the "Lama from Afar"—calling your guru or teacher and asking for inner guidance. You don't go on the Internet; you go on the "Inner-net." Source will bring you to this stage when the awareness arises and you are not in judgment. There will be no more looking at television. There will come "Tell-A-Vision." Anything you get is to be shared. It is not just for you. It is for everybody that is you. "Give me your ears and your eyes, those that will listen and those that will see. I will show you wonders beyond belief, but only when you are ready." When the student is ready, the teacher comes. When the teacher is ready, the student falls apart at the seams.

You have heard of Mother Amma, the Hugging Saint. If you were a world-class weight lifter and had to hug fifteen thousand people without a break for a day, you would win the world championship straight away or you would end up with a huge hump on your back. That is very human, yes. But that is what this woman does. She goes around the world and hugs people. I got an e-mail that said she was the devil. This was from a woman who had been told vicious things. And then I got another e-mail from someone else who said the same thing. Two people. What happened was "Amma" was the word that got people mixed up. "Amma" just means "mother," but these people reacted in fear and judgment. That is what I am saying, as the truth begins to set us free, each thing that crosses your path is a gift. You can call it a test or whatever. It is just a gift to see if you are going to sit in judgment, or will you just send love. Even if somebody is the head of a gangster pack, there is enough judgment going on the planet right now. We don't need to do that bit anymore.

I will tell you what Sai Baba says about judgment officially. "When I am in the midst of man, I am a man. And when I am in the midst of woman, I am a woman. When I am in the midst of children, I am a child. And when I am alone, I am God." Let people go around saying what they like because it is all true in their world. It may even be true in your world, but the truth may be sitting above it. The only reason that a being may come into your life would be to deliver a gift. So don't shoot the messengers. We have been doing that for most of our lives. It is just a test. Do you get it? When something happens, be still. Be alone. Be still and know that you are God. Sit there and say "That's not my slice of cake," and honor that, and that is fine. Some people don't like pickled ice cream, and some people do. The second part of what Sai Baba says is, "I am neither guru nor God. I am you and you are I. That is the truth. There is no distinction. The appearance of differences is the delusion. You are the waves. I am the ocean. Know this and be free by Divine Creed."

CHAPTER 28

MEDITATION

If you know you are in meditation, you are not. Ramana Maharshi wanted us to understand meditation. There are only a handful of people who can meditate. Most people sit in a state of contemplation. If you reach a state of meditation, there is nothing but God. If your meditation does not take you there, then you are in contemplation of getting to meditation. So please understand and distinguish the two. Otherwise, you could be stuck in contemplation, and meditation can't enter. If you believe something is something, then it becomes that something for you.

Ramana Maharshi wanted us to know why people rise to meditate at 4:00 a.m. He wanted all the people who love to stay in bed to know that is okay too. He said that most people who can't get up at 4:00 a.m. to meditate beat themselves up so badly that they run programs saying they are not worthy and not particularly as powerful as the person who gets up at 4:00 a.m. to meditate. He wanted you to know that is not true. He said that if you are programmed to lie in your bed for the rest of your days, you will lie in your bed for the rest of your days. If not, you will be awakened when you are supposed to arise. The reason that certain vibrational beings get up at 4:00 a.m. every morning is called the service of sacrifice. It is based on one of Sathya Sai Baba's teachings: "Service to Man is Service to God."

These people get up to greet the day. Then they enter into a process where they manifest the day that they want. So the truth is if these people didn't do what they do, then we couldn't sit here. The vibrational state of the other world would be so bad that we would all be in a massive state of depression. They offer the meditation away from themselves. They offer it to humanity. Then they manifest that love for the people who are required to stay in bed, to hold the energy and pick it up later on during the day.

Don't sit in meditation for yourself, sit in meditation for humanity and create love. For yourself, take some time to sit in contemplation of "Who Am I?" Don't repeat it like a mantra over and over. You only say it three times. Three is the number of manifestation. Once you say it three times, it has to manifest. Where it will manifest you don't know. Anything you put out into the universe three times has to manifest. If you are in a state of fear of not being good enough and you put that fear out into the universe three times, guess what? It manifests. After saying "Who Am I?" three times, then you wait in a state of contemplation. Usually you will then have the split personality system, which is like two voices having a conversation in your head:

"You are unworthy."

"No, I am not."

"Yes you are. I can prove it."

"Okay. Go ahead."

"Well, your mother didn't want you. Didn't she say that?"

Contemplation now drops into self-loathing and self-criticism. That voice is as good as someone in physical form saying that to you. You don't have to let anyone in this world beat you up. You are doing a fabulous job on your own. Recognize that this voice is part of you. Let the voices come. Don't attach to the voices. Your task is not to enter into the conversation. What do you say? "I AM." The energy will start to grow, then it will blow itself out. You may have entered a very deep state of contemplation saying, "Who Am I?" Then you will hear a voice come through that says, "You and I are One." When that comes through, that is the last grain of your ego. It is like a seed waiting to catch you that one last time. That is usually the time people think they are brilliant. That is when you have to say again, "Who am I?" and the voice will say, "You and I are One," or "You are God." Then for the very last time as a human being you will say, "Who am I?" And if that voice comes back and says, "You and I are One" or "You are God," I can guarantee you that they will immediately write you out of the contract and write in that you have mastered this existence and can go on.

The best meditation technique is a very simple technique called "Show up for your life and make every act that you do a sacrifice to God." Offer everything up. Never do an action without offering it up. That is a great meditation, a walking meditation. The time for meditation in the lotus position is over. The steps prior to this were: "So Hum," all meditations, and forcing yourself into knots. I know nothing about yoga. I know that the word means "communion with God." I don't know anything about the way that it is taught, but I can see energy. I see people doing a Plow Asana with legs going over the head. I assume this is taught in a lot of yoga classes, and I wonder how many teachers know the particular danger of that pose. Not many. So do you know what it does? It blows up the relationship and emotional chakras and it makes you feel good because you are flowing, but when you go home, your partner will have changed and gotten all grumpy. The teachers are not telling people to expect the processing that come afterwards.

Everything is a meditation. The simplest meditation is, show up for your life. Breathe. Watch your breathing, because when you see people in fear, they won't give themselves a full breath. If they give themselves a full breath, what would happen? Fear dissipates. So again, it comes down to that simple technique that we are already supposed to know how to do, breathe.

Meditation by sitting in caves is well and truly over on this planet. There is no cave meditation. The only cave meditations are in here, the heart. Hello. Welcome. It is all happening here—cheesecake and sex.

Meditation is where you have dropped into your heart. Contemplation is where most people are. If you think you are meditating, you are not. In other words, if you are sitting down meditating, you are not, because meditation "is." If you have had the experience, you will know what I am talking about, and if you have not, you will know when you have it.

I don't meditate, because my life is my meditation. That is because of what my destiny is in this lifetime. Sitting in a lotus position, floating six inches above the ground, didn't do it for me. I decided it was an easier reality for me to make my life my meditation and offer everything to God and never reach for the fruits of my actions. Let it all flow and watch it. I don't realize I am meditating, and when you don't realize you are meditating, you are. Otherwise, you are contemplating, or ego-elating. Just offer every action to God. It is that simple. It doesn't have to be that complicated. Offer it to God and let it go. Only you can let it go. Nobody can take it from you. Nobody. You have to let it go. Then the receiver comes, collects it, and turns it into the love that you have always been looking for.

You don't have to do anything. You just have to be awake enough to see and act on the guidance you are given. I want to explain some deeper meanings of some stuff that has been floating around the planet for centuries with half-truths and some controlled truths. There are people on the planet who have been sent to this planet for no other reason than to wake up at 4:00 a.m. and meditate. They are called the Manifestor Energies. They manifest the world and each day of the world. That is what their task is and what God has them here to do. Now, that is them. Without them, you would wake up to chaos every morning. All those monks who chant and do all that stuff for us, thank you very, very much for that is what they do. The problem is, people think that must be their path and try to follow it. But it is not their path. So, they meditate, but they never really meditate. See, if you think you are meditating, you are not. That is truth. If you think you are meditating, you are not meditating because you are contemplating. You are sitting in contemplation of life, because if you are meditating, that means being one with Source. Only a handful of people on the planet can meditate. Many people advertise that they can teach you how to do it. Only a few can meditate, and they are in a state of meditation most of the day. It is about being in your body to feel your truth. If you are not in your body, then anybody can sell you any product.

CHAPTER 29

PARENTING

P eople think that birth is the moment when the body emerges from the mother. Actually, the birthing process begins as soon as the fetus has been accepted by the "I AM" consciousness. There are all these arguments going on about "Right to Life" and abortion. The truth of the matter is this: two people come together. There might be some love in there, or there might not. Then this piece of flesh is born. That is all it is, a piece of flesh. That piece of flesh is a very fine thread. There is an egg and there are all these little fishes trying to get to the egg. Some of the fishes are confused, but then the Olympic swimmer comes along, meets with the egg, and a contract is started. Like all contracts in life, it can be annulled. At the beginning, there is a consciousness that wants to be birthed. As it goes further and further along, the contract is solidified and comes into matter. The wisdom we have been looking for has been around all the time.

You see a parent wisely talking to a child and saying, "What is the matter?" The child answers, "I am…." Now you know what the matter is. And now you know what the illusion is. It (matter) has been there all the time. You have just missed it. What is the matter with you? The child's reaction to that comes from the energy of the question. If the parent's energy is, "What is the matter with you?!!," the child's answer will come back with the same energy. You only have to watch it. As soon as a child is screamed at, what happens?

The child shuts up. "Why did you do that?" That is the next question, and it is in that moment that the Divine answers through the child, "Because." That is where the parent's human stupidity comes in and says, "Because of what?" The parent is getting the most Divine answer the child could give, because the child has created it: "Be cause."

That is what this birthing process is all about. As you go through the birthing process, the egg joins with the sperm and consciousness takes on form, or matter. Anything that manifests in this solid, or matter, from that moment on, is part of the running program that will be invented in that being. So at this stage here the woman tells the man, "You are going to be a father." The man says, "No!" Inside, the baby goes, "Oh, no!" and starts to register rejection. And this is before it even comes into physicality. So already the baby is feeling rejection. That is why it is really, really important for people carrying the "Divine Spark," a baby, to spend time communicating love to that baby. Play nice music. It really does cause a huge difference in the baby. All kinds of events happen to and around the mother, and then out pops the baby. But here is what happens: the baby only has one leg. Why? The baby only has one leg because of the rejection it felt. It says, "Reject me?! I am going to make sure you have to spend a lot of time with me." That's what is going on all the time. It's amazing, isn't it?

The cutting of the baby's cord eliminates that which may have gotten caught up in the baby's psyche. So, at the stage of conception, the bumpity-bump of the physical parents isn't bumpity-bump anymore. It is the Divine Mother and the Divine Father coming together as a Divine Being—It is two gold orbs coming together to create this seed. And now you have the Divine contract manifesting as well, instead of the clutter that the baby experienced on the way here.

An abortion is very similar. It is great. I have a lot of people who come to me wanting my permission to have an abortion. When I say "me," I mean the doctor, counselor, healer.

They say, "I just found out I'm pregnant. I am a career woman, and I'm up to be manager of McDonald's. I can't do it right now."

They are waiting for me to say, "Yeah, you are a career woman. Go on get rid of it." But I don't.

Then they think, "I have walked into the wrong office."

I say, "I tell you what… go down and ask the baby if it wants to be born now."

Many times they stand up right then and decide to have their child. If they don't, then they sit there. I know by their energy, face, and body actions what is going on.

I just say, "Open your eyes. What did the baby say?" They tell me the conversation that took place. Then I hit them with the Divine Plan.

I tell them to go down and say to that baby, "I think I can't have you right now. And if it is not part of the Divine Will that I have you, would you please leave? I promise you that when and if I become ready, I will call you in again."

At that moment, and it happened once in my office, instantaneous abortion occurs. That is how the Divine Plan works. It is the wisdom of communicating yourself with this being, a partner, who is looking to grow, and asking if it needs to grow into matter.

I learned very early on that I did not own my children, that I was just a custodian of them. I watched my son and daughter grow, and because of my own journey, I was able to notice things maybe that other people wouldn't or weren't tuned into. One of the things was that my son was never bright in school. That is on an intelligence level, yet he was the brightest light in the class. I encouraged him to leave school because I realized his gift was the gift of carpentry and that he had brought this gift with him after many, many lives. One of the lives that he had was that of the chief sacred geometry architect for Sathya Sai Baba, building the temples in India, during Sathya Sai Baba's incarnation as Shirdi Sai Baba. I encouraged my son to awaken to this, never telling him why.

I would note that when Gavin would take a piece of wood to saw, he would spill some of his chips or milk on the piece of wood. Of course, what he was doing was making an offering to the wood. He did this unconsciously at first, and then as I watched him, he began to utilize it all the time. He has built a couple of healing centers already. When he builds, he does the twenty-one sacred pujas of building. This means he does a puja, sacred prayer, mantra, or whatever you want to call it, before the land is even touched, asking the nature beings to make room or to say it is okay to build there. Then he goes through these rituals all the way through to the completion of the building. The reason I tell this story is to show how important it is for parents to get out of their children's lives and how important it is for parents to notice what they are doing.

The practical thing that I saw with my son was that he is a craftsman. I wouldn't allow him to be "head-ucated" because I realized what the educational system had done for me. It had shut me down into my head, and I forgot that I had a heart. I was lucky because God came and collected me. If you think you go to God, you have it all wrong. God comes and collects you. You don't have to do anything to get there except love all and serve all. That is all. Just be nice. When that is difficult, and it can be, there is a very simple exercise you can do. It is called "You cannot always oblige, but you can always speak obligingly."

So whether my son knows or doesn't know is totally irrelevant. He is just on a trip and loving every minute of it. He uses the five values in his life: love, peace, truth, right action, and right conduct. He runs them past everything. My son had no money, but I never encourage giving children money because I've seen what it does, even on a very hidden level, to what looks like a stable person. I encourage my children to learn how to utilize energy. I always got them to earn money. They would wash the car or whatever.

You do not have problems with your children. Your children have problems with you. Why don't you let the child be who the child is? Why do you tag your child "a problem"? Please be careful about the words you use around your children because children are hypersensitive. There is a cancer in our society. It is the cancer of parents who won't let their children walk in their children's own mess. The Lotus comes up through the mess. We try to protect our children by using compassion without detachment. The most important thing is to let them fall down. Let them know, "I am here. When you reach, I am here. I will not reach for you. You can reach for me if you wish."

Children are great teachers. The wonderful thing about these teachers is that they didn't read the same instruction book that we did. So, when we find ourselves saying things to our children, being truthful is very important. When the phone rings and you tell your children to say, "I am not in," you might want to stop and think about what you are teaching them. That is why children are our greatest teachers, because children don't like hypocrites. One of the things that is going around this planet right now is this A.D.D.-A.D.H.D. nonsense. The truth is that children incarnate at a higher vibration than their parents. Children can't stand to be around anything that is out of alignment, so they give their parents a hard time. They let the parents see that they are not happy with this criticism and stuff. You know, the educational system on this planet is based on competition, and only the best survive. That competition is an extremely effective way to stop people from stepping into their mastery.

We have reached a state where people can no longer show too much affection toward a child without fearing they will be locked up and called a pedophile. The truth is that you should hug your children every morning. Go to bed and sleep with them. Embrace them. And if there is another child in need of that, go do it for that child as well, and fear not. Fear not because if there is sexual energy there, you will end up in prison. If there is not sexual energy there, you might end up in a building that they call prison, but you will have left your body. That is the journey. This is part of the Divine Feminine energy coming in. It is part of the mother calling the children back and understanding.

I taught martial arts for thirty-two years. I have personally trained many world champions and Olympic athletes (big egos here). I stopped because they told me that I needed to take a course. This course was to instruct me in a new procedure where if any of the 300 children in my clubs fell and hurt themselves, I was to go and physically help that child.

You know what my mantra was for the child that fell? "Tae Kwon Do. Feel no pain." The children were like switches, so they just switched off. I could have become a multi-billionaire by babysitting. Their parents used to say, "If I could only have you at home." At the Martial Arts Club we taught human values. If the child wanted to join the club, he had to bring his parents. Then they had to pick out a habit that the child had that caused arguments. "Johnnie doesn't make his bed." I would say, "So, Johnnie, you want to join the club...wow." I would get him all jazzed up, then I would ask him to give me his best high kick, and of course he would give me his best high kick. Then I would turn to the home club and say, "Black belt material." I would tell Johnnie that on his first grading I would show him how to punch and kick and do all that. Then I'd say, "You only get your yellow belt if your parents say you have been making your bed." The grading had two parts: what was happening outside and what was happening inside.

The next thing that happened was that these kids started to take on those values. Teachers at the school where we had our martial arts classes approached us and said that the bullying rate went down to under five percent. That school formerly had the highest rate of bullying in the country. What was happening was that the kids were coming to the Martial Arts Club, and I was teaching them that if they hit one, they hit all. So when the bully stepped forward, the student had a greater Source that said to him, "Don't do that. That is not good for you." The bully got the message and changed his ways. And so it was. We need more of that.

Never let them go. Never ever, ever, ever, let anybody go. Wait for the natural time for it to happen, and you won't even notice it. Then you can wish them well on their journey. Don't force God's hand, or you might feel some residue. When you are in the Divine Plan, it just manifests. Just give the children to God, because that is who owns them in the first place.

CHAPTER 30

POWER

You need to stop giving other people your power. You put your parents, lovers, teachers, gurus, sheiks, preachers, and others on pedestals and expect them to solve all of your problems for you. They are your guides, not your servants. So quit giving away your power. You hold on to victim mentality because your ego wants you to think that you are helpless. You get great pleasure in telling everyone your tale of woe. Stop that! You created it, you made choices, and you are having experiences. Feeling sorry for yourself only means that you are not getting the lesson and you do not appreciate the experience.

The mantra of spiritual people these days is "Stand in Your Power!" Yet you do not understand what that means. Your power is love. Love yourself, love others, love God. Power must be held in a container, or it will leak away. The container is discipline, concentration, and focus. If you go around giving and leaking your power away, you are only proving yourself right that you are a victim. It is my greatest joy to see one of my students become my teacher. When I ran a martial arts school, I remember very well when one of my students beat the stuffing out of me. I was overjoyed. I finally was able to be his student for a while. If you seek teachers, be sure that they are teachers who push you to be more than they are. Pick teachers who love to see their students become a greater teacher than they are. Too many teachers these days are afraid of their students surpassing them. You have to look out for these teachers, for they will take your money and only give you half the teaching. Teachers are afraid of their students becoming powerful because a student might show them to be the fakes that they are.

You need to start taking responsibility. You are a powerful being in your own right. You need to speak your truth and understand that when you speak your truth, not everyone is going to like it. You may be crucified for it, but what a fabulous gift you will have given to humanity. To give your life for all humanity is the highest of all blessings. You have to stop avoiding your truth because you are afraid that someone won't like you. To speak your truth no matter what is what stepping into your power means. It is time to step up into your power, and unless you are willing to do that, you are only fooling yourself.

Be the powerful being that you are, and understand that there will be challenges. Most people on the planet will criticize people who step up into their power. You will attract far more people who will want to destroy you than people who will want to heal you. Do not worry, for if you are destroyed, you win! Fear is the only thing to fear. Fear paralyzes you and attracts more fear. Unless you are truly able to stand in your own power (love), unless you are willing to pass on a teaching and are willing to die for that teaching, you may not be ready to be a teacher. You may only be willing to be a student teacher. Most people are just not yet ready to completely commit themselves to the path. It isn't because they don't want to; it is because they still have so much to let go of.

People have trauma, memories, pains, sorrow, guilt, and many other negative thoughts and emotions that are like dust on their mirror. When they look at themselves, they can't see themselves because of all of the dust hiding their light, their power. You have to clean the dust off your mirror and let go of all the negative thoughts and emotions. When you do that, you will be able to see yourself for who you truly are. Now, if you see two people, you need to go and get medication and some psychological help. When you look into yourself, you should only see who you really are. You are the creator of the whole game.

Stepping into your power is admitting to yourself that you are the creator of your world. You have created all of what you perceive to be good and what you perceive to be bad. One of the great mysteries of life is that you are not the doer until you understand that you are the doer. Many people have experiences and then beat themselves up for having the experience. That is crazy! How can you open your arms and embrace your powerful nature when you are busy punching your lights out? That is like a wallpaper hanger trying to hang wallpaper with both hands tied behind his back. Check in and see how you have been wasting your power. Whenever you find yourself beating yourself up, criticizing your decisions, and calling yourself names, remember that you are leaking away all of your power. There are plenty of people who will criticize you; you don't have to be one of them.

The easiest way to step into your power is to let go of your past. Remember the lesson, but let go of the emotions attached to the events of your life. You judge yourselves too harshly. You do not need to judge yourself at all. Many of you want to be perfect but do not recognize the truth that you are perfect. You set up standards and meet them; then you set up higher standards. You are never good enough for yourself. This is an illusion programmed into you by your parents and teachers who wanted you to excel. That was their reality, not yours. Step into your power and realize that you are perfect, you always have been perfect, and you always will be perfect. All you have to do is stop judging yourself. Replace the judgment with love. Love is the source of all true power.

The great illusion is that there is a pedestal at all. Putting people on an illusory pedestal, and giving them all of your power, is a waste of your life. Everyone is on the same journey, back to God. Sometimes we need a guide to get us from one point to another, but you have to realize that you are a guide to others behind you. If you spend all of your time worshipping someone who is simply a human being just like you, you will miss all of the directional signs that have been left for you. Sometimes you get so caught up in looking at the directional sign that you forget to follow the directions. You have to apply these teachings in your life, or you will get lost.

Pick guides, teachers, or gurus with whom you resonate. Dig deeply into the teachings and seek deeply the understanding of the teacher's being. When you strike water, dive deeply and find pearls. When you open the oyster to find the pearl, go share it with someone else. You may find that the pearl is you. It doesn't benefit you to chase this guru or that teacher and only scratch the surface. If you dig many holes and try to serve many masters, you will only get confused. I see some who think they are smarter than their teachers, and they want to take one teaching from one teacher and another teaching from another teacher, like a great buffet table. That is great for them. They are afraid to see the truth of the teacher, and they only want a taste. So they skip across the pond of wisdom like a skipping stone and never really get to the deeper teaching. Getting to the deeper teaching is the only way that you will finally realize your own reality, which is that you created it all in the first place.

You have never been lost. You never will be lost. Nobody here was ever lost. That was an illusion. It's very simple. I was walking down the street one day, and I saw a man under a lamppost looking for something. I just sat there and watched him for about three hours.

I finally went up to him and said, "Excuse me. Have you lost something?"

He said, "Yes. I have lost the key to my car."

I immediately asked, "Did you lose them here?"

He said, "No. I lost them over there in the darkness, but there is more light here."

I said, "Didn't I meet you before, in the Himalayas?"

"Yes, you did."

"While in the Himalayas, I asked you what you were doing there, and you said, 'I have come to find myself.'" I looked at him and said, "Are you sure you lost yourself on this mountain?"

The answer is in there. You can't look for something you've already got. It is in the middle that you are lost. You have already found it. You always have and always will stand in the light. You are not lost, you are found.

Never, ever, go to your Creator as a beggar. Go to your Creator saying, "Give me the tools to do your will or leave me alone!" It is a showstopper. I tell you what, if He gives me the tool, something will happen. If He doesn't, then I just lie down and relax.

If you are disempowering yourself to God, I applaud you. However, the greatest guru lies within you. It is vitally important that you are picking this up. There are two types of teachers in the world. There is the great teacher who helps you to suffer. Then there is the great teacher that helps you to love. Both are great. The suffering teachers keep you suffering by letting you down. Aren't they doing a great job? When you see through the illusion that is when the truth will begin to set you free. As I said before, my mother was an alcoholic and she beat me morning, noon, and night. She broke plates over my head and brushes over my back. I still have scars where she stabbed me with a knife, blah, blah, blah. Thank God for sending her! Thank God for it all, because if I could love that being, I can love anyone. She was my greatest teacher, and I do Padamascar (a show of respect to a Master) at her feet morning, noon, and night now. Have you stopped thanking your teachers? Have you hardened your heart to them? If so, trick your teachers today. Love them. They won't expect it. You'll completely bowl them over. Because they are trained to take your anger, they haven't a flippin' hope if you love them.

If all of your thoughts were projected onto a screen in a movie theater, you would run out of the room. You would see the real you. When I offer you the invitation to come live with me, I am not talking about Derek O'Neill. I am talking about the Master, Teacher, and God that you have carried around with you since your moment of incarnation. This is where your teacher lies, and this is where your guru lies. These pictures of the Masters are just reminders. There is nothing funnier to me than people praying to statues of Jesus because they are praying to a lump of concrete that is just a symbol. Go beyond the symbol, go beyond the physical teachers, go beyond. That is where the truth lies. The photos, paintings, statues, and symbols are an illusion, projections of your mind, of what you want the master to be.

There is a lot of advice going around that says, "Don't give your power away to a teacher." It is really no problem. Just give it to the teachers anyway. For starters, the teacher won't be able to hold your power if it is not true power and if you are not meant to be powerful at that time. The fear of giving away your power creates more fear. The truth is, if you give your power away to a teacher and the teacher isn't standing in truth, your power returns to you usually with the teacher's powers. You awaken to every experience that is going on. One of the greatest teachers here today are the flowers. They don't go through this big ego thing. What happens is a great metaphor for life. They are a seed. God the Creator takes the seed and shoves it into manure. It grows and pushes its way up through manure. Then it just comes up, shows us its beauty, and returns to start the process all over again. It doesn't care if God, or anything not of God, is looking at it. It hasn't any concern for that, and everyone here should feel the same. If you give your heart with love, there isn't a being on the planet that can harm you. There is no such thing as a bad teacher. There are just teachers.

You are very special to me, but I don't know how much of that you believe. As you can imagine, when love flows, it attracts more love, like bees to honey. My daughter, Orla, and my son, Gavin, I don't own at all, nor did I own Linda, my wife. Now, with Gavin, Orla, and Linda the "my" is gone. Linda struggled with letting go of "my husband" so she could own me. But we understood that the only way for Linda and me to grow into the beings that we are was to take away the hump. Sai Baba came into my dream and said, "Sell your house and give me all the money." We sold the house and were about to give him all the money, then he said, "I have changed my mind." He said to go do this, and we did it. The fact was that we sold the house to give him all the money, and we were 100% sure that there wasn't a hope that God would intervene here. It was like, if that is what you want, and we have to live under rocks or die, or whatever, that is fine.

Linda finally had to get into the space where she realized a very hard lesson. That lesson was that I love everyone exactly the same. I don't have percentages. You could make me tea every morning, throw petals at my feet, punch me in the eye, and I won't love you any more or any less. I just love everybody the same. That is very difficult for people to grasp because it is human nature to want to be special. That nature comes from their past when they felt they were not special. Who made them have those feelings? That is where you find your truth that will set you free. "I AM" who "I AM" and I can't hide it anymore. I can't deny who "I AM" and people are drawn to who "I AM." When I am not being what "I AM," the two percent of me you would then see, you probably wouldn't even like at all.

Michael Jackson had the exact thing happen to him, and Sai Baba had the exact thing happen to him. There was a young Michael Jackson boot camp, and one day a young lad was praying to Michael Jackson. Michael Jackson touched his hand, and the lad said he would never wash his hand again. What he was touching in on was the innocence that Michael Jackson was. But if he'd seen the other side of Michael Jackson, he probably wouldn't have liked it. There is no competition. You don't get an extra kiss or an extra flower. You get everything that you need. I give you everything that you need. When I go see Sai Baba, I want to sit in the car beside him. As Graceful as he is, he let me do it one time and that is fine. I felt sooo special. Then the very next day he came over to me and said, "Who are you? Where are you from?" And I felt very special. Then one day he walked by and completely ignored me, and I felt very special. Then one day he wouldn't let me into his ashram, and I felt a little tinge of anger, then very special.

You observe the love that people are. I make a joke out of it because it is only through laughter that we will get this. In India, I watch people saying, "My guru gave me a flower." They are floating and not touching the ground. Then the very next day they are committing suicide because their guru didn't look at them. India's lakes are full of dead bodies because Sai Baba didn't look at them. Do you think this is Sai Baba's teaching, that if he doesn't look at you, you should go drown yourself? Sai Baba gives a good teaching. He says every being on this planet is like a road. Sometimes, when the road is being repaired, we have to divert. That diversion you might pick up as rejection, but it is God repairing the road, strengthening it.

That is what is going on here. Yes, I am approachable for a period of time, then I become that light in the sky that is unapproachable. That is why I say, "Stop, as best as you can, giving me your power. I have enough of my own." I don't need anyone's power. If you look at the awakened ones, the teachers, the Lads, the Masters, they all do that. Sathya Sai Baba, when he first came, had little groups of friends, and it was all great. Then the group got a bit bigger, and then a bit bigger, and now his official following is seventy-million people. Seventy-million people visit him regularly. That would mean seventy-million people within a turn of three years visit Sathya Sai Baba's ashram. That is why he is a dot in the distance. In another two or three year turnover, I guarantee that then you won't even get to see him physically. He will be over that mountain, behind that dip, around that corner, and behind that tree. When he shifts, everything shifts.

So, if you like, there is this thing called the lineage that is passed. What happens is a shift here, a shift there. We can't do anything but do it because the Oneness is there, and we have the lineage. You have the luxury of saying, "No, I am not going." I think you call that free will. We call it pain. That is just the progression of life. What we are hoping is that your characters will jump onto this line. Until the day that you stand in front of a group and say, "I am sorry to offend you guys. I am aware that this Irish guy is the most egotistical thing I've ever witnessed with my eyes. How does he get away with this? How can people be so stupid as to be paying this guy when all he has is this massive big ego?" I say, "I AM." Still the negativity happens. That is what you are going to do. This mission doesn't end. It gets handed to you if you are ready. And if you are not ready, that is okay as well. That is the mission.

So knock everyone off the pedestal that you put them on and you will feel empowered. You must take them off the pedestal. Not by boxing the head off them, or by screaming, roaring, and shouting at them. What you do is you say, "I am sorry for putting you up on that pedestal, and I invite you down to me." If the teacher wants to step down, fine. If the teacher doesn't want to step down, fine. I have seen many people go through their mastery by taking up the gauntlet of the teacher. It gets hard as soon as you put on that cloak, because your ego is going to be challenged in every moment now. Not once a week, not once every six months, not once a year, but in every moment. And the closer you get to the flame, the easier for your wings to be burned. Are you ready? That is the question, isn't it?

How many times have you looked at someone, seen their issues very clearly, but you couldn't see your own? You are looking for the splinter in someone's eye when you have a big plank in yours. The mastery is taking out the plank. When you do that, you notice that everything you see is a message to who you are. If you see me as this wonderful being, I thank you very much for that. The truth that will set you free is that you have to be looking at yourself. That is the absolute truth.

A great Irish saying, "If you want to know me, come and live with me." I have seen many a teacher put on a great show. I have seen many parents put on a great show, and then behind the closed door they were beating their children. It just goes on and on. You know what I do? I don't judge them. I just love them. Why wouldn't I love myself when another part of me is off doing something that is not the most loving? How am I going to rescue that part? By showing that part love, not judgment, not hate.

What you focus on is what you are manifesting. If you are giving all this time to processing negative stuff, you are creating more of it. That is the great entrapment of spirituality. The only way to stop it is a simple exercise. Stop! Ask yourself, "What is good about that? What is loving about this?" If you say, "He was in it for the money; He conned me; He did that,"—it's more pain, more pain, more pain. Congratulations and Happy Birthday to you. So focus on the positive. That is your job to reach mastery. When the Twin Towers fell, what was the positive? I don't suggest you go to someone whose loved one was in that building and tell him or her the positives of that event. So there is a time and a place for everything.

I will allow you to put me on a pedestal for a little while and hope I don't let you down too hard, but I will. When that time comes, I hope it is gentle. If you want the real empowerment of this book, let me down off the pedestal. I have put many of you up on a pedestal. You don't believe that? When I need my iPod fixed, I am looking for my God, correct? So I search, and somebody ends up on my pedestal. "My God, you learned that quickly. How did you do all that?" That is how I speak and how I address people. "How did you do all that?" So you all have mastered something. Do you know what it is? Because there is your calling. It might be as glamorous as flying all over the world doing all sorts of great and wonderful things, or it might be sitting in an office day in and day out and allowing light to emanate from you. There is no job or mission greater than another. Does the top stone in a building think it is more important than the ones at the base?

So I tell those who take my classes that they have manifested me. You, the reader, have manifested me, and don't think you have not. You people manifested me. You caused, you prayed, and you asked. I have told you time and time again, be careful what you ask for, you might get it. You are manifesting me. I can prove one hundred percent that you are manifesting me. Don't be here next week, and I won't be here either. Isn't it true? You are the stones that form my base. If you go, the pedestal goes with you, and I return to nowhere because I have never been anywhere. That is the illusion. Heaven is not here, Heaven is here. God is not here, God is here. It is so gentle. You just slide in, not climb anymore.

The interesting thing about the word disciple is it actually comes from "discipline." That is why you go to a teacher—to be chastised, to learn discipline. Without discipline, you don't get home—it is discipline dished out with love, not with a cane, and not with your parents beating you into the line they want you in. It is discipline of the teacher who comes from love to demonstrate to you that you are off target or off line.

If you declare someone to be a disciple of yours, you are declaring that it is okay for you to show him or her the way now. Take Jesus and His twelve buddies. Each of them He treated with the same love, yet differently. I think that is what I said about children. Some children need hugs and some don't, and some you talk to and some you don't. You are and never have been anything but the Atma, God, the Avatar that you are. Experiences of other people clouded your vision and you don't believe it. An experience puts something in place, and an experience takes it out of place

Truth has this special vibration about it, and you know when it is about to fall on you. When you hear a new truth, move very quickly. Don't sit with it. Most people, when they come to a signpost, analyze the signpost, instead of following the direction. My suggestion is for you to follow the direction. You can never be harmed for anything that you do in God, even if it's your teacher, or chosen teacher, who turns out to be whatever. It is of no matter. You don't look at your teacher as God. You look at your teacher as the carrier of the essence of your next step that brings you to God. Of course, those teachers can come in the strangest form. Most of you push your teachers away because of fears and misunderstandings. The whole thing is that as we progress through our journeys together, your opinion is as valid as my opinion. I have listened to you as much as you have listened to me. I listen to everything, and as you know, I don't do spiritual homework for you, but I am a man to give you a story.

God comes in all shapes and forms. Dust falls on you, and you think it is sacred vibhutti. You look up, and discover it is actually termites. Of course, the first thing you want to do is have the termites killed. Let's get rid of the termites. But what you are about to do is kill God. You are going to kill His messengers. Why would you want to do that? You are sitting in meditation, and if these creatures come, they come. I have learned to spot God in his most subtle of forms. So what are you going to do with your termites? Thank them? Have a conversation with them? Say, "Thank you for reminding me that God comes in all forms. Thank you for sprinkling me with your work. It might be good if you could contain yourselves to just ten percent of the roof." I will tell you what will happen then. They will move to ten percent of the roof. That is how you communicate.

In India, everyone complains about being bitten by mosquitoes. When I am there, I have this little room where I go into my space, and the ants are there, and the mosquitoes, the rats, and the rabbits. I just say, "Let's make a connection here. Ants, thank you for cleaning up the crumbs that I drop. You are not allowed in this space." And with my fingers I draw a space. People have come to my space and watched the ants just walking around in a perfect rectangle because the rule is, if you step into my space, I immediately put you into your next incarnation.

Sathya Sai Baba was once asked about killing animals. He said always use common sense over spiritual sense. If you are in an area that is laden with malaria and you see one of these mosquitoes land on you, you know exactly what it is going to do. It is going to stick in its syringe and infect you. What you do is say, "If you stick it in, I wish you a human incarnation." That might seem a bit cruel, but in fact the truth is that is how we communicate with our world all of the time. If you have set up the space prior, then this event should never happen, but usually you don't give it any or enough thought. Instead of killing the creatures of God and God's messengers, just ask them to leave. You will know how advanced you are in love, depending on whether they leave or don't leave. It is about being awake whilst being fully asleep and doing nothing. That is the idea of our journey. Watch. It is coming. When it is coming, it is going on all around you. You don't know who it is going to be, how it is going to come, why it has arrived. And then, you just "be" with it, and you will get your answers.

The spiritual market has become quite lucrative, and it needs to be because people need the flavor of ice cream that they need. There is no right or wrong. When I say this, I am not taking pot shots at another system. All paths lead to Rome. What begins to happen is, you get all sorts of teachers. . . . and I have a joke with the Lads all the time. I say, "Hey, Lads. Why don't we all get together and say the same thing because everybody is saying something differently." Then God came into the room and looked in, because we were having a party, and He said, "O'Neill, it is important that everyone says it differently because not everybody hears with the same vibration." Then He slammed the door.

This is what I mean, as teachers become more out there, getting name and fame like Dr. Phil, and this is not a judgment, but what begins to happen is, you watch that soul's journey into or out of entrapment. I watched Dr. Phil as an instrument of teaching, because he was a great teacher. Because he came, he had an idea, he had a focus, and he did a great job. Then he started to make so much money that he lost the plot. I can tell you the point when he lost the plot. It was when he brought his wife onto the Oprah Winfrey Show with him and made a comment. He said, "My technique is better." And there was a lot of energy behind it. That was the moment that he swirled. His techniques worked for millions of people. That's wonderful. But his spiritual journey got harder, which was all the Divine Will.

As a spiritual teacher speaks, it is vitally important for the teacher not to think, "I am the Doer," and for the teacher to be so present in the moment. I am so constantly right because I can tell the second that Derek arrives into this room, because the energy comes from the head down, and not the heart up. This is what I am saying. Teachers' words become very powerful, and they can either be guiding, or guiding. There is no such thing as misguidance. They are either guiding or guiding. They will either send you down this path or that path. There are only two paths. That is the duality that we live in.

You are going to be the lesson, and here is the Grace: you either get it going down the path of love, or you get it going down the path of pain, but one of those paths you are going to walk. If the Grace is that you have a teacher who is in a state of loving obedience with the Divine, there is a good chance you are going to go down the path of love. Sai Baba proved this very nicely. One day he was going along, stopped at a man and said, "Do not eat bananas. Bananas not good for body's health." There were enough people within ear range to hear that. The next thing, everybody, hundreds of thousands of people, stopped eating bananas. This caused a crisis for those people who made their living selling bananas. All hell broke loose. See, if these honest folks couldn't make an honest living selling bananas, the only alternative they had was to beg or steal. He was shown this lesson. A couple days later, a new photograph was issued in the Ashram. Sai Baba was sitting there eating a banana. This is what the great teachers do.

The point was, at times teachers cause confusion in order for truth to arrive at the top. Somebody later got an interview with him and asked, "Swami, why did you say bananas were bad?" Sai Baba said, "For that man. He had congestion problems in his lungs and bananas caused phlegm. It was bad for his body, and I was speaking to him."

So I am speaking to you now, and these people are going to discern whatever they are doing to discern. I answer the question from the energy it was asked. So someone asks the question over here, "Is there free will?" And I say, "Absolutely there is free will." Somebody over there asks the same question and I say, "No free will at all." Why? Because if I say there is no free will over here, they are going to shut down. Exercise over. If I transfer it, it will only cause confusion and confusion is good. Doubt is a tool to dig deeper. It is okay to have doubts.

The student never looks for the teacher. The teacher waits for the student. God has come to collect you. Not you to Him. So you were collected; you didn't come. That is why this is Grace. That is why the teacher/chela (teacher/disciple) relationship is so strong. You have to go to your teacher and offer your life, offer everything at your teacher's feet saying, "Here." That is the teacher. Your spiritual teacher is your go-between that you need at a certain time.

There is a door and the door opens and you are invited to step inside, which is the last act of surrender. You look to your teacher, and your teacher is now standing with you, not in front of you anymore. You look to your teacher for the very last time and what happens is you see the Universe in the teacher's eyes. Watch. Then he leaves and you step in through the door, and you find your teacher waiting there. Everything I offer is merely scaffolding. The building is not going to look very good to the eye with the scaffolding in front. So take down the scaffolding. Then the building stands on its own merit. When your teacher comes back and says, "That is not the way I showed you," you can say, "That is okay, teacher. I will help you with those control issues." That is all they are. People are trying to make things complicated that are not. Structure, structure, structure. The building is being built. Let the building stand on its own merit.

I have a brand new car. Speaking of rich spiritual teachers. So far I have put seven thousand miles on that car. That consists of me physically getting out of bed at 2:00 a.m., my time, to drive four hundred miles because there is some young lad about to jump off a bridge, and I have to just drive past him and say, "You don't need to do it, you know." Then I pull up to the side and wait for him to come. He comes and I say, "God sent me. Sorry if that upsets you." Then you get to watch manifestation. Do you understand? If I need a better car to keep this physical body in shape so I can drive more of those miles, that too will be given. If I don't need a good car, because I won't be doing as many of those miles, that too will be given. So that will be given and will be taken and I have no attachment to all of that. That is all just tools, part and parcel, games, and experiences. That is what it is about all the time. When you are in alignment with the "I AM," it comes. It is just that simple. I get absolutely great love watching people struggling hard rather than giving me what it is they are supposed to.

Sometimes we feel like we are betraying our teacher for another teacher. You are not going to another teacher, you are just trying another flavor of ice cream to make sure you haven't gotten stuck on one flavor. If it is God, it is then digested Grace. You'll find a flavor of ice cream that is so neutral and natural it has to settle, and it is called the rainbow ice cream. The mark of a good teacher in physical form is that once that teacher is in physical form, he or she has issues. The mark of a great teacher is a teacher that will tell you to get lost with the most compassion possible, because you are stuck and you need something more than blissful "Aahhhs."

A teacher is challenged every moment because people start to look at the teacher as if the teacher were God. When you say, "This is my teacher," your teacher has to become your God. It's not the physical form, but what is holding that teacher in place, the Source. Those teachers take on the vibration of any teacher that has ever touched your soul, or giva, or your own experience, and they suck that into themselves using an extremely powerful "Pranayama" breath (a controlled yoga breathing technique) on a physical level. When it is here, it is then digested and simulated. You know you have made a connection with a teacher when a big flash of yellowish gold shoots from his heart. What he has done is integrated every lifetime you have ever had into that moment, and he then appears as a rainbow bridge across the floodwaters of Samsara, or pain and suffering. He is only a bridge, and he knows it. When you get to the other side, the bridge disappears like the rainbow, and the sun comes out again. That is the signal.

I have never felt competitive with teachers in my life, even when I taught the martial arts. When I taught, I talked the complete reverse of everybody else. The first thing I'd say was that they should try all flavors, don't just come into Tae Kwon Do or Judo. I knew that because I have seven black belts in seven martial arts, so I understood what it was like to taste different flavors of ice cream. When people with black belts from other clubs would come to visit our club, our white belts would beat them. The black belts couldn't understand that, because black belt is a very high rank and white belt is supposed to be the lowest rank. It was because I had a philosophy that I introduced in the club. The philosophy was this: You come and you are given a white belt symbolizing all the colors spinning as one. The start and finish of your journey is in front of you, behind you, and below you. Then I would give them the yellow belt and say, "This represents the sun shining upon you to help you grow toward the light." Then you were given a green belt, which represented the plant beginning to grow toward the heavens. After that, you were given a blue belt, which represented you touching the sky. At this stage, ego manifests itself because now you think you're something. The next belt I would give is a red belt, representing the fire, representing sexuality in the physical form and spirituality in the Kundalini form. I would awaken their Kundalini before they got their black belt. When they got their black belt, I began to train them, and that was the difference.

So, I have never been competitive. I have upset other teachers to the extent that I have received very threatening phone calls saying they're going to do this or that. I'd say, "That's okay. Sai Ram." So, no fear. I am not here to be your teacher. I am here to show you how to teach because I have only one drop to drop in the ocean. That starts a wave and sometimes that wave thinks it is separate from the ocean. Then that wave crashes onto the sand and is filtered back into the ocean, and the journey continues all over again. Well done.

True power comes from within. Your greatest teacher lies within. Everyone needs a teacher, a guide, to help on the journey. Whatever teacher you may have is perfect for you at that time. Remember that you manifest your teacher, not the other way around. So if something happens that you don't like, you have to look within yourself for the lesson. It has nothing to do with the teacher who is simply holding space for you. Your teacher did not lie to you, cheat you, or mislead you. That was God showing you how you treat yourself. That doesn't mean you must allow your teacher to abuse you, it simply means you need to understand that you are doing it to yourself. Stop abusing yourself and move on.

CHAPTER 31

PRAYER

Prayer is your connection to God. Every thought, every word, is a prayer. A heart connection will have you standing in the middle of atheists and saying God is alive and well and lives through me. Until you find yourself in that situation, you don't know how strong your connection with your Creator is. I always say that when I am alone, I pray silently and when I am with others, I pray aloud. It is called the "More Truth Will Set You Free" Workshop. This is my prayer or offering. I don't ramble on. Prayer is your actions manifest through the Divine Creator. When you are alone, it is a silent banter between you and your Creator. That Creator will take any form.

There are people praying every day for miracles. They are praying with such desire, but the desire is coming from fear. It is not coming from love. If you desire somebody to get well, that desire is coming from fear, my friends. Subtle as it may seem, it is fear-based. Only God knows that next step to our path. What is illness anyway? I don't understand it. Yes, it has come through me. Yes, I had cancer. Yes, He took it away to shock the doctors. He utilizes this body again and again and then some. He has trained me for thirty-two years in martial arts. He has given me seven black belts in seven styles. I can raise my hand quicker than most people in this room. He is looking to do a job, I am here.

Stop praying for miracles. Just know they are already on the way. A fleeting thought, that is all it takes. Let it up and go, then the miracles happen.

Allow miracles to just happen. What we are looking for is real love, and real love is happening all around us. Sometimes we are just blind to it.

If you need any guidance, pray just once. Just once and then let it go. If you pray the second time, you automatically cancel it because now your prayer has become a desire, and God doesn't give desires. He gives you what you need, not what you want. So if ever you want anything, please just ask once, but say it three times. Three is the number of manifestation. If it is said three times with energy, it is answered immediately. When you hang onto it or you continue to ask for the same thing, you have gone to your God as a beggar, not as a child. So stop begging. It is already on its way, in spite of you. It is already here. It has arrived.

You need to understand that prayers for other people are answered much more quickly than prayers for yourself. Remember that desiring something will block it. Pray that God's will be done or that your lessons come quickly, gently, and easily. Then you leave open the infinite possibilities of God's Grace. However, if you are praying and you are attached to the results, you will be disappointed. Suppose your child is sick and your prayer is that he be healed. Why are you praying? Are you praying for his highest and best good, or are you praying because you do not want to lose your child? The illness may be the child's quickest way to God, and God's plans are God's plans. God's plan may be that you take the child to a doctor and let God heal the child through the doctor. There are infinite possibilities. So pray that God's will be done.

CHAPTER 32

RELATIONSHIPS

S o many of you have the belief that you need to find your soul mate. You are looking and looking. You look under rocks, on the computer, in the gym. You are searching for the lover that will be perfect for you. You may be married, and you still are looking for that soul mate. You may be divorced, and you are looking for a soul mate. Have you ever stopped to calculate how much of your energy is spent looking for your soul mate? You spend a lot more than you realize. You probably spend more than fifty percent of your life-force energy fantasizing, searching, and sizing up potential candidates. You search the faces of the crowds, the people at the workshops. You devote so much of your life to looking for that person who is perfect for you.

You project what you want onto other people. Your ego has a long checklist of qualities and quantities that satisfy your personal definition of a mate. You are always holding this checklist up to people to see if they match it or not. Then you project these things onto another person and you think you have found "the one." You fall in love and you sacrifice everything to attract this person. You get lucky, and you get married. Then what happens? The person you thought was so perfect for you has a big pimple on his bum. You didn't notice that before because you were projecting all of your desires over the pimple. You didn't see it. Then you start to see other things that you don't like. This is because the more time you spend with someone, the more their truth will start to replace your projections.

Twin flames and soul mates are all about separation. God said, "I separated myself from myself so that I can love myself more." It is about Consciousness being bored out of its tree. God was bored, doing crossword puzzles, so he said, "Hey!" and He flung a piece of consciousness forward to create. Now what He is doing is going back because consciousness can't stay away. Anybody who knows anything about electricity knows that there is a positive and a negative current. The negative always flows to positive, not the other way around. Hence, that is our journey. He threw us all out there, and now we are all coming back to Him.

The reason soul mates don't usually arrive doesn't have anything to do with an open or closed heart. It has to do with you limiting God.

If you want to cut all ritual out in one nice sweep, you just say, "God, send me a soul mate." Then forget about it. I guarantee your soul mate will arrive.

What people usually say is, "God, I am looking for my soul mate…"

The wise people stop there, but then they say, "And make her five-foot seven, blonde hair, blue eyes, big hands, preferably rich, and if possible, with no baggage."

Then they say, "Scratch that and give me someone else that I can have sex with." That is all it is, and that is all that you are doing.

Don't go to God as a beggar. You are His child. You don't beg the parent. You go as the Divine Being that you are, spawned from the Divine Being that He is, that we are and everyone is, and it is all fine. That is the problem with the whole soul mate thing. A soul is spirit, it is free, and you never know when it is going to come into a body. As long as you are clear about what you want, that clarity will send better vibes out. Otherwise, I have seen this happen; I remember teaching a man how to manifest. I am a really good teacher at manifesting instantly, and he wanted to live in a castle. I showed him this technique to manifest and there it was. He ended up living in a castle in Ireland called St. David's Castle. He was quite an elderly gentleman. The problem was, the castle had no bathrooms, it was very damp, and he got physically ill.

When we met up again he said, "What is going wrong here?"

I said, "Excuse me, you asked for a castle and a castle you got."

The same holds with soul mates. Be very careful what you are looking for, because I still haven't found what I am looking for.

All I can say for soul mates is to just say, "God, I trust you. Bring it on." And you will have great fun. Pretty soon, everyone will look like your soul mate.

Imagine you have a boy or girlfriend, and this boy or girlfriend decides he or she doesn't want anything to do with you anymore. A hook has developed on both ends, which is probably one of the most dangerous hooks. What you now have is two anglers, and both think they have caught a fish, but they have actually only caught each other. What's going to happen, there is going to be a tangle out in the middle of the line between the two. They will never see the tangle unless one or the other gives way. So one gives way, and the other angler reels in the line. The other angler is not reeling, in the sense of "I won." The other angler is reeling, in the sense of "Now that we can see the tangle, we can start to unthread it." The majority of the people have that tangle between the two boats and neither can see it. What that tangle does is send up the line to whoever is holding the fishing rod, frustration, anger, jealousy, or misunderstanding. Then what you have is both people acting out of their issues. They are probably not angry that they both are going their separate ways. What they are actually angry about is that here is that program of rejection again. Then they begin to blame the other person for that instead of following the line to the tangle.

If you are in pain because you can't see the tangle, let me tell you, and this comes direct from the "I AM" Source, just let it go. Let the other person reel in, because you are ready to let go and the other person may not be. So if you let go, the tangle lies in the other's domain, and it is there where the work must be done to untangle it. Think about that as an easy reality. Here is the thing though, if the other person refuses to untangle that knot, then the Divine, Archangel Michael, or whatever word you use for Divine, comes along with a great, big, giant pair of scissors, looks at that person and says, "Are you willing to cut this?" If they say, "No," the Divine says, "Shucks." And you remain free, and they remain tangled for the rest of their existence, or until further down that hard path that they have just chosen when they decide to untangle that knot.

Now do you understand how powerful you are by letting go? Can you understand how that goes against everything you were ever taught? That used to be called weakness and giving in. People will come at you with all sorts of angles, which is why they are called "anglers." When they come at you, you just step aside and say, "I AM." This is going to annoy them, so they will come at you even harder. And again, you say, "I AM." That is why the energy from these workshops gets used up so quickly. It is because you use that energy to defend yourself instead of saying, "I AM." When you do this, their negative thoughts and emotions are going to be standing in front of you at fifty feet tall with baseball bats flying, trying to get you. You can be assured as you are breathing, they can't get you if you believe, "I AM."

It does help to believe in past lives a little. You see, you don't have to believe in past lives, they are just true. You don't have to believe in past lives, but if you do, then you can say you were a prostitute, a pimp, a robber, a priest, a pope, or a judge. "I was this and that." All those experiences can be brought into a moment in time. It defuses the situation. Then later you can cancel the "I AM." Just cancel it. "I AM God and God in All." That is what we call taking time out or taking space. Here is the gift of using this system: if someone says something negative to you and you are in your body and you feel the feeling associated with what they said, Bingo! You have got it. You have gotten the gift of this person in your life. Somebody is screaming, shouting, and abusing you to bits, and you call them a gift because that is what they are.

As soon as somebody turns around to you and says, "I am sick of you, and you are a terrible person," you say, "I AM," because that is fine.

You do that and the hook doesn't go in, and if the hook doesn't go in, you can then watch the manifestation of who this person really is. Their pain body will step forward straight away, and you can watch it. It is quite an achievement to be able to watch that and not have negative thoughts and emotions energize another person's negative thoughts and emotions. If you want to watch negative thoughts and emotions energize another person's negative thoughts and emotions, just watch parents argue with their children. Children are experts at it. They are so intelligent—they think. "Watch now how I wind mom and dad up. Watch how I separate them in different rooms to make sure I get what I want." Everybody does that to us. I call it the secret ear.

I don't wear a wedding ring. Linda and I realized that we had bought into the contract that says, "if you look after me, I will look after you, and if you don't look after me, I won't look after you." What we decided to do was to take the rings and throw them away. We went over to India and re-engaged as two souls. The ceremony is not two people looking at each other, but rather looking in the same direction. You know that point in the marriage ceremony where they say, "You can kiss the bride." When I perform the ceremony, I say, "This is your journey." As I gently bring them forward, you will notice they come together as one and one.

The Truth that Will Set You Free is that Jesus walked around with twelve men and a woman named Mary Magdalene. This is how you break it down. If you don't know that you are doing something that you tag as wrong, there is no wrong and there is no right, except that you are tagging it wrong. You don't need me to tell you that you are happy, because you are smiling. No one needs to be told what they are feeling, because only they know how they are feeling. Like the "More Truth Will Set You Free" Workshops and the people who sit in the back and say, "I don't know if I want to be here or not." That is what it is. If you are in your body, all the feelings that you need are contained within the package. If you are not in your body, you reach out to another physical being. The only reason we do it is to make our flames bigger. Two flames come together and the flame gets bigger. Two people come together not to look at each other, but to look in the same direction. Now the flame gets bigger. Society will lock you up for doing certain acts, and if so, so what? You can get all the love you need while sitting in a box, because it is all inside you. Imagination is a great thing, isn't it? Stop your boundaries. Stop your barriers and stop everything, because nothing can come to you that you didn't attract. Yes, it all just arrives and it is more important how you deal with it than that it arrived. Be in your body, and you will know what to do.

When people have affairs, well, an erect penis has no conscience. This is because we are made up of chemical reactions when we are fired up, because we are in matter. Once those chemicals fire, you will find it very difficult to control them. It is the same system when anger fires in your body. The chemicals change and anger is there and you will now have to sit there in that anger until the chemicals change back again. If you have a good teacher, you will be shown how to defuse or get those chemicals to change and shift through faster. When two people come together, they come together not to look at each other, but to look in the same direction. If they look at each other, they will suffer. Why they suffer is because they are brought in union with a partner.

See, Jesus was a very clever teacher. He sent his twelve apostles out in pairs. He didn't send them out on their own. He sent them out in pairs because he knew when one would fall, the other would be strong. When one was strong, well, they would take turns. That is why he sent them out in twos.

Marriage is a little like that. When one is down, the other is up and vice versa. When the two go down together, crisis hits, and then your journey is over. You are no longer capable of looking in the same direction because what you have done is signed a contract of marriage. When Linda and I got married, it was really funny because I wrote out our marriage vows and gave them to the priest.

He said, "I can't say this."

I said, "Then we are not getting married in your church."

I told him there was nothing in those vows that wouldn't sit with God. The way I worded it was something like this: "I, Derek, take you, Linda, to be my wife. Do you, Linda, take Derek with his fishing, martial arts, and other activities?" And vice versa for Linda's.

What I was saying here is that "We are going to come together and you had better understand that when I get on a lake, I could be sitting on a boat for three days and not even know I am there." That was the consciousness that I had. I needed to know that she knew what she was signing. When we did, we were both in a space of understanding. At the wedding, the priest sort of brushed over it like "Duh, duh, duh," and then he said, "Do you, Derek, take this woman to be your lawful wedded wife in sickness and in health until death do you part?" And I said, "I do."

You get teachers who abuse their position. They start doing sexual activity with their students or devotees or whatever you want to call them. You may look at that as wrong, but I do not. If it is wrong, then the fruits of their actions will take place. If it is not wrong, the fruits of their actions will take place. There is no right or wrong. There is only God's Will. Even through those teachers who haven't a clue what they are doing, it is God's Will.

Husbands and wives don't belong to each other. They are support for each other. God sends us out in twos. Noah brought the animals onto the ark in twos. But if that support gets to the stage where one leans on the other all the time, then that is victim support. And if you support victim-hood, you are out of alignment. What you need to do is subtly let your partner see their victim-hood. That is it. That is really the whole thing. I mean, as a teacher, I would have no problem going to bed with you if I thought you needed that, if it was God's Will. On the other hand, if it were because there was some part of me that wanted to go to bed with you, I would probably go to prison. You see, however, you can't imprison me. It is impossible because I would say, "Okay, so obviously You want me in prison now." You would never get a letter pleading my innocence or guilt, because I would be happy just being. That is the ultimate.

You need to be out of the way of each other's lives. You can offer acceptance no matter what the other is doing, because that is the journey. Then you don't buy into the other's drama and learning. What I do the most is just be. That is how I know at any given moment what to say to you. I don't do anything. I don't give anything. I just am. It all happens through this mind/body mechanism, but I don't do anything. In other words, you don't reach for the fruits of your actions ever.

You see, if you do a healing, you want to see people getting well, don't you? The reason my healing practice never went very well was because people kept dying. They would only come because they needed that extra "poof," not from a machine. They needed it from God to say, "Poof! Time to come home now." It wasn't very good for my leaflets. "Please come. Only nineteen deaths in the last three years." The best thing you can do for people is "be" who you are. That is your ultimate gift to the world, to be who you are and everything that you are and then some. Then you will find you are far more than you thought you were. I remember when God had a bit of a graduation party for me. It was really good. God said, "Wait, I am going to give you a real mind blower. People only need to pass you on the street and their cancer will disappear." I went, "Can I collect money?" "Uh, no," God said, "but you can collect money from people who come to the 'More Truth Will Set You Free' workshops. You can take it off them, not the people who you walk by on the street." It is really simple, isn't it?

There is no such thing as right or wrong. Sometimes God uses the most unusual shapes and packages to deliver, and you don't know what form that will take. It might be you are sitting there, making yourself into a Lotus flower or something saying, "Please, God. Send me my soul mate." And down it arrives: the soul mate, love, lust, the whole package. It stands there and it is all wonderful for a week. Then comes the duality—unless the two of you can turn and face God together, you will suffer in the relationship. Because this happens, people break up, get divorced, and do all sorts of silly things. I just say, "Please, God. If you are going to send me a lesson, please let it be on ground that I understand." Far better, I would like to learn a lesson where you are sitting, rather than in the middle of Africa. This is familiar ground and this is Grace that you learn it in such an easy manner.

If you don't learn it here, it just changes overcoats, and it comes back, and back, until you get it. When you go to it, you realize God was the soul mate you were looking for, and God can manifest in any shape or form. God could manifest in a physical form and you could be very happy. Let me tell you something, living with God is not the easiest when truth enters your door and people start to live under the conduct of truth or discipline of truth. You know from the word discipline comes the word "disciple." That is why we have to be disciplined and always show respect. It's very important to show respect to others. They are God in a different form. That is all.

All you need to understand is that when you give someone permission to do something, you are also giving permission to do the opposite. If you take away anyone of my family, my friends my, my, my… I will remain in joy. Follow your heart. Your heart will lead you home. In Hollywood movies, when the man moved toward the woman or made a move to get her, there was chemistry between them. But they usually got into an argument, and she'd slap him or he'd slap her. Then they swooned into each other's arms. That was the sound of one hand clapping, or when there was the sound of slapping or hitting, then love entered. Of course, that was in Hollywood, because violence is never tolerated in the "real" world. The cosmic slap. I remember reading once, what is the sound of one hand clapping? Then I got it.

Sometimes people come and they want the bigger picture. Is there a bigger picture that I might be able to help people with if I'm asked? Well, I've got this great story from a meditation I did. I was just sitting there and a great Being of Light was picking up pebbles off the beach and dropping them into a container one at a time. He dropped the first one into the container and then sat for a while just looking at me. He saw that I didn't get it. So he picked up another and dropped it in the container and waited. I didn't get it. Then he picked up the container and shook it, then put it back down. I didn't get it. He took another pebble and dropped it in, and I still didn't get it. I was always slow. Thank God when you are slow, because you have peace. Finally, he picked up a fourth pebble, dropped it in, shook it, and immediately I got it. The first pebble was me, the second pebble was my wife, the third pebble was my son, and the fourth was my daughter. Then he really started shaking the container. The pebbles were hitting off one another, and he kept shaking and shaking it. Then the rough edges began to come off the pebbles, they started to become round, and the friction started to disappear. Then we all moved smoothly around one another. We were free to go in whatever direction we were meant to go.

You have been given a brain; you should use it. Only use it to bring upliftment to the world. Any action being taken through you, you can check to see if it is coming from you or Source. One of the ways is running it through the five human values. Does it come from love, truth, peace, right conduct, and non-violence? There is an even a greater shortcut to this. Ever feel you want to go up and tell somebody what you think of them? Then this is what you have to do. You have to ask yourself, is it truthful? Is it necessary? The most important part is, does it improve on the silence? If you say words that are hurtful, you are hurting yourself. You can't always oblige; it is not possible. But you must always speak obligingly. We just need to speak more sweetly to each other.

Whatever you don't have within yourself, you draw from the outside world. If you think you need love, you draw it from another being. If you are very blessed, that being is very loving. If you are very blessed, that being is very non-loving. You will be brought either outside or inside for the next piece of the jigsaw puzzle to come together. Usually, outside is best. It is easier than inside. You can draw to you a man or woman or whatever you are into, and this person might beat you up, but the reason this person is beating you up is he or she wants you to go inside. Unfortunately, people don't get that message. They keep returning to the beatings time and time again.

The partner thing is simply complicated. It is great to have somebody to talk to at times when you are confused. You don't have to marry that person. If marriage is meant to be, that too will happen. But you don't have to marry. Your partner may come in any shape or size. All you have to do is be awake. Bad relationships cannot happen again if you already got the message. If you are still in a bad relationship, it is because you didn't get the message the first time. The first time could have been in your last lifetime, and the game continues until you understand that love number one is God. God is the only unconditional love in Source; everything else comes with a condition. Even the most loving relationships have a condition if you go deep enough into them. The whole thing is to come away from conditions. Love somebody because you love that person, not love because you have to. That is not love. How you know you have the right partner with you is when you are never questioned about what you are doing. Your partner gives you a lift to the venue and doesn't come in to check up on you.

A relationship is a relationship. See how we put tags on them and we get confused? No matter who or what the relationship may be with, if the relationship ends against your desire, your feeling is betrayal and rejection. Your broken heart is just rejection. The only relationship worth having is between you and God. All the rest come with conditions. It is that simple. The test is to see the action taken by God for God. Blame and shame will get you nowhere. It is just another lesson on the path. God tells us very simply, "Look first to Me and then to each other, and I will send you those teachers that will teach you best." First relationship is with God, and the second relationship is with everybody else.

The problem people have in life is that they think they have free will. You don't have free will. To be gentle on your ego, you have as much free will as a donkey tied to a post walking in circles eating. As he eats and eats, at some stage he is going to merge with the pole. Welcome to the spiritual path. That is all the free will you have. The absolute truth is, you haven't any. Three questions I will run by you just to check it out.

Do you believe in a God?

That is your first question. If you do, that is wonderful, and if you don't, that is wonderful. If your God is cheesecake, that is wonderful. If your God is sex, that is wonderful. If your God is Jesus, Buddha, Mohammad, isn't that wonderful? You see, call God by any name or form. If you believe in a God, then you must believe He created the game. If you don't, then there is your first sticking point. You see, free will is like going to God and saying, "Hey, God. You got it wrong! Let me tell you my plans." Ha, ha. Another one. You are not the Doer.

If you believe in God, do you believe He created the game?

Here is the big trick question coming up. Do you believe God makes broken items?

So, our teachers come and go. It is like money. Let it go and it will flow. If you hold on tight, you will get a fright because we are going to take it from you. That is why God invented social diseases. It is called karma, amongst other things. This is the truth of life. If you sit back and watch, you will see justice equalize in that way. The dark needs the light and the light needs the dark. The light cannot exist without the dark, and the dark cannot exist without the light. It is that simple. God created the devil, and the devil is His best friend because they shine off each other. God says, "I am not feeling too good today. You go off and get them." Then you send them to the "More Truth Will Set You Free" workshops, and we will share love with them. But until then, walk in on your husband and catch him in bed with your best friend, just to make sure everything is okay. Are you getting it? Do you understand? Manure happens. Now what?

It is your reaction that is causing all the broken-heart mess. Nobody can break your heart. You have to dash it, and only you. Now it is time to put back all the parts of your heart. Ommmmm.

Here is the truth. You are your own soul mate. You are your own twin flame. You have to find yourself to find your soul mate. You have to love yourself to find love. You think you are looking for a certain kind of person, and what you are really looking for is love. It is your ego that convinces you that you have to have love in a particular kind of package. It may be that your ego has you convinced that you want love in a daddy package or a mommy package. Either you are open to receive love or you are not.

If you restrict God, you restrict yourself. If you say, "I am looking for a soul mate. Make him 5'9", black hair, a six-pack instead of a keg, you know."

Ninety-nine percent of the time that means you just shut the door to your soul mate. I have seen really interesting things happening, particularly about soul mates. Everybody is looking for a soul mate. I have seen soul mates come to these workshops and pass each other. I try to intervene. I ask God, "Is there anything to be done here before they go out that door?" He just says, "I have their names here." The most interesting interactions just happened in Phoenix. Two people came together and found each other. Then there were two more people who were on fire. They were this close. All I can say is, the bliss they would have had if they were awake to each other was amazing. The problem was, they were both female. One was a Catholic and one was not. The Catholic one shut down because the Catholic Church says homosexuality is bad. Well, you are back in the room, you two. Let's have a lesbian party!

Only ask for anything three times and then let it go. Never let it come into your consciousness again. If you do, you block it straight away. You think you might need something for yourself, and that very thing might be a message from your guidance. A lot of people don't know which is which. A thought arises like, "I want five million for an ashram. I want five million for an ashram. I want five million for an ashram." Gone! Say it three times and let it go.

Finding the love of your life is a journey. I wish you all well on this journey. It is a new journey not yet ventured by many, and it is causing bleakness and concern for most of you, as you have not yet fully experienced the journey into the unison of your soul. Your soul is complete within itself, and it is in fulfilling this completeness that you will find all you are looking for. Most of you have gone about this in the wrong way. You have looked outside yourselves for love instead of going within. This is what has caused most relationships to fail. First go within, then go without. You will find the love you are looking for, and it is going to be soooooooo much better than you could ever have imagined. This love is a love you have never known. When you find the love fully within – you have connected to the Source of all love – this is the love you are looking for. It is all within. Once it is completely fulfilled within, you may manifest it in a Divine partner on this earthly plane through the purest of intent.

What you do is look at God first. If you have looked at God first, then you will recognize God when you turn to look at your partner or child or dog or flower or house or car or whatever relationship you are having. You just have to realize that they don't belong to you. Nothing belongs to us.

When you go within to find love, the first issue that you will have to deal with is self-image. Do you think you are not attractive? That's because you are not looking through the same eyes that I am. All you have to do is adjust your vision. Instead of looking at all those advertisements for diet pills on the television, why not "Tell-A-Vision" of who you are, beauty manifest, God manifest in human form. What more motivation do you need? God gave you your package and your package works for you right now. You don't have to know why; you just have to accept it. Really what I hear you saying and the truth that will begin to set you free is, "Hey, Derek. I have no confidence in who I am. It has nothing to do with my weight, because I could be seven hundred pounds."

What name do you give your body? What tag have you put on it? Beautiful or ugly? You resonate with it. You are very beautiful as you are, but lack confidence. You have just bought into too many advertisements. You have bought into too many people telling you that you have to have a certain body shape to be happy. You may be experiencing rejection and abandonment. That is your issue. It has nothing to do with your body. Your vision is turned, and what you need to do is go out there and smile at every person you walk by.

On a scale of one to ten, how much do you love yourself? If you give yourself a one, then you are saying, "I don't love myself at all." If you give yourself a ten, well, you are a giant ice cream and you are going to lick yourself to death. Do you know where you are on that scale? You have your number now, and only you know the truth of that number. If you gave yourself a one to four, please reach out for help. Go to a massage person, a Reiki or a Rising Star person, or some professional. There are millions of different versions out there. You need to get a little lighter, that is all. Before you pick up the phone to ring the therapist, just say, "Hey, God. I know that this therapist is full of manure, as most of them are, but could you make sure you are not having a day off and overshadow them for me. Thank you." Then you will have a wonderful session.

If you are between five and seven, you are in the majority, which means you are neither here nor there, you just are. If you gave yourself a seven to nine, you are on fire and are burning through very nicely. If you gave yourself a ten, please see me … I need a healing from you.

CHAPTER 33

RESPONSIBILITY

If you put up your own roadblocks, then you have to take full responsibility for that. You have to sit down one day and say, "You know I am creating all this." Before you get to that space, you have to start over here: "It is his fault, her fault, their fault, and that God thing, and it is their fault. If she hadn't done that, then this wouldn't have happened." These are baby steps, and as you are getting closer to here, the step just before that one, is this one: "I am a Co-Creator," which is the step before mastery. You are the Creator. Are you ready? God cannot exist without your creating Him. "I now take full responsibility for any karma that I carry out." Fully Creator. It's easy to say, yes. People here say, "I am the Creator." They don't believe it, they just say it. "Here, 'I AM' the Creator and I take full responsibility for my actions." If God needs to be sexually abused, you may be the one abused or you may be the abuser because God loves you that much. If you are a master, you will willingly be the abused or the abuser and totally accept the action and the consequences of that action. The master knows there is no difference between the abuser and the abused and that they are both God. You will gladly be sentenced to a cell because you know you can't lock up light. So those are just steps along the journey, and that is what karma is.

If you look at most of the great teachers who have come to this planet to awaken people, they have all been accused of something. Sai Baba is a pedophile. Jesus is a money-grabber. Do you know the only reason that Jesus was crucified? He was taking money out of the pockets of the people who were running a bathhouse and money-changing racket. For you Jewish people, you will understand what I am talking about. Before you entered Jerusalem, you had to take a bath, and there were loads and loads of bathhouses. The guys who ran them were all high priests and they charged you a fee for using their bath. That is when Jesus went into the temple and threw everything around and said, "I will take this down in three days." That is why they crucified him, no other reason. He was taking money out of their pockets. He was a political activist and they knew they could string him up. That is why they did it. That is the world we live in.

As soon as you do good, you are going to be pointed to and charged. Money comes and goes. Love comes and grows. Anybody can accuse me of anything and I will say "I AM" and it is perfect. Does that clear up a lot of stuff? Take away the negative connotation and replace it with positive and start to arise.

"Now" is the place to be. "Now" changes everything because "Now" changes the future. I used to be an angler until the Divine had another plan and said, "You are to become a fisher of souls. No longer will you catch a fish." And then He proceeded to steal my boat and fishing rod. Funny part about it was, I met a man, and he happened to have the same name as my own, Eugene O'Neill. Only the other day I realized that Eugene had told his story, because Eugene was the water bailiff, the person that looked after the Lord's river. You know, like you have Lords of the Manor. No one was allowed to fish the river without a license. That is a water bailiff. He told this story, and I didn't realize that he put all the experiences that he had into a book. Somebody gave me a copy of the book and I just laughed and laughed. I was wondering if anyone else would get it. When you laugh sometimes, you laugh through an experience that you had. I reckon that a couple of you might get this story. So, a bailiff is someone that checks your license to see if it is okay that you are fishing on the river. This little story goes like this:

The policeman's lot is not a happy one, but neither is a bailiff's. While working as a bailiff on a certain stretch of privately owned water, I chance to come upon an Englishman fishing in the best pool without a license. On challenging him about what he thought he was doing, he replied, "I am trying to catch a salmon." Then he showed me a cane, like somebody uses who has difficulty walking. He showed me a cane with some two-pound line on it and a hook with a lump of potato, a spud. Well, I need not tell you, I needed to stifle a laugh, and feeling a lot of sympathy for him, I gave him my blessing and left. Later that same evening in the pub, whilst I was telling the story to some local fisherman, in walked the Englishman and he sat down alone in the corner.

I approached him and said mockingly, "How many did you catch then?" With that, he bent down and picked up a bag from which he took five sea trout, all about two pounds each.

Being very annoyed, I said, "You didn't catch them with a spud?"

"No," he exclaimed. "I caught you with the spud, these I caught with the worm."

It is amazing where enlightenment will come from. So that is life. He never once told a lie in the whole story. The Englishman stayed within integrity and got his fish. At the same time, he taught an arrogant Irishman a lesson. That is the way it should always be. Always stay in your integrity, but you can't be responsible for how another person will take what you are saying. There is never a need to know; just stay in your integrity.

Let go of anything that you feel responsible for because you are not the Doer. So what you do is ask Archangel Michael to come during the next set of your meditations, because he comes with the Archangels. You say, "I want your sword for a minute because I want you to give me the 'ability' to 'respond' when it is God's Will." So it is the ability to respond. That is the difference between pain and Divinity. When you feel responsible for something, you go through pain. When you know the action being taken through you at the moment is not yours, you can sit and watch it happen. So let go of all responsibility. Now, I take full responsibility for nothing. You should do the same, I think.

Let it all go. It has nothing to do with you. You think people need you? They need Divinity. You can be the instrument. That you can be. In order to do that, you need to make yourself as clean an instrument as possible. Krishna blows through the flute. That is what you are, the flute. The more you unlearn what you thought was right when you learned it, the more you shift through it quickly.

It is much easier to play the blame game. "I blame him for everything. It is all his fault. As a matter of fact, I blame him, the teacher." I was saying this to you earlier. The whole thing is to find yourself a teacher, then you can blame your teacher. "He told me. I believed him." You have no responsibility. Responsibility is not in consciousness. It is a human-made thing. You are responsible for nothing. You are nothing and from nothing you came and to vibhutti you will return and be consumed into nothingness.

In school, it took me a while to get it. I kept getting "Fs". Because my parents called me stupid all the time, I thought "F" was failure. When I went to my Divine Parent, He said, "No, no." I said, "Then what starts with F?" He said, "'F' means fabulous. You are a genius. I have been telling you that you were fabulous all the time, and you listen to those idiots that I sent as your parents."

I don't have any expectations. I had no idea that I was going to come here today. I just arrived. If my guidance tells me not to show up, you could have ten million people sitting there and I am not coming. I have no expectations. I move in the characteristic of what we call the "now." At any given moment, any event can happen, and I am there one hundred percent. I don't actually go anywhere without being there one hundred percent.

You have all the guidance you need; only you haven't let the intuition and guidance in. What do you want? Well, if you come up with what you want, that means that is what you haven't got. If you know why you are blocking your Divine Guidance, then you will know why you have taken on certain diseases, illnesses, misrepresented energies, thoughts, and experiences. Coming back to the manifestation thing, the reason we manifest people in our lives to punch our lights out is because somewhere along the line we sent up a request for them to come and punch our lights out. You have to take responsibility for that. Somewhere along the line you had to request that your father be an alcoholic and give you these tools. Now, if you want to take responsibility for that, your depression goes. If not, your depression stays. That is really what wisdom is. It is all around us.

The first thing you have to do is shift lack out of your consciousness; for example, "I have a lack of happiness." No, you haven't. You have as much happiness as anyone else on the planet, and there are buckets of it. Why have you chosen to come to your Savior with a thimble and say, "Fill that with happiness"? Why do that when you could go with a cup and fill that or a jug or a forty-foot container or the world, which isn't even big enough to hold it? That is what we are doing all the time. We are forgetting how powerful we are. That is the bit that catches most people. You are absolutely terrified to say you are powerful, because if you do, they are going to come and attack. Who are they? They are the parts of you that don't believe. If you happen to be walking out through a door and somebody on the other side happens to be coming in and smacks it just as you are going through and hits you on the nose, why would you have manifested that experience? When you understand that, then you'll take responsibility for everything in your life and un-manifest

200

that which you do not want anymore and manifest that which you do. We have the ability to fill an empty cup. You are manifesting. You take responsibility for your actions, and you are free.

CHAPTER 34

SEX

I f you start to put limitations on the Divine sexuality, then you might never experience love in this lifetime. Remember Adam and Eve, those two characters? It had nothing to do with apples. The forbidden fruit was the sexual act, because sex isn't love. Lovemaking is blissful and sex is not. Cheesecake is good. Sex can be as good as cheesecake, depending on whether you like cheesecake or not. These are given as truths, but don't believe everything I say. What you need to do, as an individual, is to make an informed choice. Go out and have an experience for yourself, and then you can decide whether it is true or not true for you as an individual.

Have you ever heard of anything in the psychological field called the Oedipal Complex? Every child on the planet is born into this complex. It is based on this theory or fact that the child's first love object is its mother. When a male child is born, the first love object is his mother. The child is there, suckling the mother's breast, just sucking away. As it is developing, it begins to notice a shadow in the background, and it fears that shadow. That shadow is the father. The mind works on the Alpha male system. The strongest is the best because he can eliminate all others. Immediately, the male child starts to project hateful thoughts toward his father. The male basically wants his father dead because he wants to mate with his mother. Now you see how it is important to have information. That "click" happens.

So most men, if they are truthful, will tell you they were obsessed with their mother.

Let's switch it now. We have a female child and that female child is you. Here you are, suckling your mother's breast, and you notice the shadow, but you fall in love with the shadow. You want to go to bed with the shadow and leave the womb of creation. That is when you become daddy's little girl. Unfortunately, this affection that is set up between daddies and their little girls can go slightly over to the other side. It is not a blame or shame thing, it is just the way nature works. Look at the animal kingdom. It is there.

The idea of this book is to really take all the teachers, gurus, and Gods off the pedestal and down from being the bright lights that you can't touch. Bring them back to the basics of who they know they are. See, they already know. You are learning. There's a young girl who lives in a family that we could call extremely loving and functional. Her father happens to be the Chief of Police. Life is wonderful. Everything is going really great. Then one day, when the girl is around ten or eleven years old, she hears loud voices downstairs. The loud voices are her parents screaming and shouting. She is sitting on the stairs listening to this. She has heard it before, but blocked it out. This time she seems not to be able to tune it out so well. So she hears these words, "Get out of my house, you pedophile!" The wife has just discovered that the father, the Chief of Police, has been interfering with children.

Now, all children on this planet, psychologically, spiritually, emotionally, and physically put their parents on a pedestal. They put their teachers up there, and anyone else who they feel is better than they are.

Next, the door opens and the mother is physically throwing the guy out. He is crying, saying he is sorry, and she is saying she doesn't care. She throws his bags and everything out through the window. You have the big picture now, don't you? That is happening everywhere in our world.

What I want to do is let people have an insight, not into the effect on the parents, but into the effect on the child. The daughter is there, and her first reaction is to protect her father, her God. She begins to blame her mother for the event. Even though the mother is one hundred percent correct in her action, she is still going to take the blame. That is what we have to do when we do something that is truthfully right. We have to be strong enough to take what is going to come because you are speaking the truth with love.

The daughter starts to blame the mother. The girl had a good outward life, a good standard of education, and she's bright. The next thing is she starts to withdraw into herself. What brings her into that withdrawal is this:

When your God falls, you are going to fall with Him. That is why it is important to take your Gods off the pedestal as soon as you get an opportunity. When you do, not only will you find out that your Gods are more human and powerful than you ever thought, but they won't have that power to drag you down with them.

So, the daughter grows up and becomes frigid. She has confusing fantasies about whether her father molested her. She becomes anorexic, or bulimic, not because the event happened, but because she isn't sure that an event happened. These are the effects of the Pedestal Syndrome. The thing is, if the girl had listened to both parents, if she had been able to take in the humanity of her parents, if she had been able to take them gently off the pedestal, it could have been different for her. That is why it is important to take them off the pedestal.

The first thing you have to do is identify how people interpret the word sexuality. Because for some people, when you ask about sexuality they think you are asking them if they are gay or straight. There is that element. Then there is the element below it: does sexuality mean that every child born onto the planet is born bisexual? The word bisexual brings up a whole set of connotations. I would be one hundred percent bisexual with no bother. What I mean by that is, when I was growing up, before I knew my lessons and what I know now, I remember looking at men and thinking, "Very nice," then having to go through the trauma of, "Am I being pulled to that side of the fence, and what is society going to do if I am pulled to that side of the fence?"

I finally realized that I was looking at energy. I wasn't looking at the people at all. I was looking at the energy and what it was manifesting. It had nothing to do with sexual orientation. I am aware that hundreds and hundreds of young men and women are taking their lives every day because they don't understand that is what they are doing. For me, what this whole package means is never limiting the Divine, ever. I have a lot of people say to me, "I am looking for a partner to come into my life. How come it hasn't happened?" I always break it down very quickly and ask for a description of the partner they're looking for. They say, "You know, I want someone to be loving, share with me, and be spiritual." I tell them what they have just done is limit the Divine Will. What to ask for is, "Give me love."

So if you start to put limitations on the Divine sexuality, then you might never experience love in this lifetime. Because who are you to say to the Divine that it has to come in this shape, package, or form? What if it is a male and you are male? What if it is a female and you are female? What if it is one hundred and nine years of age? We will have that. What is all this limitation stuff? Either you are open to receiving love or you are not. You have to take responsibility for that, and then love enters through your door. If love enters through your door, people, grab it and then share it. That is what you do. You receive and give, receive and give. To me, that is what this whole sexuality thing is all about. Two people come together, they touch, they caress, they feel, and they go into a state of being. For the male, sperm never comes, and the two of them, male and female, rise together, and they know they had an experience beyond the physicality of the meeting of two physical matters.

So, if you love, the Fire of Divine Love, from our connection with God, enters the equation and tantra is nearly there. Tantra is an eastern form of making love that incorporates all of our senses and consciousness. Tantra still is not the absolute essence. Right now I could have the most amazing thing, that we tag orgasm, with Linda, without even moving from this position. I would gain all the touch, all of this, all of that, and the "I AM," all in one gulp. Tantra hasn't gotten there yet. Tantra is still relying on matter and it hasn't even gotten beyond that. That, of course, is the "I AM." So when you really know you are the "I AM," you know that you really are the male and female.

Love goes zoooooom! Fear and Love go chug, chug-a-chug. The energy or fuel burned will determine the outcome of your journey. So when people have been sexually abused by their father, or whatever it was that happened, they start to look for their innocence back. The only reason children get sexually abused is because their abusers are looking to get their own innocence back, and they see it in this child. They are grasping for it. Hopefully, that will make it a little easier to forgive them and shows that they obviously lost their innocence as well. The chain is here.

I have been sexually abused. It is wonderful now. It wasn't then, but it is now because I understand it. If I didn't get it then, I couldn't do these workshops and be real. If you have had hardships, sit down with me and I will tell you all about it. You are listening to somebody who has had hardships and has come out the other side. That is how I can guide you, because I have seen the trauma. You have come to break that chain. Are you going to press delete, or are you just going to put the programs on a disk? Which are you going to do? I will know you pressed delete if you end up in a heap with a river of tears flowing out of your eyes. Don't try to fool me, because I am easily fooled, but you can't fool you. Ding, delete. If the delete doesn't work, then get a baseball bat and beat that computer.

We have to have sexuality to be in matter and to learn our lessons, but we have been taught sexuality is dirty in some way. I will give you an example. Sathya Sai Baba has been accused of being a pedophile, gay, or whatever it is that they accuse him of. What happened was there was a young lad in the interview room with Sathya Sai Baba and his parents had been called in as well. Sathya Sai Baba's interview room is laid out about ten feet by twenty feet. He takes groups of people in there and talks to them about spirituality and such. If he wants to do a one-on-one with somebody, he pulls a net curtain closed. By doing that, he is actually pulling a whole Universal block. He pulls the curtain closed but leaves it open a little bit. The family members of this boy have been devotees right through Sai Baba's Shirdi Sai Baba incarnation, their grandparents, their great grandparents, etc. They are well connected in, which almost doesn't exist. He takes the boy in the room and his parents are there too. There are seventy million people looking for an interview with Sai Baba, and if you get in there, it's God's Grace.

The young lad goes behind the curtain, down with his trousers, and Sai Baba starts pulling the you-know-what on the young man. The boy freaks and goes running out. Then the parents run out. There is pandemonium going on all over the place because Sai Baba has just sexually abused some young lad. A man who had once been an assistant to Sai Baba but had been barred from the ashram was the first to talk to the boy and his parents. He was the one that started the rumor about Sai Baba being a pedophile. What happened next was, the former assistant was caught in England in an apartment with two young boys. See, Sai Baba is only a mirror. It is all there. It all happened.

I was invited to a meal in India at my friend's place and sitting there was the young man whom the rumor was started about. My friend said to him, "Tell Derek the story of what happened to you in the interview room with Sai Baba." So the young man told me that he had been having difficulty at the time he was a student at Sai Baba's college. He was having trouble studying because he was constantly thinking about girls. He said, "Every time I went to meditate, I was forever seeing women's breasts and I knocked onto them and I was doing all sorts of things." The family got an interview, and when the family went in and Sai Baba did this action, he said, "I just freaked." He freaked so badly that when they caught him, they had to put him in a straight jacket and tie him to the bed in Sai Baba's hospital. What had happened was, the reason the parents had taken the boy to see Sai Baba was that he had torn the skin off his penis from masturbating so much.

They had to tie him to the bed at the hospital, and they did. Three days later he awoke, completely silent, no sexual thoughts anymore and dropping into depths of meditation that would make a Buddha jealous. That guy told me this story so I could utilize it as a tool here today to help you understand sex and sexuality. I said to him, "Why don't you go to the papers and tell them what really happened?" He said, "Sai Baba told me not to because I am only an instrument to cause a breeze in the ashram to remove the debris."

There is a fine line between what we classify as sexual abuse and what we do not. I have been sexually abused, and I have never been sexually abused, because God is the Doer. There are two paths that you can choose between, after an event happens. One is the positive path. You say, "I don't understand why it happened, but it had to be God's Will." And if you believe it was God's Will, you will get the answer to why it happened very soon. If you do not and you choose the other path, you remain a victim, you get ill, and you die of cancer. Then you come into the next life to have it done all over again.

Most homosexuals on the planet are more spiritual than heterosexuals. That is why a lot of them are very soft, because they are more spiritual. The reason they chose and signed this contract to come back as a gay person in this lifetime is to get over the anger of being judged by society. If you can get over the anger, then the enlightenment flows back into you and you realize you can have sex with this, and that, and that, and that dog, and that donkey, or whatever, and that it is all perfectly Divine Will. I have this great idea for a film that would heal a lot of promiscuity. The film is about the secrets of why God would send somebody down gay. They would be brought through a whole life sequence until they actually realized that the reason they came was that they needed to break through that final barrier of being judged by the multitudes and being able to sit on their own.

What is gay? We have to put on labels, or we would be lost. Have you ever been looking for some place and there is no signpost? You get that lost feeling. Yes, I find it interesting—the use of the word gay to describe that particular action because gay, to me, means joyous and fun. That is where the secret always lies: be happy. If you were meant to be heterosexual this lifetime, or into animalistic "riding the donkey in the back field in Ireland," guess what? Poor donkey.

Whatever comes as fruits of the actions, give to God because that too will be God's Will. I guarantee you one hundred percent that you cannot walk out of a marriage unless it is God's Will. It is a one hundred percent guarantee. It is a bit like you can't stay lying in the bed unless it is God's Will. You are just too terrified to suffer. Who are you, trying to save the world? What you are doing is called projection. You are projecting yourself onto your partner. As a matter of fact, you are so good at projecting on him that you will even be able to tell me how he will react if you leave him. I know. I've been there, and I have the T-shirt to prove it.

The truth you need to grasp here is this, just be. Say to God, "If I am meant to be here with this partner, then give me the energy to do so. And if I am meant to move on, then give me a kick to shift me through." Then let it go. If you give it more thought, you are going to block God's response. You have to let it go. People procrastinate. When you come to a signpost saying "this way," "this way" and "this way," what you are doing is analyzing the signpost instead of following the direction. Home, away, home, away, home, away.

A friend of mine lives in Puttaparthi. She had just come out of a really bad marriage, and she went to see Sai Baba.

Sai Baba comes up to her in darshan and says, "Where is your husband?" She says, "I have left him."

He says, "Very happy, very happy," and walks away.

He comes back and says to her again, "Where is your husband?" She answers, "I told you, I left him."

"Not Good!" he says and walks away.

Months went by and he never looked at her because she was in the analytical process of destroying her mind.

When she had come to a place of normality, if there is such a thing, Sai Baba came up to her and said, "Husband over here. Husband over here."

Then he gave her an interview, and he gave a man an interview. Then he brought them into the room together. He materialized wedding rings for them and earrings for her. She was so proud of them that she flashed them around everywhere. By the way, when Sai Baba manifests a chain, he is telling you that you are chained to something. When he manifests a diamond ring, he is saying to let the mind die.

So, they got married and moved to Australia. The man turned out to be what is tagged, "the biggest jerk on the planet." He beat her, drank, and did all sorts of weird and wonderful things.

Here is the problem: Sai Baba said in the interview room, "You must never leave this man, no matter what he does. Never leave this man."

So she stayed with him and went through this hell and high water. Finally, she couldn't take it anymore. She was a broken woman. She got angry, and the anger motivated her. So she flew back to India, and she sat and sat.

In a crowd of two hundred thousand people, Sai Baba picks her out and says, "Where is husband?"

She says, "I left him, Swami. I couldn't take it anymore."

He replies, "Very happy, very happy. Go!" This means go to the interview room.

She goes to the interview room and he says, "Where is husband?"

This is how he breaks you down. He will talk to you, and then the next moment he will act as if he doesn't know who you are. It is only ego that craves the attention and you have to feed it at a certain point.

So, she says crying, "Swami, I left him. He did this and this...."

He says, "Where are the earrings I gave you?"

"I lost one of them, Swami," she says.

"Oh, not balanced," says Sai Baba.

He then materializes the earring that she had lost and gives it to her and says, "Now balanced, and no more husband, only 'me.' 'Me' is your husband. 'Me' is your father. 'Me' is your brother and sister."

Then she was happy. She wrote a book, and I think I gave a hundred copies of it out at one time. She is now working to help the whole Jewish victim consciousness get back into alignment by telling her story about being a child of survivors of the Dachau experience.

So you ask me? "Very happy."

Pain and pleasure is the same thing. That is what we have come to learn. You only have to look at a man masturbating for that truth to be revealed. At that moment of exhilaration, if you took a photograph of his face, he is in complete agony, with toes curled up. That is the truth. Maybe pornography can be useful for you women who never looked into the face of your man whilst it was happening, or the men who were not looking into the face of the men, or for the women who were not looking into the face of the women. At that moment, pleasure and pain rise together because Kundalini and sexual energy are the identical energy, my friends.

CHAPTER 35

VICTIM CONSCIOUSNESS

If you see people suffering in the street, don't feel sorry for them. You are only wasting your breath. First, you are looking at them as victims and you are throwing victim thoughts at them. Then you might be pitying them, which means you are throwing pity at them. If you see people who make you uncomfortable, that is the opportunity. That person is the gift for you, not the other way around. It gives you the opportunity to see program data compared to "I AM" presence. Program data will tell you that you have to help. Program data tells you to act. With "I AM" presence, you see the picture. Have you ever had the experience where you are walking down the street and you have twenty dollars in your pocket, and someone just catches your eye? You get what is called a moment of enlightenment. In other words, there is a part of you out of alignment with the "I AM." What you have is data saying, "Out of alignment." When it all is in alignment and you have the "I AM" saying, "They are fine," what happens is you reach into your pocket to give the twenty to them and you think, "But then I won't have enough to get on the bus." Data.

There should never be a moment when you think not to give. You just go give to someone, you give twenty and you continue to walk. That is Divine Alignment. If you have a single thought that there is not enough or you pity them, then that is your gift exchange. It is showing you that there is a part

MORE TRUTH WILL SET YOU FREE

within you that needs attention. That is truth. I'll give you an example; I did a workshop in America. I was in a Starbucks, and a homeless man came nearby and started talking to a homeless woman very loudly, so we could hear. He started saying, "The truth will set you free, you know, but most people don't want to see the truth." As we were leaving, I gave the man money wrapped in a one dollar bill so that when he opened it after we left, there was one thousand dollars in there.

The amount was not important. The energy exchange was important; the Universe told me to do it. So I became the Universal facilitator again. I was just as happy to walk past the person and not do any action. But the alignment of the "I AM" has a vibration that is different from what we are talking about, which is, "Look at me. I am great. I am the Doer." In therapy form, it is called "Savior Consciousness." I want to save the world, but the truth is, the world will be saved by the "I AM." That is truth. You are going to be asked to facilitate that. How we facilitate that is by giving you little Graces of not looking at them with pity. You know how you look at somebody when you give him or her something? You are looking at them as worse than you, as broken people in need of healing.

If you are giving healings to people who need healings, then you need to go back to kindergarten. Nobody needs healing. They are going to be given it, but they don't need it. That is where it is going to be very confusing when you are running a data program. The data is everything that you would have learned. If you are in your body, you will register what you are given. So the Prema Agni becomes a living symbol, not something that you need to keep drawing. You become it, and it becomes you, and you and I are one.

God works in the balance of duality. That is why I get away with sitting in a room with people and telling jokes about physically challenged people, and there is somebody sitting in front in a wheel chair. Because you see, everything is in balance, yin and yang. When you see something of a victim nature of consciousness, you can actually help it to balance by joking about it. Jokes create laughter, laughter creates love, and love balances it. We were taught it was cruel to laugh.

Let's be truthful. Let's start out with the truth. When you go to see Sai Baba and he spins his hand and a ring appears, first things first. Is he a magician? A good magician can do that. Don't be overwhelmed by that because he knows what he is doing. He would deliberately do that to make you think he was a magician. I have seen him do it on many occasions to crack people up. All he is doing is trying to get your attention. Those things are his calling cards. Your truth, only you know. It is okay to have doubt because doubt is the tool you use for digging. If you haven't got doubt, you've stopped digging. Don't be afraid of your doubt. Accept it as part and parcel of your journey going forward. If you have doubt, there is only one being that can take that doubt away. We call the being Source. You say, "Look, I have read it all in books and I generally have it, but if only you could give me that proof. Maybe if I went back to my room and there was a rose on my pillow?" If it is your time, you can be absolutely certain there will be a rose on your pillow.

Your journey is to take yourself from this baseline and let the Divine move you. Not you move you. That is what this is about. It is not about tricks. When you laugh about it, you realize how unimportant that stuff is. That stuff is only sent to catch you. I have met people who have the most wonderful gifts, but are still full of ego. They have been caught. When you have an experience, the experience is sent to catch you. Are you going to get caught? I got caught in a part of India that is extraordinarily hot, and I don't like hot weather in particular. I was there and I was just falling apart at the seams. My body was going into some madness from lack of water.

Finally, we found this little shed that had some water. It was boiling water, but it was water. There were three of us sitting at the table and I made this statement, "What I wouldn't give for an ice cold glass of water." With that, the woman sitting across from me, her water turned to ice. Now I am looking at my water, which is still boiling nicely in my glass. So, this event is happening and next I say, "Why isn't mine like that?" and bang, mine was solid ice. I was able to turn the glass upside down and the ice stuck to it. Big deal. So what? I was able to get my nice glass of cold water when it melted. Now, either I am a complete liar or that event happened. Or, I invented that event to help me on my spiritual path.

You are the one that is manifesting all this, not some Superior Being. You are that Superior Being. You just don't know it. Are you ready to take responsibility for manifestation? If you are, then start and off you go. If something happens, you are also going to take responsibility for it. Isn't that right? The co-creator is a step before Creator. Co-creator is the one that says, "Life is wonderful." Then as soon as something goes wrong, it is your fault. That is the majority of people coming onto the spiritual path. They come on first as broken beings basically, and as they get a few workshops under their belt and they are reading the right books, they are then willing to take this leap of faith. "Co-creator? That is me!" Blessed are those that take the next step. These are your steps, your ladder. Be careful about putting the ladder up to

213

Heaven, then wanting to take one step toward Heaven. One step is much easier. Two steps? Great. I am not afraid of heights. Be gentle with yourself. Be gentle with the world. Be gentle with the Creator.

There is a secret the Creator wanted to let me in on. The Creator said, "Without Me, I don't exist. And without you, I don't exist. If I continue to push your buttons," says the Creator, "You run away from me, and I cease to exist." Notice the Creator's hand with the finger pointing out, and whenever you are ready for your button to be pushed, just jump on that. No blaming the Creator anymore. Whenever you are ready to push a button, that hand is ready and the finger is in place. Is that fair enough? Derek O'Neill doesn't push buttons for people. You jump on the finger.

At this time in man's evolution, they are still working on the shock system of awakening, it is still used. In the Shakti path, the guru comes up and boom and bang comes out, and fireworks go off, and Beings of Light come shooting forward. What is Terrorism? Fear.

When fear and love come into the same room, what do you think happens? Fear leaves. That is how I know you are all love, because you haven't left yet. Sometimes love is so overwhelming that you fear it. Unconditional love is the most powerful source of fear in you. When it arrives you will immediately start to say, "This couldn't be true. I am not worthy. He is just in it for the money. He wants to go to bed with me and have sex." You will immediately start to discredit unconditional love. While unconditional love has all that within you, there is nothing you can do about it.

I am a psychologist. President Bush was a big child trying to prove to his daddy that he is a man. So he was dangerous. Saddam Hussein and Bin Laden and these characters were hurt children looking for revenge. We, as a world, didn't look at the truth of the Twin Towers, that it would only be the start of terrorist attacks. The world would also suffer tsunamis and earthquakes. I am not talking politics—I am talking world involvement. I believe former President Bush was the absolutely perfect president for America at that time. I don't think the Divine ever puts the wrong person in place. But President Bush still had that little psychological trigger in place. You know how I found out that trigger was still in place? He was interviewed on television, and the reporter kept needling him and needling him. I was watching, and I thought Bush was not the cleverest in the pack. The next thing, this question came at him with energy. The question was, "Why are you so determined to get this man?" He whipped around with fire in his eyes and said, "He nearly killed my Pa!" That was the moment that any enlightened person on this planet would have seen, "Uh-oh."

Using the President as the terrorist, we are going to see the importance of the role of the therapist. Therapists are the greatest terrorists on the planet. They make you look at things. The President was so engrossed in this thing, he made actions happen that caused people to say we needed to get him out of there. Wasn't he doing a great job? I am not calling him on his integrity. His integrity was compassion without detachment. His religion was the way, and that was it. But it was integrity.

Terrorists are people that don't think they are getting a fair deal. There was a time in my life when if you hurt my child, I would have had no problem shooting you. Does that make me a terrorist or a murderer? Does that make me too attached to my children? Now, if you hurt my children, I love you. Because now I understand you would have only been sent to help them grow. They are big and strong enough to help themselves. If they weren't, then I would encapsulate the whole thing with love and whatever would happen would be fine. That was growth. You are listening to a person who went through the same system that you are going through. He had the lessons, etc., etc., thank God. And this is who I am.

Hurt is a tool. I felt hurt when I saw those children in India because I was those children. I looked up and said, "You want me to do something about this, give me the tools." In case you didn't notice, there was a time when we didn't do any advertising at all for these workshops. Now we do a little, but people keep coming. I know people who would love to have our advertising plan. You are just meant to be here at the right time for you to reach your destiny. Hurt is part of your destiny because you are in a physical form. As long you are in a physical form, there will always be physical hurt. At the moment of your passing from the world, hurt is the last breath into the lungs. Why do you think a child cries when it comes in? It is the first breath into the lungs, and it is very hurtful. It is the same going out. Just ask for the tools and don't put a label on what the tool is going to be.

Duality is only necessary to feel love. You were brought into duality to feel love. So God was sitting there one day, full of light, love, and all that stuff. The next thing He noticed was that He was bored. He said, "Is this it?" So He set up a board game, like Monopoly. That is it. That is God's story. No more complicated than that. Then He said, "I need to feel something." So He blew again and here we are. Then He said, "We have a boring game, so let's create wars." And he blew and created wars. God created wars? "Let's confuse people," he thought. "Let's make them think I don't have anything to do with wars. Let's create Satan." And he blew again. That is the duality. So, who created the whole game? God. So, where is the suffering? It is in feeling separate from God.

I had a group in Ireland, and I said, "Eeny Meany Miney Moe, catch a nigger by the toe. If he screams, then let him go. Eeny, meany, miney, moe." I knew exactly what was going to happen. It was going to bring up all these issues about color. I needed them to get into this. There is ancient wisdom in the old saying, "Sticks and stones may break my bones, but words will never hurt me." If those words are hurting you, then you have an issue, and that issue needs to be addressed.

Before that workshop, I was explaining to the people who came to collect me from the airport that there was a big debate happening on Irish radio about colored people, and how they were fed up with being called colored. "Ireland is very racist and da-dee-da." You know those great radio talk programs? I love them. But when the radio switches itself on and it is not even plugged in, then you think, "I have to hear this on this level." I decided I would ring the station and lo and behold they put me through.

I said, "I would like to talk to the colored gentleman. I don't know his name, but I would like to talk to the colored gentleman."

He comes on and says, "This is what I am talking about with white people."

I said, "Excuse me, sir. When you stop calling me white, I will stop calling you black."

There was silence on the phone. I said, "That is the stupidity of this whole debate."

There was more silence. I said, "I know what I am talking about. My name is Reverend Farmer."

I was channeling him at the time. I said, "God made the rainbow, and He put every color in it. Where is the debate here? It is only fear-based. It is only aggressive-based and all it is doing is keeping alive that which you are trying to get rid of. I love you all. Goodbye."

At the end they said, "Well, how do we sum this up? I guess we give it to Reverend Farmer, who has it absolutely correct when he says that we are all just colors of the rainbow."

There is a great change happening on this planet. Barack Obama was elected President of the United States. There is a great hope around him, and he has promised to change many things about the troubles that plague not only his country, but also the world. This is a sign that all of the cataclysmic prophesies of 2012 could be misplaced if he could be surrounded by light and love of all of the beings of light on the planet. However, do not fall into the trap of thinking that he is the polar opposite of his predecessor. They are all God, they are Satan, they are light, and they are the darkness. They are simply the aspects of ourselves playing out the age-old inner struggle of our positive values versus our negative values. As I have said before, you are creating this reality. When you let go of your separation consciousness, fear, and victim-hood, then we will shift further into the light.

Here's a great story about victims. God is looking down on earth and sees this old man in India. This old man is one hundred percent devoted to Him. He calls Him Hanaman, which is the Monkey God. But all names and forms belong to God. So you can call Him a "dummy" and He will still respond. It is amazing. He is sitting there, looking down at this old man who is completely devoted to Him. The old man only owns a single, very skinny cow that gives him just enough milk to live on. Then God looks over and sees a really rich man who has hundreds of cows. The rich man decides he is going to be charitable.

"Watch me be charitable," he says.

He gives away a hundred cows. The old man just takes the single drop of milk that he has and drops it to Mother Earth. God then gives the rich man a thousand more cows, for the hundred that he gave. He then turns to the old man and kills his only cow.

The angels say, "What is that, God?" It is confusing.

The angels turn to God and say, "We thought you were God, but now we have to leave you. It seems you were just playing God. You are not God."

God says, "Okay, but before you go, you might have a question for me."

One says, "Yeah, I do. Why did you kill that poor man's cow? He was devoted to you and this rich man has all this money. He only gave it out of big ego and 'look at me.' Still you gave him all the rewards."

God turns around and says, "No, no, my friend. You have it wrong. This rich man has nine hundred lifetimes left before he can come home. This poor man, his last attachment in this worldly life before he could come home to me was his cow. I removed the object to bring him home."

The angels exclaim, "Oh! You are my God again."

God says, "Not any more."

CHAPTER 36

DEATH, AN ILLUSION

There is absolute proof that death is an illusion and that we go on, helped on across by elders, family members, friends, masters, angels, and the gods. This story is the story of a great being passing, my wife, Linda O'Neill.

The events began to unfold one day when I was in the healing center in Wexford. The phone rang, I picked it up, and it was my daughter, Orla, ringing to inform me that Linda had had a severe headache, a sharp pain in her head, and she was feeling unwell—very unwell. Linda and I had not been to a doctor for many years, maybe twenty years or so, and I felt it very strange that my first response was, knowing of course that all can be healed through meditation or mind acts, my words, "Call a doctor." So Gavin and Orla called a doctor, and when they described to the doctor the symptoms, the doctor says, "No, this is not a doctor case, you need to go straight to the hospital. I will send an ambulance." The ambulance took Linda to the hospital.

Upon her arrival in the hospital, after a period of waiting, Linda was seen by some doctors, and the diagnosis was that it was just stress, or a migraine of some sort. Linda was then told to go home for rest and not to worry; over the next couple of days she began to deteriorate really badly. This deterioration led me to come up from Wexford to see how she was doing. As I was there for a few days, I watched as Linda began to recover slightly and then deteriorate, recover slightly and then deteriorate, until one morning I was making her a cup of tea, and I asked her a question, and just for a moment she spoke with a lisp, or strangely disorientated kind of speech, and then I realized that the symptoms were that of a stroke. Knowing that Linda might begin to panic slightly about this event, I went to my daughter Orla and said, "Please go down and ask your Mum if you could bring her to a doctor, that you're worried about her, so that she would do it, because she would relieve the worrying of her daughter far quicker than she would relieve her own pain." This is the type of being she was.

So Orla brought her to our GP, the family doctor of thirty years or so. It turned out that the doctor actually wasn't there when Orla brought her to the surgery, but another doctor was there, and strangely enough this doctor had once been in the super specialty hospital, Sai Baba's super specialty hospital in Putti Parti India. Orla explained that whilst there Linda had quite a severe reaction, and the doctor noted this and said she needed to go back to the hospital. He began to write a letter in order for Orla to bring her to the hospital. Strange, of course, that the doctor never called an ambulance, which you imagine would have been the more appropriate response. So as Orla was taking Linda, who was very weak at the time, out to the car, she was stopped and asked by the receptionist for the payment before she could leave, even though Linda was in quite a weak state and leaning on Orla. So Orla paid and then went to the hospital, and on the way to the hospital rang me to inform me that Linda had taken another turn, and that she was on the way back to the hospital. I decided I would meet them at the hospital.

I arrived at the hospital, and to explain—the system in this hospital now was what's called a triage nurse system, which basically is a failure of the medical community, in that instead of seeing a doctor when you go to the hospital, you see a nurse. And then that nurse has to assess as to how serious the accident or event is and then put you on a list of who would be seen first and last.

As I entered the triage nurse's room, she was stating that Linda was perfectly fine because.... she was either just having a migraine or the condition was stress-related as per the week before.

And I got quite annoyed and I said, "Please, you need to understand that this is a stroke."

I mentioned the word "stroke," and the nurse said, "No, this is not a stroke because..." her coordination would be this, that or the other.

I said, "No, my father had taken a stroke, and his coordination was perfectly fine until it was too late, and in fact, also passed away from the same associated symptoms."

So I began to plead with the nurse to at least monitor her heart again or blood pressure, that this was a stroke, and just to appease me, she took Linda's blood pressure, which actually turned out to be extremely low at the time.

Then she said for us to wait outside, that a doctor would see us as soon as possible. This wait ended up taking something in the region of six to eight hours as Linda vomited, went in and out of conscious, and became more and more weak. I had to go and attend to some important business, and by this time was convinced I was wrong, and they were right, and Linda would be fine. So Orla stayed with Linda and kept me informed over the phone. Then when Linda was seen again by the doctor after whatever, six or eight hours, the doctors again agreed that it was only stress-related and nothing to worry about, and Linda was once again sent home for the second time.

This time when Linda was sent home, I wanted to keep my eye on her, but I also had my duty in the healing center in Wexford to attend to, so we brought Linda down to Wexford and looked after her there for several days. During those days she began to recover; I am absolutely sure this had to do with the energy of the healing center in Wexford.

As Linda recovered, we brought her back up to Dublin, and there in Dublin the phone rang, and it was the nurse saying could we bring Linda in on a Monday (this was a Friday), for tests, blood tests, et cetera, and I said to the nurse, "Please could we not bring her in now? I believe this is very serious, and in fact she may not be with us by Monday," but the nurse insisted that we go in on Monday.

So Orla once again brought Linda to the clinic on the Monday where they took blood tests. And then they took a CAT scan or an x-ray, and it showed some sort of little disruption or patch, which caused them to begin to worry, and this worry then led to a doctor to say that it would be best for Linda to stay in the hospital for a day or two to undergo more tests. The problem was that there was no bed for her, so Linda ended up sleeping on a trolley with no pillow or anything for 24 hours whilst they tried to locate a bed for her. But things deteriorated a little further, and finally they ended up locating a bed for Linda on the second day, and she was admitted to the ward.

There they undertook more tests with Linda, and then she was generally just left in the bed for five days on aspirin tablets, and no other medication was administered during this time. We saw Linda in several different states of being during these days.

Then a sequence of occurrences began where Linda began to complain of chest pains and the likes, and so we informed the staff of the hospital. And the doctor then had a monitor applied to Linda. This monitor was to monitor her for 24 hours to see if there were any irregularities.

After just several hours of this monitor being on, the nurse came to take the monitor off Linda. Orla said for it to be left on for the 24 hours, at which the nurse said that it was needed for another patient who was sick, more or less indicating that Linda was some form of malingerer. This obviously caused great, great distress to my daughter, and then when they informed me, I also made note to the staff about this event.

The next big event was that Linda was to have a lumbar puncture, and the lumbar puncture was to happen at 11 o'clock, but in fact I arrived at the hospital at 8 o'clock on the Friday morning, and when I arrived Linda was lying very flat on her back looking very pale and weak. I asked her what had happened and she said "Nothing," nothing had happened and nothing was wrong. I said to her, "Please, Linda, you and I can see that something is wrong. You need to tell us if something is going on." It was at this stage that she informed me that the lumbar puncture had not gone to plan, that in fact there was great difficulty and instead of the procedure taking its normal period of time, it took much, much longer. I believe that this particular technique is extremely painful, and it should take only eight minutes, but it took something like twenty minutes in Linda's case, so she was in quite an uncomfortable state. So I sat with her that day, and then my son and daughter and daughter's boyfriend arrived at the hospital, and Linda motioned or gestured to me that I should go and look after whatever business I needed to look after, that she would be ok.

During the time that my son and daughter and daughter's boyfriend were at her bedside, a speech therapist came to assess her speech, and in fact Linda's coherent speech was not good, i.e., when asked something like who was the president of America she said "Bill Clinton," but it was in fact at that time President Bush. When asked what her date of birth was, she took a long time to remember this type of thing.

But she was getting stressed, according to Orla and my son Gavin, and she was getting more and more agitated. So much so, that when the test was over, she said to Gavin and Orla, what are now famous words in our family, "When this is over, there will be big changes." At this time Orla and her boyfriend Colin went to get something to eat in the cafe downstairs.

Gavin stayed with Linda reading a magazine when Linda said to him, "I feel really tired but don't want to go to sleep."

Gavin said, "Don't be silly. Go to sleep, and I'll be here when you wake up."

Orla came back a while later to see how Linda was doing, but she was asleep by now, so Gavin and Orla went outside the room for a few minutes so as not to wake Linda. A while later Gavin went back into the room to see if she was still asleep, and while he was there the doctors came in to check on her. Gavin tried to wake her, but when she woke up she was totally disorientated and could not speak or understand the doctors. At this time the doctors asked everyone to leave the room. Orla then rang me and said, "Please, Dad, please, Dad, come, something seriously is wrong."

So when I arrived at the hospital my sister and Linda's mother also had come to the hospital and were not allowed to see her. I said, "They won't stop me from seeing her," and I went in and went behind the curtains. The doctor asked who I was, and I said Linda's husband. The doctor then said, "Linda, your husband is here." Linda had no recognition of what he was saying. He then took a pen from his pocket and he said, "Linda, Linda, what is this?" And Linda just babbled and babbled and babbled—no coherent thoughts. The doctor then informed me that all would be fine, that there was no problem. It was just a little turn, and that they would bring her down now immediately for an MRI scan to see what was going on in her brain in order to fix it.

I asked could we go down with her and was informed "No"—but one of us could, so it was deemed then that I would be it. So we went down to the MRI section of the hospital. When there, the staff were not quite ready for her appearance, so Linda was just left outside the door and the nurse went to accommodate. I was holding Linda's hand, and her eyes were closed, and next she just opened her eyes, and at that moment, with great compassion, I saw that Linda was potentially about to leave this world. She squeezed my hand just at the moment that the nurse arrived and wheeled her into the MRI.

I then rang Orla and Gavin who were upstairs and told them to come downstairs to sit outside and just support their mother while she was getting these tests, knowing full well that something very dramatic was about to happen. That drama happened when, all of a sudden as we were sitting outside, we began to hear screams of Linda's name in a very frightened and fearful tone from the doctors and the nurses. Then a bit of panic started to set in with the nurses and then with us, as Orla went into a complete and utter shock listening to the events unfolding. As I held her close in my arms, comforted her, I realized what was happening.

Then the nurse came out and was in quite a state of shock, which was quite surprising because, as you know, nurses are sometimes quite used to these events. But, in some way, I'm sure Linda had touched them with her energy as she had many people during this event. The nurse was there with a tear in her eye saying that all would be ok, that the doctors were looking after Linda. Next, what looked like a crash team went in, and I believe Linda had had a heart attack in the MRI machine. Then the doctor came out and said that there was no problem, that all was fine, that Linda had just vomited or something in the machine, but because of the vomiting, some swelling had began to occur in her head, and that she was now being transferred to the ICU unit.

As Linda was transferred, we all made our way up to the ICU unit. I began to ring all of Linda's family, her brothers and sisters, to come because I realized once again that this was the beginning of the end. When we had all gathered in the ICU, the doctor came, and he was in a great state of shock. He just kept saying that he didn't know what happened, he didn't know what went wrong. Everything would be fine, he said, but there was some swelling and he was making arrangements to have Linda sent to a specialty hospital in Ireland for this type of stroke or injury. They would take Linda and reduce the swelling, and then she would come back to Tallaght Hospital where they would then give her care. He was in quite a highly agitated, sorrowful state. I held his hand, looked him in the eye and said, "This has now gone out of your hands and has gone into a hand greater than that of yours or mine, i.e., the hand of God." But he kept insisting that all would be ok.

Then the ICU nurse came out and asked did we have a religion, and as I was about to say, "The religion of love," her sister said, "Yes, she's a Catholic."

The nurse then said, "You should send for a priest." It was at this stage that the whole family realized that Linda was in grave danger.

So I said, "I am a priest, I am a minister; I will administer the Last Rites."

The nurse looked at me as if I had two heads because in Ireland ministers/priests aren't married and definitely don't have wives or children. So I explained that I was a minister in an organization that allowed this. After a couple of moments, she said that it was ok to come in and carry out the Sacrament. So I called Gavin and Orla to come in with me, but the nurse said that they couldn't come. This was beyond belief for me, so I just said, "They are coming," and put my hand across to block the nurse from preventing them from walking in. They came in and we all arrived at Linda's bed. She was wired and tubed up to every machine possible. At that moment I began to administer the Last Rites in a lineage that Linda and I had spoken of many times, called the Bardo Todal, which is the preparation for the leaving of the body in this life, to administer and get ready for your next life.

After this Linda was transferred to the specialist hospital, and all the family and I followed. As we waited for Linda to be made comfortable, the doctor asked to speak to her husband and children. We were brought into a room and the doctor, who was an American woman, asked us what we knew about what was happening. So we explained that the doctor in the other hospital had said that she had got sick in the machine, that there was some swelling in her head, that the idea of sending her to this hospital was that you would relieve the pressure, and then she would be sent back to the original hospital and nurtured from there.

The doctor then became quite irate, nearly to the point of frustration or anger. And without thinking, said, "Are you kidding me? You must be joking. This woman will more than likely not make the night. And you should prepare yourself for this."

The shock of this once again for my daughter Orla was great, and I found myself holding Orla all night, trying to console her, as she just wept at the potential loss of her mother—not only her mother, her absolute best friend and absolute support in this life. So three days began to pass with all sorts of "maybe she'll make it, maybe she won't" scenarios that go on in these situations. In that time Orla could not sleep and stayed awake in the waiting room for the whole three days.

Then came the most relieving or what we would now class as miraculous event that gave us all peace of mind and heart. Gavin, my son, had noticed that there was no picture of Linda's spiritual teacher, Satya Sai Baba, over her bed. He asked somebody, who was going home to get fresh clothes, to bring a special picture that he had in his bedroom. This person brought the picture, and Gavin put it over Linda's bed.

Moments later, as Gavin was at the bedside on his own, an Indian doctor arrived into ICU, came to Linda's bed, picked up Linda's chart, looked at it, looked up at the picture of Sai Baba, and said to Gavin, "Do you know this man?" or "Who is this man?"

Gavin replied, "Oh, this is Satya Sai Baba."

The doctor then asked, "How do you know this man?"

Gavin replied, "My mother and father and family are devotees of Satya Sai Baba," and said that they had gone to him many times and received his Darshan, and that he was their guru.

So the doctor then said, "Very happy, very happy." Then the doctor said, "I will examine your Mother." Taking out her stethoscope, she began to draw on Linda's body the symbol of Prema Agni, which is the symbol associated with divine love that is also used as the logo for the charity work that we do building schools and orphanages all over the world, but especially in India. So Gavin watched this in sort of two minds. On one hand he realized what was going on, but on the other hand, he didn't have a clue.

Then the doctor said, "She will be fine, very good woman, very blessed woman to have been to this man Sai Baba," and that she would be fine. Then, taking up the chart, she said to Gavin something like, "Wrong medicine." Then she said, "I will be back in a moment, I'm just going to check something," and walked round to the nurses' station to monitor all the machines.

After five or so minutes Gavin was waiting and there was no sign of the Indian doctor returning. So Gavin walked to the nurses' station. The doctor wasn't there, so he said to the nurses, "When will the Indian doctor be coming back?"

To which the nurses said, "What Indian doctor? There is no Indian doctor." And even if there were an Indian doctor, she wouldn't have been allowed to examine Linda because doctors have to have permission from other doctors in order to examine their patients.

At this stage Gavin had a realization that Linda had potentially received a visit from her guru, her teacher, Satya Sai Baba, in a different form. As crazy as this all seems, these things happen all over the world all the time.

So coming out of the room, Gavin came into the waiting room and shared the story of what happened with Orla and me and one or two others. At this, Orla became very excited, very up beat, and said, "I knew he would come. I knew he would come." She had written him a letter the day before, stating that if he came and looked after her mother that she would be a good person and dedicate her life to the service of others. This caused great relief and great joy.

And so that evening we all had a good night's rest, Orla for the first time was able to sleep. I remained in a state of meditation rather than sleep. Then at 7 o'clock in the morning the nurse came into the room where I was and said, "Derek, I have some bad news. Linda had a very restless night. She had a severe heart attack and won't make it."

I thanked her for her work, and she looked at me with amazement, that I was taking this news with such grace and not anger or shock. I asked her if it was ok for us to go in and see Linda, and she said, "Sure." So I woke Gavin and Orla gently and told them to get dressed.

When they came out I said, "Your Mother had a heart attack and she will be passing away in a short time, if you would like to go in and talk to her." So we rang once again all the family to come, because a lot of the family had returned to their homes.

And so we went in. Linda was lying there in a very glowing and yet weak state. So I went to the nurse and said when she starts to go into her death, would it be possible to knock off the machine before we heard that beep that you hear when somebody has died, that I didn't want my children's last memory of their mother to be a beep. She agreed.

As Linda deteriorated and began to drop more and more into the lower and lower heartbeats, it was a very dull, dark, cloudy, miserable day in Dublin. And Linda's bed was beside the window of the hospital and the curtains were open, but there was no light of any significance because it was such a dark, quiet, miserable day. Then, at the moment of Linda's transition, the machine began to drop and gracefully the nurse's hand came around and just switched off the machine.

And as we stood there, the people who had made it to Linda's bedside, her sister, her daughter, her son, her daughter's boyfriend, the manager of Creacon Lodge, Jonathan, and I, I said to Orla, "Your mother will be passing. Now if you would like to put your hands over your mother's heart, she will say to you her last goodbye." I also asked Gavin if he wished to do this, so he did his own goodbye.

So as Orla placed hands over her mother's heart, the most amazing event unfolded. At this stage two nurses had come to the bedside, the one who had switched off the machine and another. Just at this moment a massive, clear light, the clearest light that I had ever experienced, broke from the clouds and began to descend in through the window, and the light narrowing from a wide light to a narrow light, resting on the back of Orla's hand and going through her hand into Linda's heart charka. At that stage I saw many beings: Jesus, Buddha, masters from all religions, angels, friends, and family coming from the light down to stand by Linda's bed.

I thought that I was the only one witnessing or seeing this. But as I looked around me I began to realize that Linda's sister and everybody, even the nurses, were witnessing this event. As we all looked in awe, I watched as Linda lifted from her body, was greeted by all these beings of light, and began to walk with them away from her body. At that moment Orla said, "I witnessed, I felt her last heartbeat..." with joy and yet great sadness. Then, as quickly as the light came, it began to leave, but leaving in a quick and yet slow way. It lifted from the back of Orla's hand; you could nearly touch it, as it went to the window. From the window it began to go up, up, up into the clouds, and just before the clouds closed over once again, I could see Linda just turn and, with a great smile on her face, I heard her say, "Great changes are coming." The light disappeared. And we stood at her bedside in awe.

Believers and non-believers alike had just witnessed a great event, possibly one of the greatest events that we will ever be given to witness in this lifetime or any lifetime…the death of a soul happily returning home to its creator to serve as a guide from the other side in the heavenly realms. To me and now to Linda's sister, Orla's boyfriend, to Orla, my daughter, and Gavin, my son, and Jonathan, the manager, our lives have been touched forever, and we know, without a shadow of a doubt now, not to fear death, that death is just a happening, and that God is always with us, even if we deny God.

Hopefully this story brings you some relief, that should you have to go through this event or have already, that there is nothing to fear.

SUMMARY

This book will bring you from doubt to proof that we are more than just what we see ourselves as. Reading about the extraordinary journeys of the people in this book will give you hope and comfort about your own ability to heal yourself and others. This book is an inner and outer journey of great benefit to all walks of life.

Derek O'Neill is a master spiritual teacher, healer, philanthropist, and practicing psychotherapist based in Dublin, Ireland. He holds the position of Supervisor of Ireland's Association of Hypnotherapists and Psychotherapists, is a Martial Arts Sensei, and is a loving parent of two young adults.

Derek is founder of SQ-Worldwide LP, a multifaceted company (Wellness, Foundation, and Fortune) committed to teaching both individuals and corporations how to use consciousness, compassion, and cooperation to transform not only themselves but also the world.

Derek is also founder of Creacon Prema Agni Healing Centre, a spiritual teaching and retreat center in Wexford, Ireland. His popular More Truth Will Set You Free™ workshops have helped thousands worldwide to free themselves from longstanding obstacles and step into love, joy, and empowerment.